FROM EQUITY TO GROWTH

INITIATIVE FOR POLICY DIALOGUE AT COLUMBIA:
CHALLENGES IN DEVELOPMENT AND GLOBALIZATION

INITIATIVE FOR POLICY DIALOGUE AT COLUMBIA: CHALLENGES IN DEVELOPMENT AND GLOBALIZATION

JOSÉ ANTONIO OCAMPO AND JOSEPH E. STIGLITZ, SERIES EDITORS

The Future of Work in Developing Countries, Arjun Jayadev, Akbar Noman, and Joseph E. Stiglitz, eds.

The Great Polarization: How Ideas, Power, and Policies Drive Inequality, Rudiger L. von Arnim and Joseph E. Stiglitz, eds.

The Quality of Growth in Africa, Ravi Kanbur, Akbar Noman, and Joseph E. Stiglitz, eds.

International Policy Rules and Inequality: Implications for Global Economic Governance, José Antonio Ocampo, ed.

The Welfare State Revisited, José Antonio Ocampo and Joseph E. Stiglitz, eds.

Efficiency, Finance, and Varieties of Industrial Policy: Guiding Resources, Learning, and Technology for Sustained Growth, Akbar Noman and Joseph E. Stiglitz, eds.

Too Little, Too Late: The Quest to Resolve Sovereign Debt Crises, Martin Guzman, José Antonio Ocampo, and Joseph E. Stiglitz, eds.

Macroeconomics and Development: Roberto Frenkel and the Economics of Latin America, Mario Damill, Martín Rapetti, and Guillermo Rozenwurcel, eds.

Industrial Policy and Economic Transformation in Africa, Akbar Noman and Joseph E. Stiglitz, eds.

New Perspectives on International Migration and Development, Jeronimo Cortina and Enrique Ochoa-Reza, eds.

Development Cooperation in Times of Crisis, José Antonio Ocampo and José Antonio Alonso

Reforming the International Financial System for Development, Jomo Kwame Sundaram, ed.

Taxation in Developing Countries, Roger Gordon, ed.

Growth and Policy in Developing Countries: A Structuralist Approach, José Antonio Ocampo, Codrina Rada, and Lance Taylor

Privatization: Successes and Failures, Gérard Roland, ed.

Escaping the Resource Curse, Macartan Humphreys, Jeffrey D. Sachs, and Joseph E. Stiglitz, eds.

The Right to Know: Transparency for an Open World, Ann Florini, ed.

FROM EQUITY TO GROWTH

Social Discontent in Developing Countries

José Antonio Ocampo, Jonathan Malagón, and Andrés Narváez

FOREWORD BY

Michelle Bachelet Jeria

COLUMBIA UNIVERSITY PRESS

NEW YORK

Columbia University Press
Publishers Since 1893
New York   Chichester, West Sussex
cup.columbia.edu

Cataloging-in-Publication Data is available from
the Library of Congress.

ISBN 9780231222914 (hardback)
ISBN 9780231564441 (epub)
ISBN 9780231566322 (PDF)

LCCN 2025051561

Cover design: Noah Arlow
Cover image: Shutterstock

GPSR Authorized Representative: Easy Access System Europe,
Mustamäe tee 50, 10621 Tallinn, Estonia,
gpsr.requests@easproject.com

INITIATIVE FOR POLICY DIALOGUE AT COLUMBIA: CHALLENGES IN DEVELOPMENT AND GLOBALIZATION

JOSÉ ANTONIO OCAMPO AND JOSEPH E. STIGLITZ, SERIES EDITORS

The Initiative for Policy Dialogue (IPD) at Columbia University brings together academics, policy makers, and practitioners from developed and developing countries to address the most pressing issues in economic policy today. IPD is an important part of Columbia's broad program on development and globalization. The Initiative for Policy Dialogue at Columbia: Challenges in Development and Globalization presents the latest academic thinking on a wide range of development topics and lays out alternative policy options and tradeoffs. Written in a language accessible to policy makers and students alike, this series is unique in that it both shapes the academic research agenda and furthers the economic policy debate, facilitating a more democratic discussion of development policies.

Is it possible to build fairer societies without undermining economic growth? Combining economic theory, political analysis, and real-world case studies, *From Equity to Growth* offers new perspectives on one of the defining challenges of the era. Rejecting simplistic binaries between equity and growth, the authors argue that inclusive development is not only possible but essential. They highlight specific policy choices that can reconcile social demands with macroeconomic stability. Clear, timely, and rigorous, this book offers both a diagnosis of many countries' current predicament and a hopeful vision of how to move forward.

CONTENTS

FOREWORD

The countries of Latin America and the Caribbean have been shaped by narratives and promises of wealth and development. This vision fueled the struggle for independence and later the pursuit of greater well-being for their people. The path to full development has been far from linear or complete, however; instead, it has been marked by setbacks and subject to contradictory interpretations. Today, many of these doubts remain valid.

Politics and economics have served as the primary arenas for debating alternatives, agendas, and unifying visions. It would be naive to assume, however, that decisions have been made solely through rational deliberation. Periods of democratic stability were achieved only in the 1990s, following the rise of dictatorships and the gradual consolidation of the rule of law. After enduring civil wars, agrarian reforms, nationalizations, and coups d'état, Latin American societies appeared to be on an upward trajectory of economic progress, inching closer to the long-elusive goal of development. The data on rising wealth, improved educational levels, and reductions in poverty and infant mortality serve as evidence of this progress.

We know well that these advances were insufficient. Beyond the unique circumstances of each country, the so-called lost decade of the 1980s gave way to a new period of stagnation beginning in 2014. What happened to us? Why does this cycle continue to repeat itself?

We continue to lag behind in critical aspects of our countries' development. First is the so-called middle-income trap. In other words, there is a structural weakness in deepening the foundations necessary for full development: we remain emerging economies constrained by globalized markets or reliant on raw material exports, with the volatility this entails. Second, democracies have also failed to meet societal aspirations fully, opening the door to authoritarian and/or populist movements. Our governance systems have struggled to keep pace with societies that are increasingly informed, demanding, and prone to rapid shifts in expectations. Today, more than ever, we face the challenge of advancing economic and political systems that, instead of reinforcing stability and fostering confidence, tend to exacerbate tensions. As always, the most vulnerable groups bear the brunt of this uncertainty, suffering the most from the lack of clarity and the inability to establish medium- and long-term horizons.

This book deliberately positions itself within this complexity and its most evident manifestations: the frustration over unmet progress and the discontent fueled by accumulated setbacks. It offers an analytical framework, supported by data and examples, to reflect on two concepts often perceived as opposing forces: equity and growth.

Of course, these two objectives sometimes appear antagonistic—what the authors refer to as anti–growth equity and pro–growth inequality. It is also true, however, that when we broaden our perspective and conduct comparative analyses, we find examples of public policies that achieve a virtuous balance. What is desirable can indeed be possible. This book provides guidelines for reaching states of pro–growth equity.

To achieve this, it is necessary to shed some of the heavy burdens that prolonged debates have carried, in one direction or the other. This is why it is crucial not to overlook the fact that, in addition to the middle-income trap, two other traps are evident in the analysis. In fact, it could be argued that they are two sides of the same coin. First is the trap of bad politics, embodied by populism and the temptation to offer solutions to deep problems through the irresponsible use of institutions and public finances—effectively mortgaging public trust to seek political gain. Second is the trap of conceiving growth in a way that is decoupled from social cohesion. This is another form of irresponsibility, one that seeks retribution within closed macroeconomic circles while turning its back on the majority who bear the costs of shock policies or rigid dogmas on a daily basis.

Without falling into simplism or mere redistributive formulas, this text advocates for a long-term commitment; for good economics, hand in hand with good politics; for informed and vigilant societies; for functioning, rather than disappearing, states—where shortcuts, as we have seen time and again, prove futile; where social mobilization, an essential part of any healthy democracy, can be channeled effectively. Although many forget it, the very essence of politics is to serve the people: to listen to their aspirations, address their demands, and implement effective solutions that prioritize their present and future well-being.

An economy cannot remain relevant if it fails to recognize that expressions of discontent—whether in the streets, in the virtual world, or at the ballot box—are symptoms of malfunctioning within our institutions, and, why not say it, within our elites.

In the ever-renewed need to think more deeply about how to combine ethical horizons with the pragmatism demanded by responsibility, readers will find a valuable contribution in these pages.

Michelle Bachelet Jeria
President of Chile, 2006–2010 and 2014–2018
Former United Nations High Commissioner for Human Rights
Former Executive Director of the United Nations Entity for Gender Equality and the Empowerment of Women

PREFACE

Since the time of Adam Smith (1723–1790), who is considered by many to be the founder of modern economics, the primary goal of economists has been to understand how scarce resources are allocated to meet people's needs. Thus, economists explore how goods and services are produced and distributed in societies. Empirical evidence suggests that they have done a relatively good job when analyzing what happens on the production side: it is enough to review the historical behavior of real gross domestic product (GDP) per capita worldwide (figure 0.1)—the indicator most commonly used to reflect a country's production levels—to see that humanity has managed to increase its production by 1,281 percent from 1820 to 2018 and by 579 percent from 1920 to 2018. If we were to take production levels as a measure of well-being, we could confidently say that the world has never been a more prosperous place to live than it is today.

We cannot say the same if we analyze the issue from the distribution side. In this area, economists have significant outstanding debts. While it is true that real GDP per capita provides important information about the size and evolution of an economy, it does not specifically assess distribution. Consider the following example: a country may have a high real GDP per capita, but its wealth could be concentrated in a small segment of the population, while the majority earn low incomes.

To discuss distribution, the most commonly used indicator is the Gini coefficient. This index ranges from 0 to 1, where 0 indicates absolute equality (all individuals receive the same income), and 1 reflects extreme inequality (a single individual concentrates all income, while the rest receive nothing). Thus, the higher the Gini coefficient, the greater the

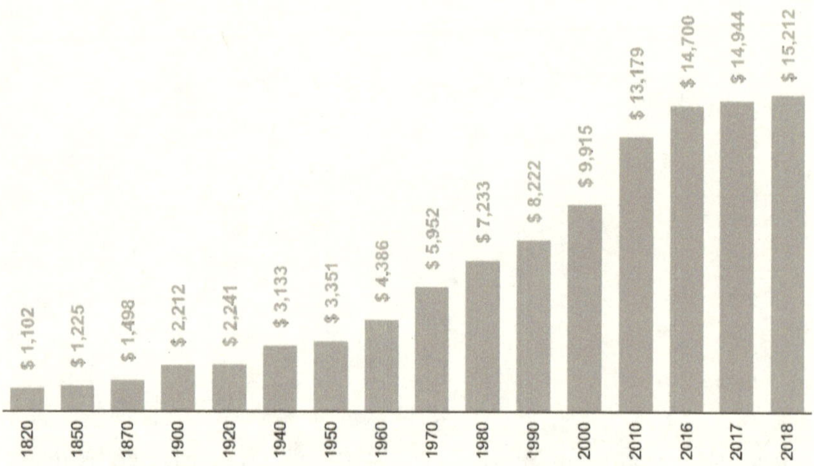

Figure 0.1 Evolution of real gross domestic product (GDP) per capita worldwide from 1820 to 2018, expressed in constant 2011 US dollars. The bar chart shows significant growth in per capita income over the last two centuries, with especially rapid increases since 1950.

Source: Author's elaboration based on data from the Groningen Growth and Development Centre, "World GPD pc," Maddison Project Database 2020, https://www.rug.nl/ggdc/historicaldevelopment/maddison/releases/maddison-project-database-2020?lang=en.

inequality levels. As shown in figure 0.2, the global Gini coefficient has remained close to 0.70 over the last four decades, indicating a highly unequal world, albeit with a slight improvement in the current century. If we were to use income distribution rather than production levels as a measure of well-being, we could conclude that the world is a place lacking prosperity.

The conclusion is clear: we have learned how to generate greater production and wealth, but we have not yet mastered how to distribute this abundance of resources among people equitably. This situation should be alarming for everyone because inequality brings with it a series of problems that are impossible to ignore. Here, we will mention three, although it is important to note that the list is much longer.

First, inequality leads to higher levels of poverty and social exclusion because individuals with lower incomes often struggle to access essential resources such as health care, education, food, and housing. Second, high inequality tends to perpetuate over time, leading to inequality of opportunity and limited social mobility. As a result, those from low-income

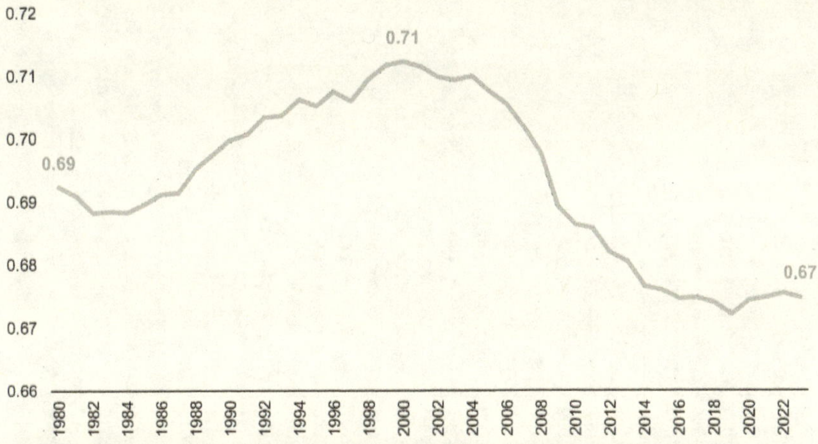

Figure 0.2 Evolution of the global Gini coefficient from 1980 to 2023, calculated on pretax income. The line chart shows a rise in inequality from 1980 to the early 2000s, peaking at 0.71 in 2000, followed by a steady decline to 0.67 in recent years.

Source: Author's elaboration based on data from the World Inequality Database, "Gini Coefficient," https://wid.world/data/.

families face additional barriers to accessing quality education and decent employment—both of which are essential for prosperity. Third, greater inequality can undermine social cohesion and solidarity within a society. When the gaps between socioeconomic groups are large, trust and cooperation among them often erode.

Overall, greater inequality translates into increased poverty and social exclusion, limited opportunities, restricted social mobility, and a lack of trust and cooperation among members of society. Because inequality is often seen as the result of inadequate economic policy management, it is expected that societies with inequitable resource distribution will experience heightened social and political tensions, political polarization, and distrust toward government institutions and the political system as a whole. These factors can lead to widespread discontent when members of a society demand better living conditions and a more equitable distribution of resources from their leaders. These demands are just and necessary for achieving real change in current conditions, but they often escalate social conflict, leading to riots and violent protests.

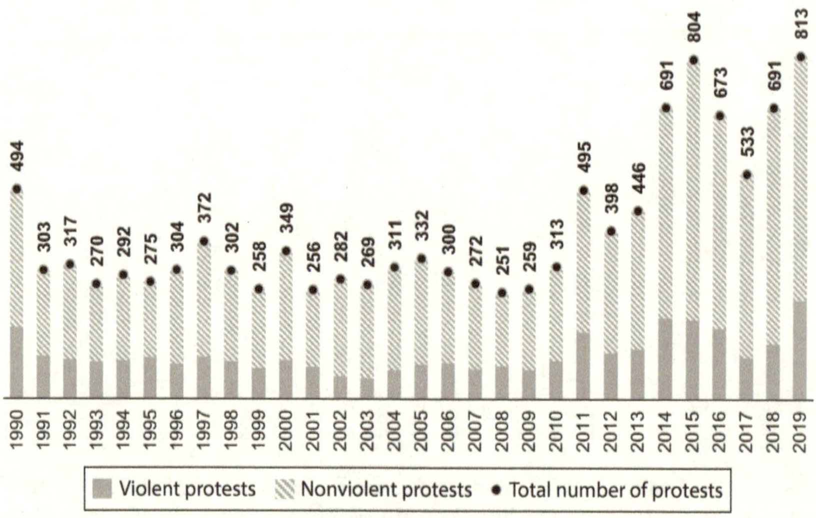

Figure 0.3 Number of antistate protests worldwide, disaggregated by type: violent protests (solid bars), nonviolent protests (patterned bars), and total number of protests (black dots), from 1990 to 2019.

Source: Author's elaboration based on data from David Clark and Patrick Regan, *Mass Mobilization Protest Data* (Harvard Dataverse, 2016).

The data presented in figure 0.3 support the idea that we live in a much more discontented world today, where people across various societies are demanding better living conditions from their governments. Between 1990 and 2019, 11,925 protests against governments were recorded worldwide, with 3,206 of these involving acts of violence by demonstrators. In other words, one in four protests includes acts of violence against the state. In 2019 alone, there were 813 protests, representing a 214 percent increase compared to the 259 protests recorded in 2009.

Considering what we have discussed so far, we can reformulate our earlier conclusion as follows: today, we live in a world with unprecedented levels of wealth and income, but we have failed to distribute these resources equitably. This failure has, in part, led us to the current era of social discontent.

Faced with this scenario, several political actors are committed to capitalizing on the situation by promising what appears to be a correct interpretation of popular demands. These demands range from valid social needs in areas such as health care, education, and employment to ill-timed welfare states and overly welfare-oriented social policies. While it is imperative to address the deep-rooted deprivations of part of the population and the ethically unsustainable inequalities plaguing our economies, the policy response can often result in temporary relief measures that are difficult to sustain over time. The consequences of such measures can be devastating for the productive apparatus. Desperate and improvised actions aimed at promoting equity can lead to significant distortions in labor markets as well as unhealthy fiscal policy situations. These in turn can result in unsuitable public sector finances or the imposition of tax burdens that undermine the business climate and discourage investment.

This book presents two types of scenarios to address the growing social discontent. The first explores the theoretical mechanisms and recent evidence of how a poorly designed short-term pro-equity agenda can lead to lower levels of economic growth, compromising the state's ability to generate wealth. The second, in contrast, explores theoretical mechanisms and recent evidence of how a pro-equity agenda can be designed to align with increasingly higher levels of economic growth. In this sense, the first scenario examines situations of anti–growth equity (what we call frustrations in the era of social discontent), while the second analyzes situations of pro–growth equity (what we call aspirations in the era of social discontent).

Note that both scenarios are based on the same premise: that there is a causal relationship running from equity to growth. This is a striking aspect because economic analyses have commonly been conducted under the assumption that growth generates equity. It is paradoxical that this relationship dominates research agendas given that the economist who introduced the analysis of the relationship between equity and growth into the economic debate—Nobel Prize winner Simon Kuznets—was emphatic in correctly identifying that the causal relationship between these two variables could operate in both directions.

We have divided the book into five chapters. Because the general purpose of the book is to analyze the possible relationships between equity and growth, chapter 1 begins with an in-depth review of what has been introduced and discussed so far on this topic. The objective of this chapter is to examine the approaches that have been developed regarding the relationship between equity and growth. This leads us to explore one of the most important economic models ever formulated: the Kuznets curve. We start with the original framework proposed by Kuznets in 1955, which suggests an inverted U-shaped relationship between growth and inequality. According to this model, growth initially generates inequality but eventually leads to distributive improvement beyond a certain income level. While this model has faced numerous criticisms, such as those articulated by Thomas Piketty, it has also been empirically supported by other studies. We review both the criticisms and endorsements of the Kuznets curve as well as its various applications over the past few decades, including what are known as the environmental Kuznets curve and the financial Kuznets curve.

Once we have reviewed the relationships between equity and growth, our next step is to incorporate the concept of social discontent into the analysis. The primary objective of chapter 2 is to examine this concept: its definition, potential causes, means of expression, and evolution. Building on the previous discussion, this chapter highlights that the number of social protests worldwide has increased significantly in recent years because of growing social discontent. When analyzing the causes of this phenomenon, we find it necessary, based on a rigorous review of the data, to provide a general description of the main socioeconomic variables. From this analysis, we arrive at two scenarios, one positive and one negative. On the positive side, we find that, compared to previous years, we now live in a world with greater wealth, with fewer people in poverty, improved living conditions, better access to education, and higher levels of human development. On the negative side, which is closely linked to the rise in social protests, we observe that today's world is highly unequal, with insufficient job opportunities for young people, persistent gender gaps, an ongoing environmental crisis, and often democratic crises.

Having documented a world that has achieved great things but remains largely mired in social discontent, chapter 3 analyzes the consequences that public discontent can have on the politics of societies. We begin by clarifying that social discontent can have both positive and negative effects on politics. It would be a mistake to categorize social discontent simplistically as entirely good or bad because the relationship between social discontent and politics is ambiguous. Its impact depends largely on various factors, such as the nature of the protests, their objectives, the response of political leaders, and the context in which they occur. With this in mind, the first section of chapter 3 examines the numerous positive effects of social discontent, including fostering greater political awareness among people and facilitating necessary changes in established power structures. The second section of the chapter focuses on the negative effects. Broadly speaking, social discontent can lead to opportunistic practices that threaten societal well-being. The opportunistic practice we emphasize most is the one in which politicians transform public indignation into votes in their favor. This is achieved, for example, by promising a short-term pro-equity agenda that provides immediate responses to the problems of outraged citizens but is unsustainable over time. To conclude the chapter, we outline some of the political and economic consequences of power exercised by political opportunists. Among the political consequences we document are the deterioration of democracy and even an increase in social discontent itself. One of the main economic consequences, which is explored in chapter 4, is the emergence of scenarios characterized by anti–growth equity.

To capitalize on widespread dissatisfaction, political opportunism often involves promising citizens immediate solutions to the problems causing their discontent. While these quick fixes may alleviate the targeted issues temporarily, they can also have a negative impact on economic growth. In chapter 4, we explore the potential repercussions of social discontent on economic growth. We argue that political opportunism can temporarily generate higher levels of equity but at the cost of negative effects on economic growth. This inverse relationship between equity and growth, arising in a context of social discontent, can be explained through various channels: the investment channel, the ill-timed welfare states channel, and the market interference channel. The investment channel highlights that social protests have a negative impact on both components of investment: autonomous investment and investment dependent on interest rates. The ill-timed welfare states channel refers to governments implementing welfare measures that are misaligned with their revenue and tax collection levels. The market interference channel describes governments enacting policies that prevent markets from allocating resources efficiently. Regarding the obstacles to transitioning to high income, the idea we propose in this book is that social discontent can be an additional barrier to escaping what the economic literature calls the middle-income trap—a problem particularly critical in Latin America.

The book concludes with a vision for avoiding anti–growth equity scenarios and instead promoting equity-with-growth scenarios. It is undoubtedly challenging to move beyond the persistent social protests fueled today by both interest groups—who have found in the discourse of collective dissatisfaction a shortcut to advancing their private agendas—and political actors outside power who see conflict as a strategy to discredit the incumbent government and position themselves as agents of change. The purpose of chapter 5 is to provide readers with a positive and realistic vision of how countries can achieve pro–growth equity conditions, even in an era of social discontent. To this end, we begin with a general review of how equity can serve as a significant foundation for economic growth. We demonstrate how equity can foster advancements in both the market and institutional frameworks—two key dimensions for driving a country's economic growth. From a market perspective, our analysis shows that more equitable countries exhibit higher levels of human capital, technological innovation, consumption, financial deepening, and environmental protection. From an institutional perspective, we observe that more equitable countries enjoy better institutional quality, regulatory quality, rule of law, and transparency. Next, we narrow the analysis to explore how the problems associated with the three anti–growth equity channels discussed in chapter 4 can be addressed. In the third section of chapter 5, we present conclusions and offer a potential answer to one of this book's central questions: How can pro–growth equity help countries escape the middle-income trap? Developing this response will lead us to identify the fundamental characteristics of policies that treat greater equity and greater growth as complementary objectives rather than opposing ones.

We are fully aware that the forces underlying the relationship between equity and growth are complex and extend far beyond the realm of social discontent. In a world where there are increasing reasons for widespread dissatisfaction with political, economic, and social systems, we hope that the discussions proposed in this book will provide policymakers and governments with a useful foundation to design policy agendas aimed at achieving real change. Such change should be rooted in building societies that foster growth equity.

It should be noted that, because of the nationality of the authors, there are several specific references to the case in Colombia in several chapters of this book.

FROM EQUITY TO GROWTH

CHAPTER 1

The Dilemma Between Equity and Growth

Over the past two centuries, humanity's progress in income distribution has been, at best, limited. As highlighted in the *World Inequality Report 2022*, the global Gini coefficient was approximately 0.60 in 1820, whereas today it stands at around 0.67.[1] This suggests that, rather than improving, income inequality has actually worsened. The same report indicates that since 1910, the Gini coefficient has remained stable at around 0.7, implying that high levels of inequality have been a persistent feature of the global socioeconomic structure. For this reason, reducing inequality is a central objective in most political agendas. However, this goal raises an inevitable question: What must be sacrificed to achieve greater equity? Both theoretical analyses and empirical studies suggest that, in public policy, achieving one objective often requires at least a partial trade-off with another.

The Russian economist Simon Kuznets, in his analysis of the economies of the United States, the United Kingdom, and Germany, was a pioneer in observing that the pursuit of greater equity could come at the expense of economic growth. This observation gave rise to the renowned Kuznets curve, a fundamental model in the debate on the relationship between equity and growth. According to this theory, in the long run, a country experiencing strong economic growth may become more egalitarian. In the short term, however, a trade-off emerges: rapid economic expansion may be accompanied by rising inequality, while more equitable economies may experience lower growth rates.

This chapter focuses on the economic debate surrounding the relationship between equity and growth, with particular emphasis on the Kuznets curve model. We first define the concept of trade-offs in economic policy and explain why the Kuznets curve can be understood as formulating one of them. We then examine the data and arguments Kuznets used in the mid-twentieth century to explore the potential link between equity and growth, as well as how his theory was synthesized into the model now known as the Kuznets curve, which does not necessarily reflect all of his original ideas. Finally, we review and assess both the theoretical and empirical foundations of this model, and some of its applications in other fields, such as environmental economics and finance.

THE DILEMMAS WITHIN ECONOMIC POLICY

Practically every rational decision implies at least one renunciation. In economic theory, this idea is captured by the concept of opportunity cost, which states that the cost of making a certain decision is giving up the opportunity to pursue another one (or another set of decisions) and the benefits it would provide. For example, in standard microeconomic theory, consumers must decide whether to work or dedicate their potential working hours to leisure. In this scenario, the salary received in exchange for work can be seen as the opportunity cost of leisure because choosing leisure means forgoing the monetary compensation that constitutes the salary.

Beyond theory, dilemmas between different choices are part of daily life. Should I get to work via route A or route B? Should I buy the cell phone I want in cash or on credit? Should I invest the money I have saved over the past year in equity or fixed-income assets? Governments are not exempt from the obligation to choose between different sets of alternatives, which often conflict with one another in terms of the policy objectives they seek to achieve. Numerous examples of economic policy decisions illustrate this point.

Every day, it is common to find news in the media about the latest economic policy decisions made by authorities in response to a particular situation or simply to achieve a preestablished objective. The importance given to such policy decisions stems from a fact that is now practically irrefutable: what happens to the economy affects, in one way or another, all the inhabitants of a country. The state of a given economy can even have an impact on people in other countries, a reality that is increasingly evident in a world that is becoming more and more economically globalized.

Consider, for example, a scenario in which one of the world's most important suppliers of fertilizers for food production ceases to supply other economies. In this case, these economies would almost certainly face a rise in agricultural production costs, leading to an increase in food prices that would ultimately harm the inhabitants of countries that can no longer access the fertilizers they previously imported from the supplier country.

Readers may recall that, during 2022, one of the most widely reported news topics in the media was the rapid increase in monetary intervention interest rates worldwide. Central banks made this decision because, after the COVID-19 pandemic was brought under control, a widespread rise in inflation occurred because of Russia's invasion of Ukraine in February 2022. As a result, the near-consensus approach among economic authorities worldwide to combat this inflationary surge was to raise intervention interest rates.

For example, in Colombia, inflation in December 2022 reached 13.12 percent, the highest level of the twenty-first century for the country and significantly higher than the 5.62 percent recorded twelve months earlier. In response to rising inflation, the Banco de la República (the central bank of Colombia) raised the intervention rate to 12.00 percent in December 2022. Like the inflation rate, the intervention rate in December 2022 was well above that of December 2021 (3.00 percent).

This economic policy decision potentially affects everyone because an increase in the intervention rate leads to higher interest rates for purchasing a home, a car, an appliance, clothing—essentially any good or service acquired on credit. In general, a rise in the intervention rate translates into higher borrowing costs, which can halt several investment plans.

Although inflation began to decline after March 2023—falling to 9.28 percent by December 2023—the monetary authority, in an effort to continue controlling inflationary pressures, raised the intervention rate to 13.25 percent in May and began to reduce it only moderately in December 2023, lowering it to 13.00 percent (figure 1.1).

In this situation, policymakers deciding whether to increase the intervention rate to counteract inflation must consider that such a measure could have serious repercussions on the economy and its inhabitants because it may lead to a decline in investment and consumption levels. Thus, at first glance, one might be tempted to think that the opportunity cost of implementing a policy that raises the intervention rate is lower investment and consumption levels.

However, a deeper exploration of the possible effects of an increase in the intervention rate brings to light one of the most heated economic debates in recent times—whether lower inflation levels are associated with higher unemployment.

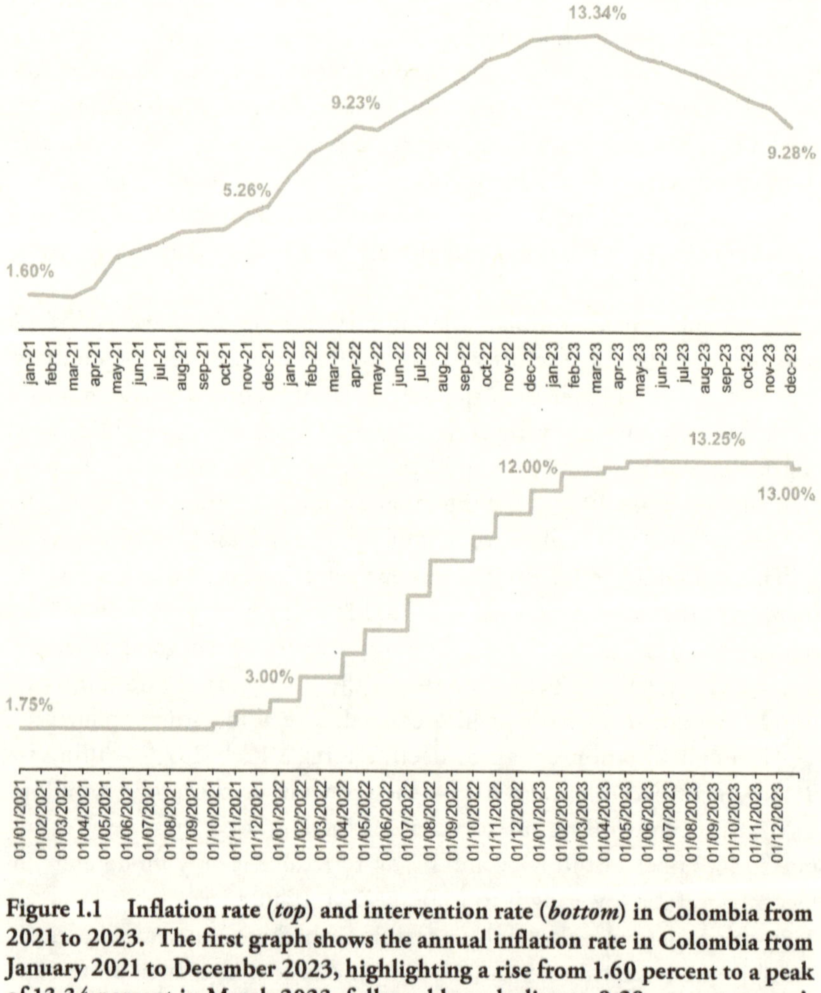

Figure 1.1 Inflation rate (*top*) and intervention rate (*bottom*) in Colombia from 2021 to 2023. The first graph shows the annual inflation rate in Colombia from January 2021 to December 2023, highlighting a rise from 1.60 percent to a peak of 13.34 percent in March 2023, followed by a decline to 9.28 percent at year's end. The second graph presents the Central Bank of Colombia's monetary policy intervention rate for the same period, showing a steady increase from 1.75 percent in early 2021 to a peak of 13.25 percent in 2023, with a slight reduction to 13.00 percent by December 2023.

Source: Author's elaboration based on data from Departamento Administrativo Nacional de Estadística (DANE) and Central Bank of Colombia.

In 1958, Alban William Phillips demonstrated that, in the case of the United Kingdom, there was an inverse relationship between nominal wage growth and the unemployment rate. Phillips's explanation for this inverse relationship was based on workers' bargaining power.[2] According to this view, when labor demand is high (low unemployment), workers have greater bargaining power and can negotiate higher nominal wages. Conversely, when labor demand is low (high unemployment), workers have less bargaining power, causing wages to decline. This relationship forms the basis of the inverse correlation between nominal wages and the unemployment rate.

Paul Samuelson and Robert Solow conducted an analysis similar to that of Phillips in the case of the US economy. However, instead of studying the relationship between nominal wages and the unemployment rate, they examined the relationship between the inflation rate the unemployment rate. In line with Phillips's findings, Samuelson and Solow discovered an inverse relationship between inflation and unemployment—lower inflation rates are associated with higher unemployment rates, and vice versa (figure 1.2).[3] This approach by Samuelson and Solow is now known as the traditional Phillips curve.

One of the key implications of this curve is that economic policymakers have a menu of possible inflation and unemployment combinations.

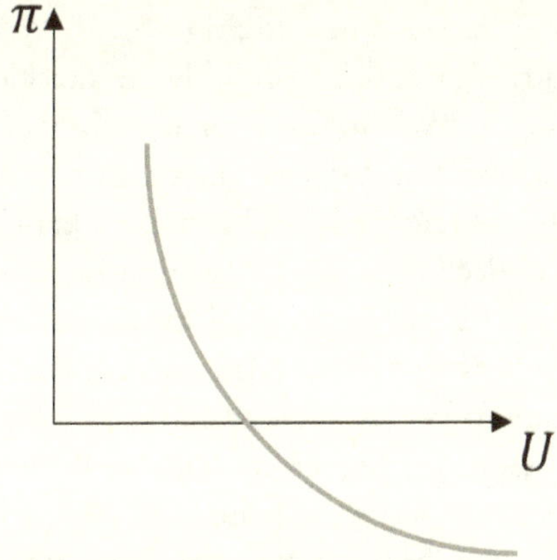

Figure 1.2 Standard downward-sloping Phillips curve illustrating the inverse relationship between the inflation rate (π) and the unemployment rate (U).

Source: Author's elaboration.

Decision makers are responsible for selecting a point on the curve to position the economy. Thus, if inflation is to be reduced, a higher level of unemployment must be accepted.

Consequently, when deciding whether to increase the intervention rate, economic policymakers must also carefully consider the potential effects of this decision on the unemployment rate. The primary goal of raising the intervention rate is to reduce inflation, but according to the traditional Phillips curve, this would lead to higher unemployment. An increase in unemployment has a direct impact on all inhabitants of a country.

At the same time, based on the traditional Phillips curve approach, one could argue that the opportunity cost of low inflation is low employment. In other words, choosing a low inflation rate means forgoing a high employment rate.

Economic trade-offs, such as the one between inflation and unemployment, are of paramount importance to policymakers. In modern economic thought, other significant economic dilemmas have also been analyzed. A notable example is the theoretical approach introduced in 1974 by Arthur Laffer on a napkin during a dinner with Donald Rumsfeld, Dick Cheney, and Jude Wanniski. This dilemma was later named the Laffer curve by Wanniski.[4] The curve illustrates the relationship between a given tax rate and the level of tax revenue.

The logic of the dilemma is as follows: if the tax rate is 0, tax revenue will also be 0. The same outcome would occur if the tax rate were 100 percent because, in this case, there would be no taxable base because no one would be willing to work for an after-tax salary of 0.[5] Using Rolle's theorem, it can be shown that between these two points, tax revenue initially increases as the tax rate rises, but beyond a certain maximum point, tax revenue begins to decline as the tax rate continues to increase.

Thus, contrary to the traditional Phillips curve, where there is only one scenario (lower inflation is associated with higher unemployment), the Laffer curve presents two possible scenarios: (a) higher tax rates lead to higher tax revenue, or (b) higher tax rates result in lower tax revenue beyond a certain point. Therefore, if the Laffer curve is accepted—particularly its second scenario—policymakers face a trade-off between the tax rate and tax revenue, where increasing the former eventually leads to a decrease in the latter (figure 1.3).

Up to this point, two of the most famous economic policy dilemmas have been discussed. However, it is important to remember that policy

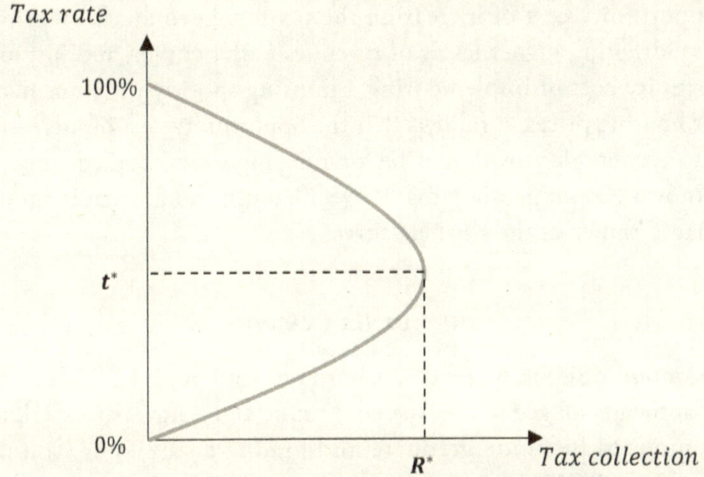

Figure 1.3 The Laffer curve illustrates the hypothesized relationship between the tax rate and tax collection. It suggests that tax revenue first increases with the tax rate, reaching a maximum at the rate t^*, beyond which revenue declines. R^* denotes the maximum tax collection that can be achieved and the level of the tax rate that leads to the collection of the amount t^*R^*.

Source: Author's elaboration.

dilemmas are not exclusive to the field of economics. For example, consider those responsible for a country's housing policy. They often face the dilemma of balancing mass access to housing with housing prices: a subsidy that makes housing more accessible could, by increasing demand, also drive prices up. Thus, a direct relationship can be proposed between housing subsidies (a housing policy decision) and housing prices. In this way, when housing subsidies are granted, maintaining low housing prices is at least partially sacrificed.

On the other hand, in education, we could assume that a policy aimed at improving the quality of education might involve tightening student evaluations. This could result in more students failing the school year, potentially leading to higher dropout rates. Thus, at least in this hypothetical case, a dilemma arises between policies to improve educational quality and school dropout rates. In this scenario, prioritizing the improvement of education quality may come at the cost, at least partially, of higher dropout rates.

Just as the opportunity cost of maintaining a low inflation rate may be sacrificing a high level of employment (Phillips curve), and just as the opportunity cost of increasing the tax rate beyond a certain point may be forfeiting higher levels of revenue (Laffer curve), and just as the opportunity cost of implementing a housing subsidy program may be higher housing prices, it follows that the opportunity cost of increasing a country's economic growth may be forgoing higher levels of equality. This well-known economic dilemma between equity and growth is captured by what is known as the Kuznets curve.

THE KUZNETS CURVE

The economist Simon Kuznets was born on April 30, 1901, in Kharkiv, a city that then belonged to the Russian Empire and is now part of Ukraine. He completed his undergraduate and graduate studies at Columbia University. In 1971, his ideas and contributions to economic growth and income distribution earned him the Nobel Prize in Economics.

Kuznets's two major works on growth and income distribution are his 1953 book *Shares of Upper Income Groups in Income and Savings* and his seminal 1955 article "Economic Growth and Income Inequality." Until the publication of his 1953 work, it was nearly impossible to find an economic study analyzing income distribution based on a sufficiently reliable and extensive data set. Kuznets produced the first historical series on income distribution, focusing on the United States for the period from 1913 to 1948.[6] Based on these data, he concluded that income inequality in the United States declined significantly during this period.

More recently, Thomas Piketty confirmed the quantitative findings presented by Kuznets.[7] As shown in figure 1.4, there was a significant decrease in inequality between 1913 and 1948. Although inequality peaked in 1928—when the top decile's share of national income was nearly 50 percent—by 1948, this share had fallen to 35 percent, marking a 15-percentage-point reduction in the top decile's share of national income.

In 1954, Kuznets, as president of the American Economic Association, delivered a lecture at a conference in Detroit, Michigan, where he presented a possible interpretation of the findings from his 1953 book. This lecture was later published in 1955 under the title "Economic Growth and Income Inequality."[8] In this seminal article, Kuznets developed the hypothesis that gave rise to the theoretical mechanism known as the Kuznets curve. This hypothesis states that in the early phases of economic

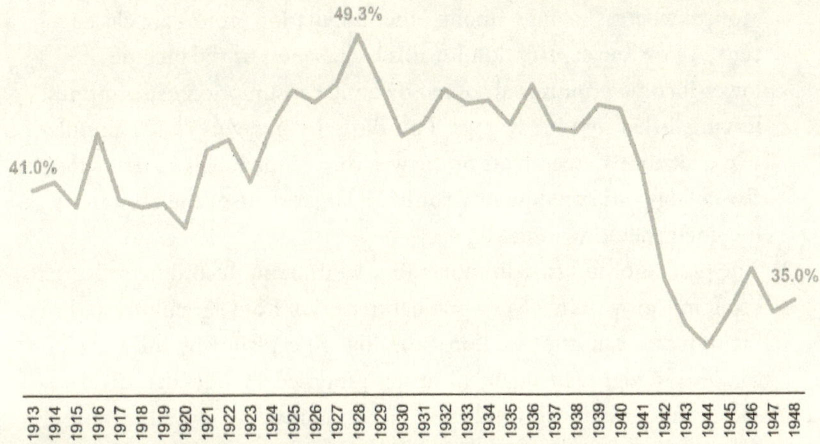

Figure 1.4 The share of total US national income held by the top decile of earners between 1913 and 1948. The share fluctuated around 40 percent during the 1910s; rose steadily to a peak of 49.3 percent in 1928; and then declined sharply during the 1940s, reaching 35.0 percent by 1948.

Source: Author's elaboration based on data from Thomas Piketty, *Capital in the Twenty-First Century* (Harvard University Press, 2014).

growth, income inequality (measured before taxes and excluding government transfers) tends to increase, but in more advanced phases of economic growth, income inequality decreases. Thus, the Kuznets curve represents an inverted U-shaped relationship between a country's level of economic development or income and its level of income inequality. Given this hypothesis, we should have two explanations for the Kuznets curve: one to account for the ascending section of the curve (where higher levels of income are associated with higher levels of inequality) and another to explain the descending section (where higher levels of income are associated with lower levels of inequality).

THE ASCENDING STRETCH OF THE KUZNETS CURVE

In the early stages of economic growth, two main forces contribute to increasing income inequality:

1. The concentration of income among the wealthiest population groups. Kuznets stated that savings are typically concentrated in the wealthiest

groups, whereas savings among other population groups are close to zero. A possible explanation for this is that most of the income of lower-income groups is absorbed by basic consumption expenditures, leaving little room for savings. This disparity in savings has a cumulative effect: the descendants of the wealthiest individuals inherit substantial savings and consequently control a larger share of the economy's income-generating assets.

2. The process of industrialization and urbanization. According to Kuznets, economic growth involves a gradual transition from agriculture and rural life to industrialization and urbanization. To explain why this transition can lead to higher inequality, Kuznets proposed a model that divides society into urban and rural areas. In this model, the overall income distribution of society is understood as a combination of the income distributions of rural and urban populations. In addition, the model assumes the existence of two economic sectors: agriculture (located in rural areas) and industry (located in urban areas). The model is based on three key assumptions:

    - The average per capita income in urban areas is higher than in rural areas, prompting migration from rural to urban areas in search of higher earnings.
    - Income inequality tends to be higher in urban areas than in rural areas.
    - Per capita productivity in industrial activities increases at a faster rate than in agriculture.

Based on these assumptions, the process of industrialization and urbanization can lead to higher levels of income inequality through two mechanisms. First, as more people transition to industrial activities in urban areas, overall income inequality will increase because the expanding urban population represents a growing share of the more unequal of the two income distributions (urban versus rural). Second, the gap between per capita income in rural and urban areas will tend to widen because productivity in industry increases at a faster rate than in agriculture.

These two factors illustrate how the process of industrialization and urbanization—both inherent to economic growth—contribute to rising income inequality. This forms Kuznets' second argument to explain the upward segment of his curve.

THE DESCENDING STRETCH OF THE KUZNETS CURVE

At a certain level of economic growth, the previously direct relationship between growth and inequality reverses. This marks the transition to the downward section of the Kuznets curve, where higher levels of economic growth are associated with lower levels of income inequality. To explain this downward trend, Kuznets poses two key questions:

1. Why does the income share of the wealthiest individuals not continue to increase over time despite the cumulative effect of savings concentration?
2. Why does the income share of the lowest-income population groups rise, even though both the weight of urban income distribution (which is more unequal than rural income distribution) and the gap between urban and rural per capita income continue to grow?

Answering these questions requires identifying forces that counteract the initial drivers of rising inequality in the early stages of economic growth. These new forces are shaped by the following two groups of factors.

First, certain factors counteract the cumulative effects of the concentration of savings. Regarding the first question, Kuznets argues that the dynamism of a free and growing economic society offsets the increase in the income share of the wealthiest individuals, which would otherwise result from the accumulation of savings. His reasoning is that in free-market economies experiencing growth, four key factors emerge:

1. State intervention: Many consider state intervention the most effective tool for counteracting the cumulative effects of wealth concentration. The state can intervene directly by imposing taxes on inheritances and high-income earners, redistributing wealth through social policies funded by these taxes. It can implement expansive monetary policies, such as lowering interest rates, which indirectly reduce returns on assets predominantly held by the wealthy.
2. Demographics: In general, wealthier individuals tend to have fewer children than those in lower-income groups. Over time, the composition of the wealthy class shifts because only a small fraction of today's rich are direct descendants of the wealthy from fifty years ago. Instead, many of today's affluent individuals come from middle- or lower-income backgrounds, demonstrating a process of social mobility that gradually redistributes wealth across generations.

3. Technological change: In dynamic economies, technological advancements diminish the relative importance of wealth accumulated by older industries. As new industries grow at a faster pace, the wealthy must either invest in these emerging sectors or face declining returns on their traditional assets. According to Kuznets, this shift contributes to reducing inequality because "the great and successful entrepreneurs of today are rarely the children of the great and successful entrepreneurs of yesterday."[9]
4. Income from the service sector: Kuznets highlights that disparities in income stem more from earnings in professional and business services than from property ownership. Lower-income individuals have greater potential for upward mobility in the service sector, whereas high-income individuals have less incentive or opportunity to increase their earnings further because (a) wealthy individuals may lack the motivation to engage in high-income service sector jobs, as their predecessors did, and (b) they already occupy high-paying positions, limiting their ability to move into even more lucrative roles. Sectoral mobility is ultimately more accessible to lower-income groups because their opportunity cost of entering higher-paying industries is relatively low.

The second group of factors counteracts the unequal effects of industrialization and urbanization. To answer the second question, we revisit the previously mentioned model, which assumes two regions: the rural area, where the agricultural sector is located, and the urban area, where the industrial sector is based. It is important to remember that the overall income distribution of the population can be understood as a combination of the income distributions of both rural and urban populations.

If income inequality decreases at a certain point in the process of industrialization and urbanization, this implies that an improvement must have occurred in the distribution of income in either the urban or rural areas—or both. However, Kuznets rules out the possibility that the overall improvement is primarily because of advancements in the rural sector for the following two reasons:

1. Because of the rapid decline in the rural sector's weight. The urbanization process leads to a continuous migration from rural to urban areas, reducing the overall weight of rural income distribution in the total population. As a result, any potential improvement in income distribution within rural areas would have a limited impact on overall inequality. Kuznets also points out that, in the case of the United States, a reduction in rural inequality was unlikely because industrialization and technological advancements enabled

larger-scale production units, exacerbating the divide between large, successful commercial farmers and small-scale producers.

2. Given the author's assumption—based on the US experience—that income inequality levels are lower in rural areas than in urban areas, a significant reduction in inequality is more likely to occur in urban areas than in rural ones.

Thus, if income inequality decreases at a certain stage of industrialization and urbanization, it must be the result of a significant improvement in income distribution within urban areas. Kuznets identifies at least three factors that explain why higher levels of economic growth are associated with lower levels of inequality in urban settings:

1. More opportunities for new generations born in the city. The children of rural migrants are native to urban areas, unlike their parents and grandparents. This gives them better access to opportunities such as improved health care and education systems. As a result, they are better equipped to benefit from urban life, securing a larger share of income than their predecessors, who arrived as immigrants and often started from scratch.
2. Increase in production efficiency. Although rural migrants initially struggled to adapt to urban life, over time they acquired skills, knowledge, and experience that enhanced their productivity. As a result, this older urban population, originally from rural areas, gradually increased its share of income as its efficiency in economic activities improved.
3. Growing political power of lower-income groups. In the free and democratic societies Kuznets envisioned, low-income urban residents and their descendants would gain greater political influence over time. This would enable them to advocate for laws and policies that mitigate the inequalities caused by rapid industrialization and urbanization, ensuring a fairer distribution of the country's growing income and preventing wealth from being concentrated in just a few hands.

Considering these two groups of forces, it follows that in advanced stages of industrialization and urbanization, income inequality decreases as economic growth rises. The factors driving the downward stretch of the Kuznets curve influence both ends of the income distribution: they reduce the share of the highest-income groups while increasing that of the lowest-income groups. For instance, state intervention plays a crucial role. Taxes on inheritances and high incomes reduce the wealth concentration among the richest, while protective policies and economic support for low-income groups help increase their share of total income. This was precisely the temporal pattern Kuznets observed in the developed economies of the United States, the United Kingdom, and Germany: a decline in the income share of the richest and an increase in that of the poorest.

For instance, in the United States, the share of the two lowest-income quintiles rose from 13.5 percent in 1929 to 18 percent in the years leading up to World War II, while the share of the richest 5 percent fell from 31 percent to 20 percent over the same period. Similarly, in Great Britain, between 1880 and 1947, the income share of the bottom 85 percent increased from approximately 40 percent to 55 percent, while the share of the richest 5 percent declined from 46 percent to 24 percent.

Kuznets also noted that progressive taxation and government transfers benefiting low-income groups have been a defining feature of developed countries. The implementation of these policies has further reinforced the downward trend of the Kuznets curve.

Figure 1.5 summarizes the factors highlighted by Kuznets that explain the two phases of his curve.

THE STANDARD MODEL OF THE KUZNETS CURVE

Figure 1.6 illustrates the key elements of the standard Kuznets curve model. First, we define a two-dimensional plane: the vertical axis (ordinate) represents income inequality, typically measured by the Gini coefficient, while the horizontal axis (abscissa) represents economic development, usually measured by per capita income. Second, for a given set of countries, we plot the relationship between these two variables, adopting a cross-sectional approach rather than a time-series analysis. Third, we assume a causal relationship where economic growth (represented by per capita income) is the independent variable, and income inequality (represented by the Gini coefficient) is the dependent variable. Finally, we assume that this causal relationship follows a stable pattern with two distinct phases:

1. Both per capita income and inequality rise together initially, indicating a positive relationship between economic growth and inequality.
2. After reaching a certain level of economic development, inequality begins to decline while per capita income continues to rise, reflecting a negative relationship between the two variables. This shift marks a

turning point at which the relationship between economic growth and income inequality reverses.

The implications of the model in figure 1.6 are both encouraging and controversial. On the one hand, the downward stretch of the curve suggests that, beyond a certain point, higher levels of economic development lead to lower levels of inequality. These two elements—economic growth and reduced inequality—are desirable in any society. However, the controversy arises when the ascending stretch of the curve is closely examined.

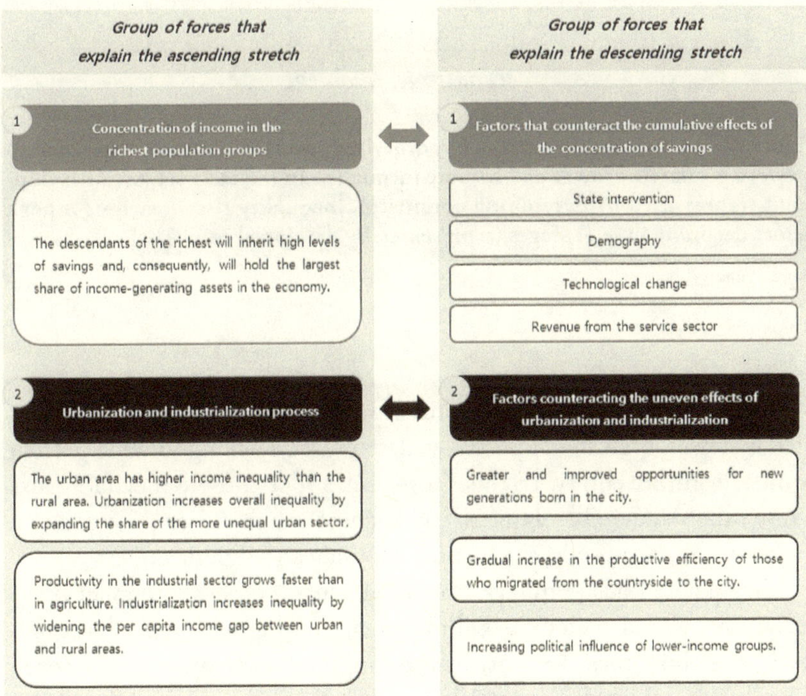

Figure 1.5 Two groups of structural factors associated with the shape of the Kuznets curve. The left panel shows the drivers of rising inequality during the early phases of development: (1) concentration of income in the richest groups and (2) urbanization and industrialization. The right panel shows factors that counteract this trend in later stages: (1) policies and structural changes that mitigate income concentration and (2) forces that reduce inequality generated by urbanization.

Source: Author's elaboration.

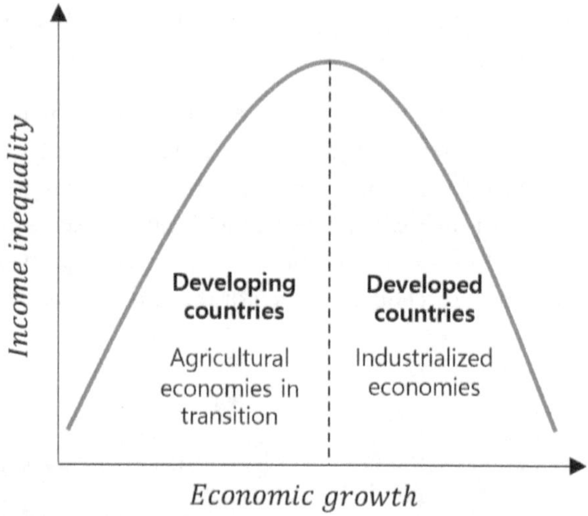

Figure 1.6 The Kuznets curve, a hypothesized inverted U-shaped relationship between economic growth and income inequality. In the early stages of development (represented by developing countries), inequality rises, reaching a peak before declining in later stages (represented by developed countries).

Source: Author's elaboration.

To achieve the desirable situation of higher levels of growth accompanied by lower levels of inequality, society must be willing to trade present equity for future equity. In this short-term process, some inevitably lose while others inevitably gain. A few become much richer than the vast majority and, as a result, the income gap increases significantly.

If inequality leads to misery, disease, violence, crime, and human rights violations, would society be willing to endure higher levels of inequality in the short term so that, in the long term, the dilemma between growth and equity disappears? Is it worth enduring the social sacrifice that inequality brings? This may be too high a cost for society to accept. This also raises an ethical and political debate from the perspective of those responsible for a country's economic policy: Would the leaders of a country be willing to plunge society into greater levels of inequality in the present to sustain future economic growth?

Another implication of the Kuznets curve is extremely important in the current context—where the majority of the population demands that their governments implement pro-equity policies. This implication emerges when reexamining the ascending stretch of the curve. An alternative interpretation of this segment is that lower levels of inequality go hand in hand with lower levels of growth, meaning a situation of equity without growth.

This issue is one of the central themes of this book: to analyze under what circumstances pro-equity policies lead to a scenario where greater equity results in lower growth. But how is it possible that equity could be synonymous with lack of growth? This claim is subject to several counterarguments. For example, studies such as that of Raghuram Rajan and Luigi Zingales conclude that greater equity translates into higher growth.[10] Their findings suggest that more equity creates greater opportunities for poorer population groups to accumulate human capital, ultimately leading to higher economic growth rates.

The findings of Rajan and Zingales illustrate only one possible relationship between equity and growth. In general, a well-designed pro-equity policy agenda fosters a positive relationship between equity and economic growth.[11] However, a poorly designed pro-equity agenda can lead to lower levels of economic growth.

Consider the following examples of how an excessive focus on redistribution can reduce growth. The most common issue in this regard is fiscal policy, where higher tax burdens intended to expand social programs end up discouraging investment and employment—but it is not the only issue. Productivity, growth, and employment objectives can be constrained by poorly designed social policies. For instance, permanent unconditional transfers based on income create a perverse incentive for lower labor market participation or even encourage voluntary informal employment to underreport income, leading to significant distortions in the labor market and social security systems.

Similarly, eliminating negative credit histories while providing public guarantees to facilitate loan access could create a perverse incentive to default on credit obligations. This in turn would ultimately undermine efforts to democratize credit and put the public good of financial stability at risk.[12]

Note that the above interpretation of the Kuznets curve arises from altering the specification of the model discussed in figure 1.6. If higher levels of equity hinder economic growth, then the causal relationship does not necessarily have to flow from growth to distribution.

Kuznets himself was aware of this controversy regarding causality between the two variables. However, economic history ultimately attributed to Kuznets the conclusion that growth affects distribution rather than the other way around. Under this premise, the model in figure 1.6 was proposed.

We prefer to call this model, in which growth influences distribution, the standard model of the Kuznets curve—the version that remained in economics textbooks, even though it does not fully reflect Kuznets's original ideas. As a result, arguments have been introduced in economic policy debates that Kuznets never actually developed. The following analysis by Jorge González, Clara Ramírez, and Alfredo Sarmiento clarifies this point: "It is not appropriate to interpret the Kuznets curve as a causal relationship in which income distribution depends on growth. This approach leads to an erroneous generalization that countries must first grow and only then distribute."[13]

For these authors, based on Kuznets's own approaches, it is also possible to argue that the causal relationship runs in the opposite direction—that a better distribution of income drives economic growth because, "in my [Kuznets's] view, a prerequisite for modern economic growth—the basic philosophy on which it is based and which conveys its great dynamism—is the belief that equal political and economic opportunities must be extended to all groups in society."[14] An unequal distribution of income would be a serious obstacle to economic growth if higher incomes are secured through means that society generally considers illegitimate and unjustified, if these incomes are used to strengthen monopolistic positions or are squandered on frivolous luxuries, if rigid barriers prevent the advancement of the most capable individuals from lower-income groups, and if there is no real consensus on the best way to achieve economic growth and the most effective use of present income.[15]

With these approaches in mind, there is no doubt that, for Kuznets, a better distribution of income generates greater economic growth. In fact, it is a necessary condition for economic growth to occur. This invalidates the previously discussed interpretation of the curve, which suggests that society must be willing to trade present equity for future equity. Renouncing present equity would mean worsening tomorrow's growth—or, in line with Kuznets's perspective, "tomorrow's growth is based on today's equity."[16]

CRITICISMS OF THE KUZNETS CURVE

Kuznets was the first critic of his own ideas. Although his work is considered by many to be the first to analyze the relationship between growth and inequality with a significant degree of statistical rigor, he was aware of the limitations of his analyses and conclusions: "I am well aware of the scarcity of reliable information presented [in this document]. The document is perhaps 5 percent empirical information and 95 percent speculation, part of it possibly contaminated by illusions."[17]

Undoubtedly, the Kuznets curve was bound to face numerous criticisms—and it did. Multiple studies have questioned both its theoretical and empirical validity. Some of the main criticisms are presented below.

THOMAS PIKETTY'S CRITIQUE: A DILEMMA BETWEEN ANALYTICAL RIGOR AND THEORETICAL SPECULATION

Perhaps the most comprehensive critique of Kuznets's ideas comes from Thomas Piketty in his book *Capital in the Twenty-First Century*. Piketty identifies two entirely different profiles of Kuznets in his works from 1953 and 1955. Piketty argues that Kuznets's 1953 book was a rigorous and objective work, establishing the first US national accounts and the earliest historical series on inequality. Kuznets demonstrated "a true research ethic."[18]

In contrast, the Kuznets that Piketty sees in the 1955 article is a speculative one, abandoning rigor and objectivity in favor of gaining recognition and influence by proposing the overly optimistic Kuznets curve. According to this view, Kuznets sacrifices investigative rigor and is more influenced by political considerations.

In line with Piketty's approach, Ivan Lyubimov argues that Kuznets's transition from 1953 to 1955—from scientific analysis in data interpretation to intellectual speculation—was primarily politically motivated.[19] Lyubimov states that "the aim of Kuznets' speech to the American Economic Association in 1954 was to support efforts aimed at keeping developing countries under the influence of developed capitalist states."[20] Thus, the Kuznets curve was presented as a way to convince developing countries that economic growth would ultimately reduce inequality. In the long run, higher levels of growth would lead to lower levels of inequality. Thus, if developing countries prioritized economic growth, they would eventually achieve greater internal political stability and strengthen the legitimacy of their governments. In this effort to boost economic growth, developed countries were willing to assist developing nations, particularly through financial institutions such as the World Bank. Given this context, Piketty asserts unequivocally that the Kuznets curve was a product of the Cold War.

In addition to questioning the theoretical foundations of the Kuznets curve, Piketty offers an explanation based on observable data regarding the evolution of inequality over time and its causes.[21] According to Piketty, the reductions in inequality observed by Kuznets between 1914 and 1945 were not the result of a dynamic of intersectoral change, as suggested by the Kuznets curve mechanism. Instead, he argues that inequality evolved as a result of factors related to economic policy decisions and external shocks rather than the free development of the economic system.

In line with this, Piketty proposes the following hypothesis: if the average rate of return on capital—which includes elements such as land, real estate, equipment, profits, dividends, and intellectual property—exceeds the gross domestic product (GDP) growth rate (which also accounts for population growth), then inequality will tend to increase. To support this argument, Piketty constructs a century-long series on income inequality in the United States, spanning from 1910 to 2010. Two particular periods stand out: (1) from the late 1920s to the end of World War II, when inequality declined (as documented by Kuznets), and (2) from the 1980s onward, when inequality surged (figure 1.7).

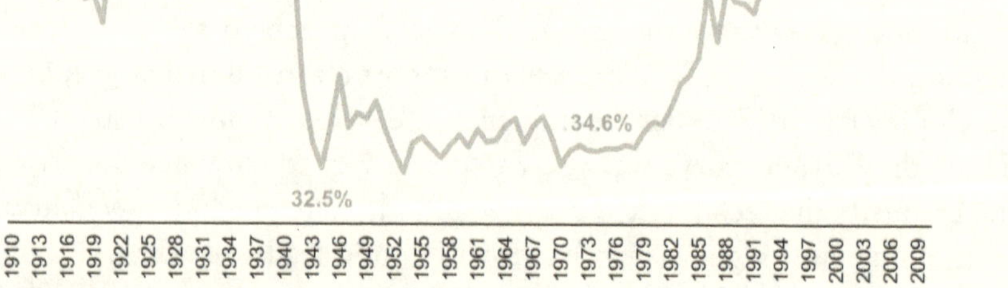

Figure 1.7 Share of US national income held by the top decile from 1910 to 2010. After peaking at 49.3 percent in 1928, the share declined sharply during the 1940s, reaching 32.5 percent, remained stable through the mid-twentieth century, and rose again from the 1980s onward, reaching 49.7 percent in 2007 and 47.9 percent in 2010.

Source: Author's elaboration based on data from Thomas Piketty, *Capital in the Twenty-First Century* (Harvard University Press, 2014).

According to Piketty, the reduction in inequality during the first period was not driven by market forces or the intersectoral transition proposed by Kuznets.[22] It resulted instead from the world wars, the Great Depression, and the severe economic and political shocks these events triggered, particularly for those holding large fortunes. For example, the high tax rates implemented to finance government spending during wartime played a key role.

These factors simultaneously reduced the rate of return on capital and increased the GDP growth rate, leading to a decline in inequality. Beginning in the 1980s, however, with the adoption of deregulation and privatization policies, the rate of return on capital once again exceeded the GDP growth rate, causing inequality to rise.

It should also be noted that the trend of inequality in the United States from 1910 to 2009, as shown by Piketty, closely mirrors the global inequality trend during the same period. As presented in the *World Inequality Report*, the share of the top 10 percent of earners worldwide followed an inverted U-shaped curve from 1920 to the early twenty-first century, starting and ending the period with a share close to 60 percent and reaching a minimum of approximately 54 percent.[23]

Readers should also be aware that some works challenge the ideas put forward by Piketty. These works argue that Piketty manipulated data in his book to obtain results that support his claims.[24] This criticism is unfounded, however, because Piketty's data come from the extensive database of the *World Inequality Report*, which will be used extensively in other sections of this chapter and in subsequent chapters of this book.

Beyond Piketty's criticisms, which challenge the theoretical foundations supporting the Kuznets curve, it is also important to consider empirical studies that have refuted the inverted U-shape of the curve.

A TRADE-OFF BETWEEN EQUITY AND GROWTH THAT SEEMS DIFFICULT TO VALIDATE

Since the emergence of the Kuznets curve, numerous studies have been conducted to test its empirical validity. In reality, more studies refute its validity than support it. Three main lines of research challenge the Kuznets curve: (a) the curve does not exist; (b) the curve appears only when certain countries that create distortions are included in the analysis; and (c) the causal relationship may run from inequality to growth rather than solely from growth to inequality, as suggested by the standard model.

THE KUZNETS CURVE DOES NOT EXIST

A PROBLEM OF ECONOMETRIC APPROXIMATION

In his 2011 book, *The Haves and the Have-Nots*, Branko Milanovic argues that, given the limited data available to Kuznets at the time, he relied on cross-sectional data to support his ideas.[25] When using time-series data, however, Kuznets's conclusions lose validity. Along these lines, the work of Laura Policardo, Lionello Punzo, and Edgar Sánchez compiles a database of thirteen Latin American and Caribbean countries containing information on GDP per capita, the Gini coefficient, and the human capital index for the period from 1970 to 2011.[26] The results of this time-series analysis show that economic growth has little effect on changes in income inequality. More important, there is a threshold of income inequality beyond which inequality itself determines its own changes—that is, differences in income inequality are explained by previous levels of inequality once a certain threshold is surpassed. Specifically, the estimated threshold suggests that when the Gini coefficient exceeds 44 points (a considerably high level of inequality), only past Gini values explain income inequality. At no point does GDP per capita or the human capital index significantly account for changes in inequality.

A SPURIOUS RELATIONSHIP BETWEEN GROWTH AND INEQUALITY

Changes in income inequality, rather than being driven by economic growth, are influenced by the type of country under consideration and the policies implemented there. Gary Fields analyzes various studies that examine structural and political factors alongside economic growth and notes that these works attribute changes in inequality to factors such as urbanization, education, and government intervention.[27] Years later, Fields reaffirms that there is no significant relationship between economic growth and inequality, stating emphatically, "The Kuznets curve is neither a law nor a central trend. The pattern is that there is no pattern."[28] Following this perspective, some studies, using panel data analysis, find that GDP per capita does not explain the behavior of inequality.[29] Instead, inequality is shaped by country-specific characteristics such as natural resources, political systems, and social structures, among other factors.

To highlight that economic growth may not be a determinant of inequality, let us consider a comparison between the United States and Sweden. These two developed countries have exhibited a similar trend in

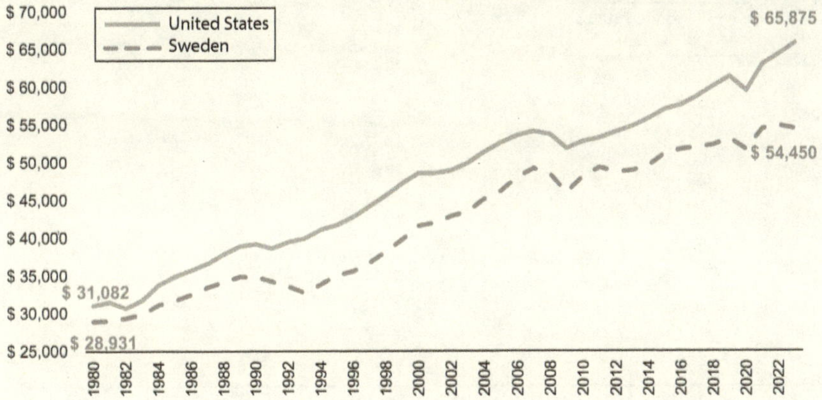

Figure 1.8 Comparison of GDP per capita in the United States (solid line) and Sweden (dashed line) from 1980 to 2023, measured in constant 2015 US dollars. Both countries experienced sustained growth over the period, although the United States maintained higher income levels, increasing from $31,082 in 1980 to $65,875 in 2023, while Sweden rose from $28,931 to $54,450.

Source: Author's elaboration based on data from the World Bank, "GDP Per Capita (Constant 2015 US$)," Data360, https://data.worldbank.org/indicator/NY.GDP.PCAP.KD?locations=US-SE.

GDP per capita over the last forty years, as shown in figure 1.8. Today, both countries rank among the highest in the world in terms of income, with the historical difference in their GDP per capita averaging around $5,700 in favor of the United States.

If the Kuznets curve were an accurate reflection of reality, we would expect to observe very similar levels of inequality in the United States and Sweden between 1980 and 2023, with US inequality slightly lower than Sweden's given its higher income. However, this is not the case. Figure 1.9 demonstrates that, despite comparable levels of economic growth, the disparity in inequality between the two countries is both significant and increasing. Even though the United States has consistently maintained a higher level of income than Sweden, Sweden has exhibited lower levels of inequality at all times.

In short, figures 1.8 and 1.9 underscore that economic growth alone does not determine inequality. Many other variables play a more significant role, further suggesting that the Kuznets curve does not provide a reliable approximation when comparing, for example, the United States and Sweden.

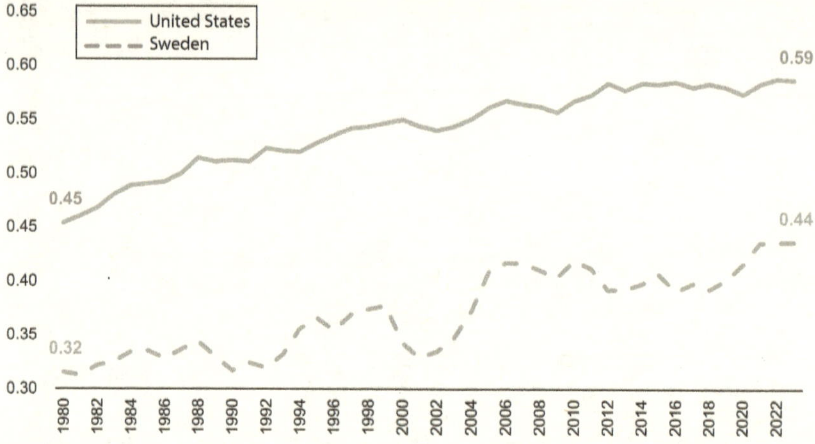

Figure 1.9 Comparison of the evolution of the Gini coefficient in the United States (solid line) and Sweden (dashed line) between 1980 and 2023, calculated using pretax income. The Gini index rose steadily in the United States from 0.45 in 1980 to 0.59 in 2023, indicating increased inequality, while Sweden's Gini increased from 0.32 to 0.44 over the same period, showing a milder upward trend.

Source: Author's elaboration based on data from the World Inequality Database, "Gini Coefficient," https://wid.world/data/.

AN UNOBSERVABLE APPROACH IN DEVELOPED ECONOMIES

The standard theory of the Kuznets curve suggests that developed economies should be in the lower part of the curve—where higher rates of economic growth are accompanied by lower levels of inequality. Numerous studies have documented that this has not been the case in recent decades, however, because developed countries have experienced increasingly high levels of inequality. These nations have achieved high levels of economic development, yet the expected process of reducing inequality has not occurred since the 1980s. Inequality reduction in these countries appears to have reversed (figure 1.10).

In the case of the so-called club of rich countries, better known as the Organisation for Economic Co-operation and Development (OECD) countries, Federico Cingano shows that, at the beginning of the 2010s, the richest 10 percent of the OECD population earned 9.5 times the income of the poorest 10 percent.[30] In the 1980s, this ratio was 7 to 1, and it has been increasing ever since.

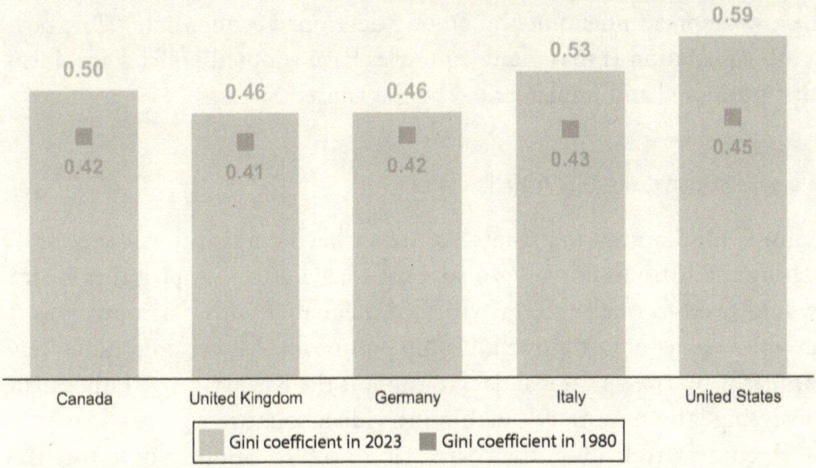

Figure 1.10 Comparison of the Gini coefficients of five developed countries (Canada, the United Kingdom, Germany, Italy, and the United States) for 1980 (squares) and 2023 (bars), calculated using pretax income. In all cases, income inequality increased over time, with the highest level observed in the United States (0.59 in 2023) and the lowest in the United Kingdom (0.41 in 1980).

Source: Author's elaboration based on data from the World Inequality Database, "Gini Coefficient," https://wid.world/data/.

In several instances, the Kuznets curve has been associated with the so-called trickle-down theory, which suggests that policies favoring the wealthy and large entrepreneurs should be implemented to stimulate investment and thus economic growth. According to this theory, higher growth over time will ultimately reduce inequality, aligning with the Kuznets curve. Authors from the Marxist tradition, such as Donald Harris, argue that the trickle-down theory lacks analytical validity and historical basis. Harris contends that capitalist economies do not possess an automatic mechanism that naturally reduces inequality alongside high rates of economic growth.[31]

Perhaps the most emblematic case is the United States—the very country where Kuznets developed his key ideas. Since the early 1980s, the United States has seen its Gini coefficient rise by more than 30 percent, making it the most unequal country among developed economies.[32] Joseph Stiglitz further notes that this trend of rising inequality appears to be a widespread phenomenon among developed economies.[33] One possible explanation is that many countries have adopted policies and ideas first promoted and implemented by the United States.

A U-SHAPED CURVE, THE ANTI-KUZNETS CURVE

John Gallup argues that there has never been empirical evidence validating the Kuznets curve.[34] To support such a claim, empirical evidence would need to track the trajectory of inequality within a country as it experiences economic growth. Gallup points out that existing studies rely primarily on cross-sectional data to support the Kuznets curve rather than analyzing long-term trends within individual countries.

According to Gallup, the correct approach to empirically testing the Kuznets curve is through time series analysis. In line with this, Gallup conducted the first study to assess the Kuznets curve using consistent time series data on inequality across a substantial number of countries (eighty-seven).[35] By estimating two nonparametric models to examine the relationship between inequality and income, the study finds that the relationship follows a U-shape rather than an inverted U-shape. This contradicts Kuznets's original hypothesis and supports what Gallup terms the "anti-Kuznets curve": a strong tendency for inequality to decline with economic growth at low- to middle-income levels, followed by a weaker tendency for inequality to increase at middle- to high-income levels.[36]

The anti-Kuznets curve can be understood as a resurgence of inequality—a phenomenon observed in several countries. Equity gains are reversed beyond a certain point, often leading to an eventual level of inequality that is the same as or worse than at the outset. The United States serves as a clear example of this resurgence, raising doubts about the empirical validity of the Kuznets curve. If one of the world's most developed economies continues to experience high and rising inequality, the notion that economic growth naturally leads to lower inequality becomes increasingly difficult to support.

As previously shown in figure 1.7, the resurgence of inequality in the United States is evident from data on the share of the top decile in national income. Figure 1.11 illustrates the same U-shaped trend in the US Gini coefficient: (1) in 1913, the Gini coefficient stood at 0.56; (2) from 1913 to 1974, despite fluctuations, it reached a low of 0.44; and (3) since then, inequality has resurged, with the Gini coefficient climbing to 0.59 in 2023—a level even higher than that recorded more than a century ago.

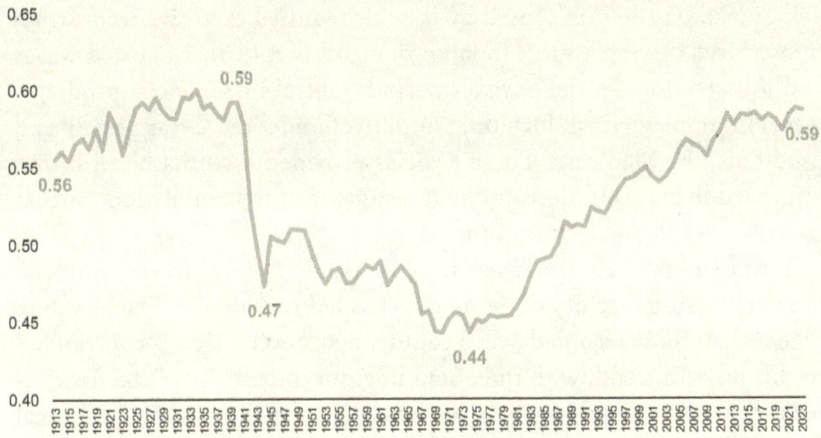

Figure 1.11 Evolution of the Gini coefficient in the United States from 1913 to 2023, calculated using pretax income. Inequality fluctuated around 0.56 in the early twentieth century, declined after World War II to a low of 0.44 in the 1970s, and then increased again, stabilizing near 0.59 in recent years.

Source: Author's elaboration based on data from the World Inequality Database, "Gini Coefficient," https://wid.world/data/.

Figure 1.11 allows us to explore the factors behind both the decline and resurgence of inequality throughout the twentieth and early twenty-first centuries. Between 1939 and 1974, the US Gini coefficient dropped from 0.59 to 0.44, marking a significant decline in inequality. As previously noted, Piketty attributes this downward trend in part to the economic and political shocks caused by World War II.[37]

At least three key factors help explain why World War II contributed to reducing inequality in the United States. First, wartime tax policies were highly progressive; the government imposed steep tax rates on the highest incomes to finance the war effort. Second, the massive destruction of capital during the war disproportionately affected the wealthiest individuals, leading to a temporary decline in wealth concentration and inequality. While these two factors played a role during the war, a third major factor emerged primarily in the postwar period. After World War II, socioeconomic conditions improved significantly, leading to a notable reduction in inequality. One key factor was the growing power of labor unions, which strengthened workers' bargaining positions and contributed to higher wages, thereby narrowing wage gaps. In addition, the widespread destruction caused by the war required extensive reconstruction efforts, driving a surge in labor demand that further boosted wages and job creation. In the postwar period, several major social programs were also implemented, including initiatives under the Great Society and programs like Medicare. These policies provided essential benefits and improved living conditions for large segments of the population, further contributing to the decline in inequality.

From the mid-1970s, when inequality reached its lowest point, a dramatic resurgence began—one that has led to Gini coefficient values higher than those recorded over a century ago. Several factors contributed to this upward trend, with three standing out in particular. The first factor is the widening wage gap driven by skills inequality and technological advancements. The technological progress of the late twentieth century increased the demand for specialized jobs, leading to a growing disparity in wages. Those with the necessary education, training, and skills were able to secure high-paying positions, while those without these qualifications faced limited opportunities and stagnant wages, exacerbating income inequality.

The second factor focuses on the negative effects of globalization. While globalization has provided opportunities to reduce inequality—particularly by facilitating the diffusion of new technologies—its adverse effects have largely prevailed. The second wave of globalization has contributed to rising inequality through several key mechanisms. The first is increased global competition: to remain competitive, many companies have prioritized efficiency and cost reduction, often by cutting labor costs, which has led to wage stagnation or decline. The second is the greater mobility of capital: wealthier individuals and corporations have been able to invest internationally and accumulate more wealth, while lower-income groups have not had the same opportunities. The third is job relocation: many companies have moved low-wage jobs to countries with cheaper labor costs, reducing employment opportunities and exerting downward pressure on wages in high-income countries like the United States.

The third and perhaps most decisive factor behind the rise in inequality in recent decades is the shift in economic policies since the 1980s, particularly the adoption of neoliberal policies under Ronald Reagan in the United States and Margaret Thatcher in the United Kingdom. These policies contributed to rising inequality through several key measures: (1) tax cuts for the wealthy: the reduction of tax burdens on high incomes and capital gains, including the elimination of certain wealth-related taxes, disproportionately benefited the richest individuals; (2) financial deregulation: the loosening of financial regulations led to severe crises, most notably the 2007–2008 real estate crash, which resulted in mass job losses and widespread home foreclosures, disproportionately affecting lower- and middle-income households; and (3) cuts to public spending: reductions in government expenditures, particularly on social welfare programs, weakened support systems for lower-income groups, exacerbating income disparities.

It is important to emphasize that the trends discussed above apply specifically to the United States and do not necessarily reflect the experiences of other developed economies. A notable contrast is France, where inequality has followed a different trajectory. Unlike the United States, where inequality today surpasses levels observed a century ago, France has seen a decline in its inequality index over the long term. As shown in figure 1.12, the Gini coefficient for France stood at 0.60 in 1915, but it had fallen to 0.46 by 2023. Although inequality reached a historical low of 0.43 in 1945, it experienced an upward trend afterward, peaking

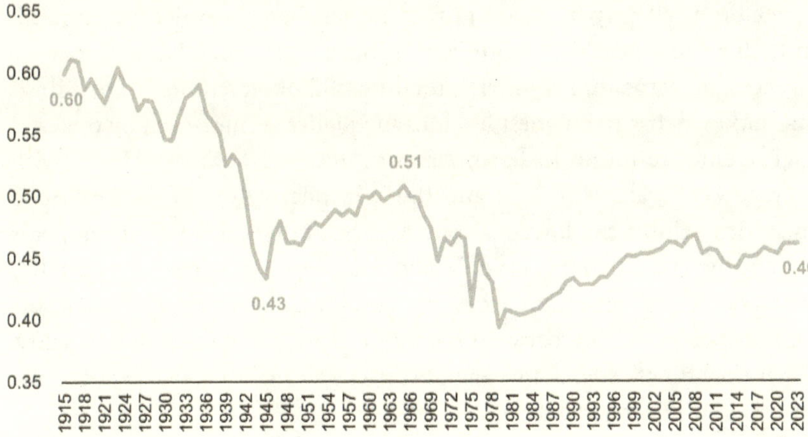

Figure 1.12 Evolution of the Gini coefficient in France from 1915 to 2023, calculated using pretax income. The coefficient was around 0.60 in the early twentieth century, declined notably after World War II to about 0.43, rose moderately in the mid-twentieth century to around 0.51, and then decreased again, stabilizing near 0.46 in recent years.

Source: Author's elaboration based on data from the World Inequality Database, "Gini Coefficient," https://wid.world/data/.

at 0.51 in 1965. However, this year marked a turning point. Since then, France has generally seen a decline in inequality. Notably, the student mobilizations of 1968 triggered political responses that led to the adoption of programs aimed at reducing inequality, contributing to a decline that continued into the early 1980s.

THE KUZNETS CURVE EXISTS, BUT ONLY IF CERTAIN COUNTRIES THAT GENERATE DISTORTION ARE INCLUDED

Some studies fault the Kuznets curve approach for failing to account for what Diya Rattan terms the "Latin America effect."[38] This effect refers to the distortion introduced in empirical analyses by the combination of upper-middle-income levels and persistently high inequality in Latin American countries. As a result, these countries create a pattern that seemingly validates the Kuznets curve, even though their inequality dynamics may be driven by structural and institutional factors rather than economic growth alone.

Klaus Deininger and Lyn Squire argue that economic growth does not drive the evolution of inequality.[39] Instead, historical factors play a more significant role in shaping inequality trends. Their research suggests that inequality itself may influence growth rather than the other way around. In their 1996 study, they compile a comprehensive database on income distribution across 108 countries, totaling 682 observations.[40] Their findings indicate that the highest levels of inequality, as measured by the Gini coefficient, are found in Latin America and sub-Saharan Africa (with average Gini values of 0.50 and 0.45, respectively), while developed countries exhibit the lowest levels. At first glance, this pattern appears to support the Kuznets curve. When examining changes in inequality over a decade of significant economic development, however, the authors find no systematic link between economic growth and shifts in inequality. What they do observe is a strong positive relationship between economic growth and poverty reduction.

Two years later, Deininger and Squire expanded their research by analyzing a database on income inequality that includes at least one Gini coefficient observation for 108 countries, along with data on income distribution across population quintiles for 103 countries.[41] Their study covers a diverse range of nations and yields three key findings: (1) their data provide no support for the Kuznets curve, (2) they identify a strong negative relationship between initial asset inequality and long-term economic growth, and (3) they find that the Kuznets curve appears to hold only as a result of the influence of Latin American data. However, when they control for a regional dummy variable representing Latin America, the Kuznets curve effect disappears. This suggests that cross-sectional analyses are skewed by middle-income Latin American countries, which tend to exhibit high levels of inequality. This phenomenon aligns with what Rattan terms the "Latin America effect," an issue also highlighted in José Gabriel Palma's work.[42]

Palma argues that the inverted U-shaped Kuznets curve emerges primarily because of the inclusion of certain outliers in the data sets.[43] In particular, some Latin American countries distort the analysis, and when these atypical cases are excluded, the empirical validity of the Kuznets curve disappears. This poses a significant challenge to Kuznets's original framework because his model was intended to describe a universal transition from developing to developed economies. If the existence of the curve is contingent on the specific type of economies included in the analysis, it undermines its validity as a general model of economic development.

THE CAUSAL RELATIONSHIP CAN BE FROM INEQUALITY TO GROWTH

As the previous analysis highlighted, Kuznets did not establish a clear causal relationship suggesting that economic growth directly causes inequality. In fact, Kuznets himself acknowledged the possibility of the reverse—that inequality could influence growth. Despite this, the standard model that prevailed in economic history is the inverted U-shaped Kuznets curve, which assumes that growth leads to changes in inequality. In this context, several studies not only challenge the existence of the Kuznets curve but also question the direction of the relationship Kuznets proposed (assuming the standard interpretation of his model). Instead of economic growth driving income inequality, these studies suggest that inequality shapes economic growth.

Roland Bénabou's work significantly deviates from the Kuznets curve hypothesis.[44] His study, both theoretical and empirical, demonstrates that income or wealth inequality is not influenced by the level of economic development. On the contrary, Bénabou argues that inequality, when coupled with a certain level of political power, acts as a major constraint on economic growth.[45] As a corrective measure, he suggests redistributing wealth to the poorest households, which could be achieved through mechanisms such as subsidies or the implementation of a minimum wage.

Philippe Aghion, Eve Caroli, and Cecilia García-Peñalosa explore the relationship between inequality and economic growth in their study, which is divided into two sections.[46] The first section examines the impact of wealth inequality on economic growth and finds that higher levels of inequality have a negative effect on growth, particularly when capital markets are imperfect and agents are heterogeneous. In addition, inequality is detrimental when some agents face institutional constraints limiting their access to investment opportunities. The second section shifts focus to the impact of economic growth on wage inequality. The authors conclude that wage inequality is driven primarily by technological changes rather than by economic growth itself.

A more recent contribution to the study of inequality and growth is the work of Andrew Berg, Jonathan Ostry, Charalambos G. Tsangarides, and Yorbol Yakhshilikov in 2018, which delves into the complex relationship between the two.[47] According to the authors, the optimal distribution of income can be a crucial factor for growth, but determining whether a more equitable distribution supports or hinders growth remains an empirical question. On the one hand, reducing inequality might require substantial redistribution efforts, potentially leading to lower investment and thus slower growth. On the other hand, improving distribution—such as through taxes on activities with negative externalities primarily paid by the wealthy, or transfers aimed at improving school attendance in developing countries—could foster growth. To test this hypothesis empirically, Berg et al. focus on net inequality, which accounts for inequality after taxes and transfers.[48] Their findings, based on a sample that includes both developed and developing countries, suggest that the causal relationship between inequality and growth is indeed valid. They find specifically that lower net inequality is strongly correlated with faster and more sustainable growth.

A body of literature also suggests that income and wealth inequality can influence voters' decisions, which in turn may have significant implications for economic growth. Drawing on studies like those by Alberto Alesina and Dani Rodrik and Giuseppe Bertola, one could argue that societies with high levels of inequality are more likely to elect governments that implement redistributive policies.[49] If these policies are financed by taxes that have a negative impact on investment, however, the result could be slower economic growth in more unequal societies. In this context, the political channel—through the impact of redistributive taxation—becomes a key transmission mechanism through which inequality negatively affects economic growth.

Figure 1.13 summarizes the arguments discussed in this section, including both conceptual and empirical arguments. The empirical arguments

A curve resulting from speculation

Its own author, the first great critic

Kuznets himself stated: "I am well aware of the scarcity of reliable information presented [in this document]. The document is perhaps 5% empirical information and 95% speculation, some of it possibly contaminated by illusions."

Theoretical speculation on analytical rigor (Piketty)

The Kuznets of 1953 was rigorous and analytical in interpreting the data, but the Kuznets of 1955 was influenced by political factors: the curve became a product of the Cold War.

The evolution of inequality is not explained by intersectoral changes but rather by the dynamics of the average rate of return on capital and the rate of GDP growth.

For Lyubimov, the objective of Kuznets's 1955 work was to support the control of developed capitalist countries over developing countries.

A curve that is difficult to validate empirically

The Kuznets curve does not exist

Econometric approximation problem: under time series, the curve disappears.

Spurious relationship: growth has no impact on inequality.

Curve absent in developed economies: in these economies inequality has increased.

Anti-Kuznets curve: U-shaped relationship between growth and inequality.

The Latin America effect

The Kuznets curve is empirically valid only when upper-middle-income countries with high inequality are included in the sample because they generate distortion and alter the results. These countries are typically from Latin America.

Reverse causation

Contrary to what the standard curve model suggests, numerous studies find that the causal relationship runs from inequality to growth rather than the other way around.

Figure 1.13 A typology of criticisms of the Kuznets curve organized into two sections. The upper section presents theoretical critiques, including Kuznets's own doubts and later objections related to analytical rigor and ideological bias. The lower section compiles empirical critiques, highlighting challenges such as the lack of robust econometric results, regional effects associated with Latin America, and reverse causality.

Source: Author's elaboration. Kuznets's quote comes from Simon Kuznets, "Economic Growth and Income Inequality," *American Economic Review* 45, no. 1 (1955): 26.

are divided into those that refute the existence of the Kuznets curve; those that support its existence because of the Latin American effect; and, perhaps most intriguingly, those that suggest causality runs in the opposite direction—from inequality to growth.

SUPPORTS AND ANALOGIES OF THE KUZNETS CURVE

SUSTENANCE

From the previous section, it was clear that numerous studies argue that the Kuznets curve does not hold on a general level. This suggests that the curve cannot adequately describe the transition from developing to developed economies, as it intends to do. It is not an economic law with empirical support. However, other studies suggest that, while the Kuznets curve may not hold universally, it does appear to be valid for certain countries or groups of countries. Research supporting the existence of the Kuznets curve points in this direction.

BRAZIL, RUSSIA, INDIA, CHINA, AND SOUTH AFRICA (BRICS)

For the period from 1990 to 2015, Moheddine Younsi and Marwa Bechtini studied the relationship between economic growth (measured by GDP per capita) and income inequality (measured by the Gini coefficient) for the following five countries: Brazil, Russia, India, China, and South Africa (BRICS).[50] The econometric analysis was conducted using a panel-type database, and the result shows that the Kuznets curve holds for this group of countries. The authors also controlled for a measure of financial development in their regressions and found an inverted U-shaped relationship between financial development and income inequality.

A PARTIAL SUSTENANCE

Using a sample of 162 countries from 1960 to 2011, and employing various estimates from a panel database, the results of Donghyun Park and Kwanho Shin show that the Kuznets curve is partially fulfilled.[51] In what sense is it partial? The authors find an inverted U-shaped relationship between growth (GDP per capita) and inequality (measured by the Gini coefficient), but they also observe that, as growth continues to increase, income inequality begins to rise again. This result is robust, especially when using the income shares of the richest 1 percent instead of the Gini coefficient as the measure of inequality.

SPAIN YES, LATIN AMERICA NO

Leandro Prados de la Escosura conducted one of the most important analyses of inequality in Spain.[52] Examining the period from 1850 to 2000, the author found that the Kuznets curve adequately describes the evolution of inequality in Spain. During times of political instability, inequality levels rose, while in periods of economic growth, inequality decreased. Prados de la Escosura also demonstrates that, from colonial times until about the mid-twentieth century, inequality in Spain followed a pattern similar to that observed in Latin America. In 1950, however, a shift occurred: while inequality in Latin America continued to rise, Spain's inequality began to decrease and converged toward the patterns seen in more developed countries (the United Kingdom, Italy, Norway, Denmark, the United States, and Japan). This decline in inequality in Spain coincided with sustained economic growth. Given these observations, Prados de la Escosura concludes that Latin America remains on the upward slope of the Kuznets curve and has not yet reached the inflection point where further growth would lead to reduced inequality.[53] Therefore, it is not yet possible to validate the existence of the Kuznets curve for the region.

THERE IS ALSO EVIDENCE FOR THE CURVE FOR A HETEROGENEOUS GROUP OF COUNTRIES

Robert Barro focused on the period from the 1960s to the 2000s, using data primarily from the World Income Inequality Database.[54] The number of countries available for analysis varied by decade: for example, data for 54 countries were available in the 1960s, for 120 countries in 1990, and for 92 countries in the 2000s (until 2004). Barro's main findings can be summarized in the following four points: (1) the data confirm the existence of an inverted U-shaped relationship between growth and inequality, which remains stable throughout the study period; (2) globalization has a positive effect on inequality, although it is not of significant magnitude; (3) while international integration may increase inequality, it also boosts economic growth and reduces poverty; and (4) inequality has a negative effect on growth, but this effect diminishes as GDP per capita increases and can even become positive for wealthier countries.[55]

THE COLOMBIAN CASE

Using quarterly data for Colombia from 1977 to 2005, Julio Alonso and Ángela González evaluated whether the Kuznets curve holds for the country.[56] They collected data on the Gini coefficient and GDP per capita for thirteen major cities. The analysis covered both the short and long term: for short-term effects, they used time series data and applied an error correction model; for the long term, they employed cointegration tests and autoregressive vector models. The results of their econometric analysis revealed that inequality worsens in the short term compared to economic growth, but in the long term, greater economic growth translates into less inequality. Based on this evidence, they conclude that, for Colombia, the Kuznets curve is valid.

Analysis by José Antonio Ocampo and Carmen Astrid Romero presents different trends.[57] Their work concludes that there was a distributive deterioration between the 1940s and the mid-1970s, a period of rapid economic growth. This could be considered the upward part of the Kuznets curve, but as a long-term rather than a short-term relationship. Since then, the Gini coefficients have fluctuated between 0.5 and 0.6, some of the highest in the world, in a context of lower growth, with patterns that do not follow any clear relationship with income levels. The distribution improved between the mid-1970s and the 1980s, and improved slightly again between 2009 and 2019, amid strong economic cycles in both periods. Deterioration occurred, however, especially after the market reforms of the 1990s.

ANALOGIES

KUZNETS ENVIRONMENTAL CURVE

The most widely used analogy of the Kuznets curve is related to the environment. Gene Grossman and Alan Krueger are credited with formulating what is known today as the Kuznets environmental curve.[58] This curve explains the relationship between economic growth and the state of the environment. Similar to the standard Kuznets curve, the independent variable in the Kuznets environmental curve is economic growth, while the dependent variable is some measure of environmental deterioration. The focus is on how the dependent variable changes as a country experiences greater economic growth or as it advances in industrialization.

In the early stages of industrialization (or preindustrial stages), primary production and natural resources predominate. These are characteristics of low-income economies, which typically have less of an impact on the environment. Once industrial production takes shape and scales up, however, this increased production leads to higher levels of pollution and environmental degradation. This represents the ascending section of the curve: higher growth results in higher levels of pollution.

At a certain turning point, the economy will shift toward a greater emphasis on the service sector, accompanied by significant technological advances. These changes help reduce the environmental impact of production, resulting in a reversal of the trend. In this phase, higher economic growth translates into lower levels of environmental deterioration, as seen in high-income or developed economies (figure 1.14).

Grossman and Krueger analyzed the relationship between economic growth and air quality by taking a sample of urban areas from

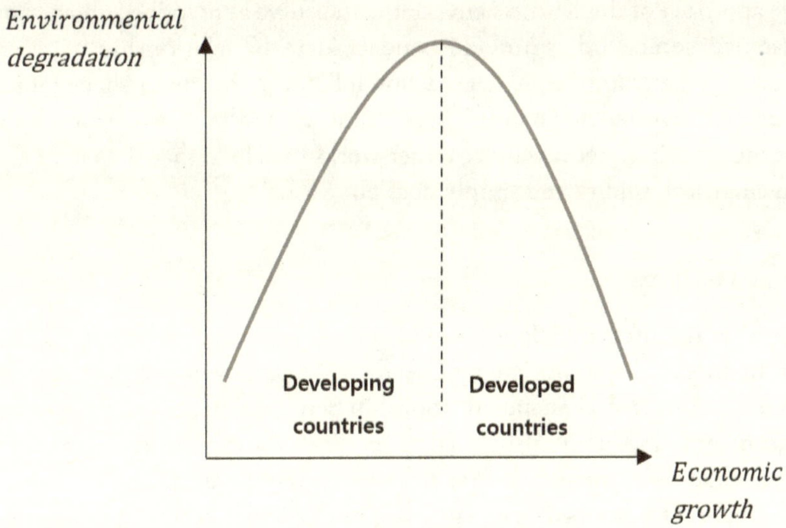

Figure 1.14 The environmental Kuznets curve, which hypothesizes an inverted U-shaped relationship between environmental degradation and economic growth. In the early stages of development (developing countries), environmental degradation increases, but after reaching a turning point associated with higher income levels (developed countries), it tends to decline.

Source: Author's elaboration.

42 countries.[59] They found that for two major air pollutants—sulfur dioxide and smoke—their concentrations in the air increase in the context of low-income countries with lower GDP per capita. As GDP per capita increases in higher-income countries, however, the concentrations of these pollutants decrease.

Several factors could explain the functioning of the Kuznets environmental curve. Patricio Crespo summarizes them as follows: (1) technological and scientific progress, (2) changes in sectoral compositions, (3) increased efficiency in production processes (resulting in less pressure on the environment to improve product quantity), and (4) stricter environmental regulations.[60] The latter is often framed within an institutional approach. In the presence of high growth rates, governments may show greater responsibility toward the environment, which could translate into more stringent environmental regulations. In this regard, Kuheli Dutt studies a set of developed countries known for their better environmental regulations and finds empirical support for the existence of an environmental Kuznets curve in this type of country.[61]

Just like with the standard Kuznets curve, several studies have refuted the approach of the Kuznets environmental curve as described above. For instance, some studies provide evidence that the relationship between growth and environmental degradation follows an inverted J-shape rather than the inverted U-shape.[62] This is known as the weak form of the Kuznets environmental curve. Other works conclude that the curve has no empirical validity and simply does not exist.[63]

KUZNETS FINANCIAL CURVE

Another important analogy to the logic of the Kuznets curve is related to the financial system. Jeremy Greenwood and Boyan Jovanovic established an inverted U-shaped relationship between financial development and income inequality.[64] Inequality increases during the early stages of financial development, but once a certain level of financial and economic development is reached, inequality begins to decline. In the initial phases of economic development, the poorest segments of society lack access to banking services, and the financial sector is underdeveloped. At this point, only the wealthiest individuals have access to banking services, specifically for financing their investment plans. As a result, greater financial development in these early stages leads to greater income inequality. As the economy grows and develops further, however, the poor gain more

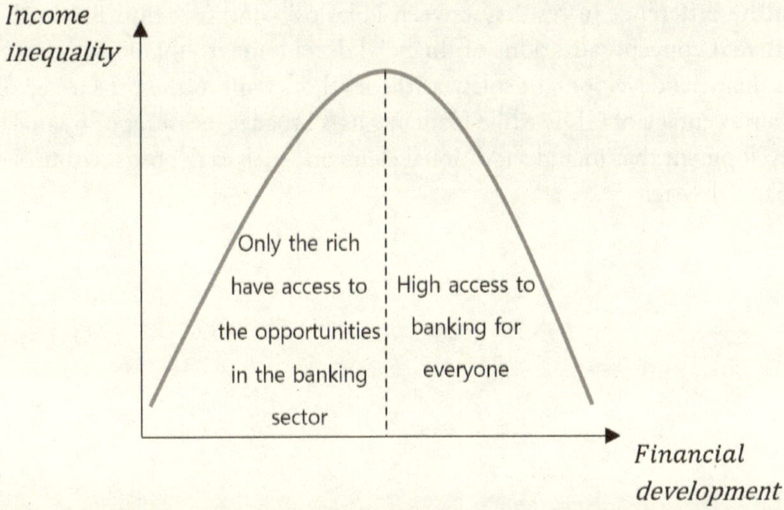

Figure 1.15 The financial Kuznets curve, which proposes an inverted U-shaped relationship between economic development and income inequality. In the early stages of development, financial services primarily benefit the wealthy, but as development progresses, access to the banking system expands, contributing to reduced inequality.

Source: Author's elaboration.

access to banking services and resources. At a turning point, the incomes of the poor eventually begin to rise as they access the opportunities provided by banking, and income inequality begins to decrease with higher levels of financial and economic development. This relationship between financial development and income inequality is graphically represented, as shown in figure 1.15.

The theoretical analyses of Greenwood and Jovanovic are supported by the results obtained from the empirical analysis of Zlatko Nikoloski, who, for a sample of both developed and developing countries during the period 1962–2006, found that there is an inverted U-shaped relationship between financial development and income inequality.[65] In contrast to this result, the work of Onur Özdemir offers a different conclusion.[66] Using a sample of developed and developing countries for the period 1993–2013, Özdemir found that there is a U-shaped relationship between financial development and inequality, meaning that in the long run, more financial development leads to greater inequality. A possible explanation for the difference in results between Nikoloski and Özdemir lies in the different conceptualizations of financial development. Nikoloski considers financial development solely as the level of credit to the private sector as a percentage of GDP, while Özdemir uses broader measures of financial development that include additional elements, such as deposits within the financial system.[67]

CHAPTER 2

The Era of Social Discontent

During the 2010s, conflict in the emerging world has increased dramatically. Both politicians and analysts have agreed on a diagnosis that can be linked to a stretch of the Kuznets curve: although economic growth has occurred and poverty has been reduced, improvements in equity have been minimal or nonexistent. The prevailing sentiment in society is that well-being has reached only a few, generating widespread frustration and genuine concern about the future of certain population groups, such as youth—the segment that most actively participates in social protests.

In many of the protests that have taken place in Latin American countries, young people have been seen wearing T-shirts, waving flags, and holding banners with the same message: "They took everything from us, even our fear." The bearers of this slogan are young people who, unlike their parents and grandparents, had access to universal basic education and health systems capable of addressing any medical situation. Some had not yet entered the labor market for the first time because they were still studying, while many others were just beginning their first work experiences when they came to accuse a society that, in their view, had definitively failed them.

This chapter documents the conflict caused by social discontent. We begin with a description of this concept and the ways in which it is expressed. Based on observable data, we then undertake the task of understanding the world we live in. Data suggest that we are in a situation very similar to the ascending part of the Kuznets curve: we live in a better world in terms of income levels and other variables such as education and health, but it is also a world with significant unresolved issues. These unresolved issues are at the root of current social discontent. They include situations perceived as negative by the majority of the population, such as the unequal distribution of income, the lack of opportunities for young people, and the gender gap disadvantaging women, among others.

Finally, we move from data analysis to case studies. We examine a series of events that have occurred in certain emerging countries, reflecting the dissatisfaction of specific social groups in response to situations they perceive as negative. For example, in the case of Latin America, we will see that the region encompasses all the sources of discontent identified in our analysis of observable data.

SOCIAL DISCONTENT

WHAT IS SOCIAL DISCONTENT?

In an ideal world, everyone would agree and feel comfortable with the economic, social, political, and environmental context in which they live. No one would demand a better distribution of income or greater environmental protection, or express dissatisfaction with gender wage gaps. That would be an ideal world, however; in reality, such a scenario becomes more removed by the day.

In the real world, it is nearly impossible for all citizens to feel satisfied with every aspect of their living conditions. What some may see as unjust economic policies, others may perceive as fair and necessary measures. When a social group views a particular aspect of its environment negatively, we describe this as a situation of social discontent. The Economic Commission for Latin America and the Caribbean (ECLAC) describes it as follows:

> Social unrest is linked to a negative perception of various aspects of social life. It can stem from disapproval of elements within the socioeconomic structure, the political and institutional framework, or social relations. This unrest manifests as dissatisfaction with the exercise of public power, political representation, and the distribution of well-being, as well as distrust toward institutions and individuals, and feelings of insecurity.[1]

Because a given situation may be perceived negatively by some but positively by others, discontent must be analyzed by considering different population groups rather than applying a generalized perspective to an entire society. For instance, in the case of the United States, Joseph Stiglitz explores the impact of taxes on large corporations and the wealthiest individuals.[2] For many, such measures are beneficial because they provide the state with additional resources for social investment. From the perspective of large corporations and the wealthiest, however, higher taxes may be seen as detrimental, potentially leading these groups into a state of discontent.

The key point is that social discontent has significant political and economic repercussions. Population groups experiencing discontent demand changes in power structures to influence policy decisions in their favor. Stiglitz argues that, in his bid for the presidency in 2017, Donald Trump capitalized on the discontent of the wealthiest individuals and large corporations, assuring them of policy changes in exchange for their support during his campaign:

> Some of Trump's supporters acknowledge that his policies are far from perfect, yet they defend him by saying: at least he is paying attention to those who have long been ignored; at least he has given them the dignity and respect of being heard. I would put it differently: he has been shrewd enough to recognize the disgruntlement, to fuel the flames of discontent, and to exploit it ruthlessly.[3]

Once in office, Trump implemented a tax reform that granted a series of tax exemptions to the wealthiest individuals and large corporations, following the logic of trickle-down economics—the idea that greater investments would indirectly benefit other social sectors.[4] At the same time, however, taxes were raised for the middle class. In addition, to protect national companies, a series of protectionist measures were introduced, echoing the principles advocated by mercantilists in the distant past.

The chapter discussion so far represents discontent from the perspective of the wealthiest individuals and large corporations—a relatively small but highly influential group. Stiglitz also examines the discontent among lower-middle-income groups and marginalized populations that have long been overlooked in US economic policy, such as young people, Blacks, and women.[5] Inequality in the United States has risen dramatically. As discussed in chapter 1, most of the gains from economic growth have benefited the wealthiest, leaving most of US society increasingly fragmented and unequal. There remains a stark divide between Black and white communities; securing employment has become increasingly difficult for young people, leading to relatively high unemployment rates in this group; and real wages for lower-middle-income individuals have remained stagnant for years. These unfavorable conditions have fueled widespread social discontent across much of the US population.

The discontent of the middle classes and minorities is neither a recent phenomenon nor exclusive to the United States. Stiglitz documented this in his 2002 book, *Globalization and Its Discontents*. While globalization has brought significant economic benefits—such as the opening of new markets and improved living standards for some—Stiglitz argues that, for hundreds of millions of people worldwide, globalization has failed to deliver positive outcomes and has instead fueled discontent among certain population groups.[6] According to Stiglitz, this discontent arises when globalization occurs without adequate state support, leading to job losses, weakened democracies, and the erosion of cultural identities.

In addition to the work by Stiglitz that we reviewed earlier, we can also refer to Nesrine Malik's 2019 book, *We Need New Stories: Challenging the Toxic Myths Behind Our Age of Discontent*.[7] In this work, Malik argues that for years we have been told various narratives that do not align with reality and have instead served to obscure the harsh political, social, and economic conditions in which we live. These narratives, which she calls myths, have fueled the widespread discontent we see today and have been crafted and disseminated by the groups that hold power and control over the means of communication.

Among these myths, Malik highlights the myth of gender equality. This myth leads society—particularly women—to believe that their conditions and opportunities are more than adequate and better than ever before. Malik argues that this narrative falls apart when one considers evidence showing that women today face increasing insecurity, a persistent and even widening gender wage gap, the reversal or lack of recognition of abortion rights, and the growing prevalence of sexual harassment. Given these realities, it is entirely understandable that women are among the key groups driving the current wave of social discontent.

Social discontent is a concept that must be carefully analyzed, always specifying the perspective from which it is being examined. What constitutes discontent for some may not be the same for others. It has also been shown that discontent is not confined to any particular group: both the richest and the poorest can experience it.

WHAT DIMENSIONS CAN BE THE CAUSE OF SOCIAL DISCONTENT?

People can feel dissatisfied with multiple dimensions of the society they live in. For example, they may perceive as negative the high levels of pollution caused by large companies that dispose of toxic waste in the open

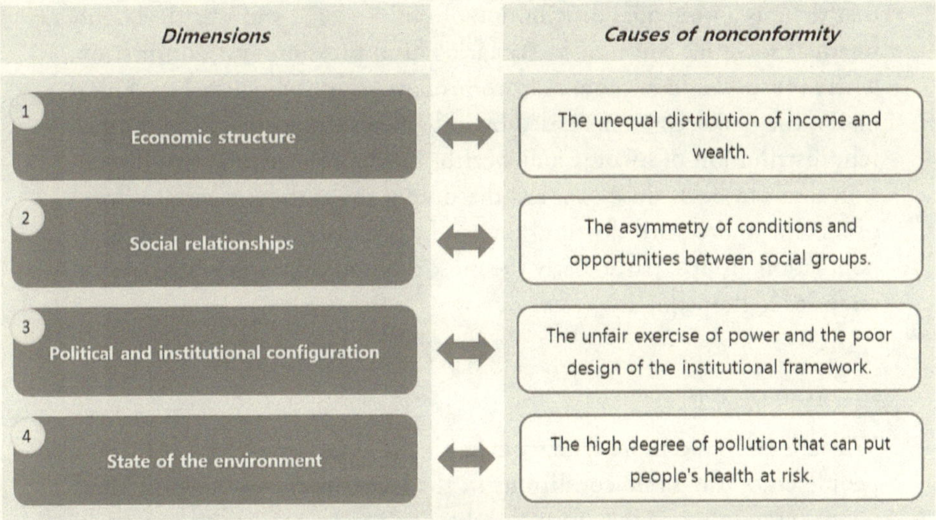

Figure 2.1 Four structural dimensions that contribute to social discontent: economic structure, social relationships, political and institutional configuration, and the state of the environment. Each dimension is associated with specific sources of nonconformity, including unequal income distribution, social asymmetries in opportunities, institutional failures in the exercise of power, and environmental risks affecting public health.

Source: Author's elaboration.

air or in bodies of water without facing any penalties or being required to compensate society in some way for their actions. A population group may feel dissatisfied with the institutional structure of its society, arguing that it is poorly designed and managed, leading to harmful situations such as electoral fraud. The examples are numerous, but in general terms, we can group the negative perceptions of social groups into four major dimensions. The dimensions we propose in figure 2.1 are based directly on the classification presented by ECLAC, but we have added additional dimensions and elaborated on some of the existing ones in greater detail.[8]

ECONOMIC STRUCTURE

Why do some people earn very low salaries while others earn very high ones? Or why are some very poor while others are very rich? A significant number of people ask themselves these questions every day, believing that there is an unequal distribution of both income and wealth. Highly unequal societies can lead to scenarios of oppression and domination, where those who have more exert control over those who have less. This is one of the major concerns raised by individuals dissatisfied with the current distribution of income and wealth. In this context, the first dimension that can be a cause of social discontent refers to how certain forms of income and wealth distribution can be perceived as negative by some population groups, particularly the most economically vulnerable in situations of high inequality.

SOCIAL RELATIONS

Why are men paid more than women for the same job? Why don't young people enjoy the same conditions in the labor market as adults? Many people argue that serious forms of discrimination against certain social groups still persist in society. For example, it is often pointed out that men's salaries are still relatively higher than women's, meaning that both groups do not operate under the same conditions, which in turn indicates strong discrimination. But beyond that, society itself appears to have created and reinforced mechanisms that prevent everyone from enjoying the same opportunities. Much of today's social discontent is expressed by young people, who find themselves in a frustrating dilemma: they need experience to get a job, but they cannot gain experience because no one will hire them. These are just a few examples of how deep asymmetries emerge within the same society. Thus, this second dimension encompasses the discontent of those groups that perceive these asymmetries as a significant source of discrimination and lack of opportunities.

POLITICAL AND INSTITUTIONAL CONFIGURATIONS

If the goal of exercising political power is to generate higher levels of well-being in society, how can people's quality of life worsen over time? Why does the institutional framework that governs society become increasingly opaque and facilitate acts of corruption among those in power instead of promoting transparency in political actions? Electoral fraud, abuses of power against citizens, policy decisions that go against the interests of society—especially the most vulnerable—are some of the undesirable outcomes when those who rise to political power prioritize their own well-being over that of society as a whole. This type of behavior is further exacerbated by weak institutional structures that fail to provide the necessary safeguards to control and penalize misconduct by those in decision-making positions. Socially undesirable policy configurations and fragile institutional frameworks that enable corruption fuel a growing sense of discontent in the modern world—one where more and more groups are aware of the consequences of policies designed for the few rather than the many.

STATE OF THE ENVIRONMENT

If the resources provided by nature are scarce, why do companies continue to destroy the environment without facing any consequences? Why do we allow companies to increase their profits at the cost of polluting the water we drink and the air we breathe? Perhaps today more than ever, people have become aware of and raised their voices about an issue that for many years remained outside the public interest: the state of the environment. Actions that recklessly harm the environment have been increasingly condemned. This fourth and final dimension aims to clarify the extent to which the interests of a few can exceed the limits of what our environment can sustain. People express their discontent with practices that threaten the preservation of natural resources and the quality of life that the environment provides to humanity.

WHAT MEANS ARE USED TO EXPRESS SOCIAL DISCONTENT?

When a social group perceives a particular situation as negative, it is expected that what Mancur Olson called the logic of collective action will emerge.[9] Collective action refers to the coordination of efforts among individuals to achieve the group's shared interests while simultaneously seeking personal benefits from collective achievements. Thus, social discontent can act as a catalyst, driving those facing similar issues to act collectively to address what they perceive as harmful, based on their historical experiences, cultural values, and normative principles.[10] Grounding his analysis in economic rationality, Olson argues that there is a direct relationship between the perceived personal benefit and an individual's willingness to contribute to the group: the greater the personal benefit of participating, the higher the willingness to contribute, and vice versa. According to this logic, Olson asserts that shared interests do not necessarily guarantee collective success because individual benefits may not always justify the costs of contributing to the group's objectives. Olson also highlights that smaller groups tend to be more effective than larger ones in coordinating their efforts because individual contributions are more visible and the perceived benefits for each member are more directly linked to the group's overall achievements.

Individuals who choose to engage in collective action as a result of social discontent typically do so with the expectation that the benefits they receive will be sufficient to compensate for the costs involved. Their actions generally aim to design and implement mechanisms to achieve the following objectives: (1) to strengthen ties and build consensus among members of the group that feels disadvantaged; (2) to convey their message of discontent and demands to the rest of society—that is, to make their grievances and claims visible; (3) to direct their demands specifically toward those who have some degree of influence over the situation that has caused the group's dissatisfaction, with the goal of bringing about meaningful change in the current state of affairs. The means by which social groups pursue these objectives—in other words, the mechanisms for expressing social discontent—can be classified into three main categories. Based on the classifications developed by Sidney Tarrow and Víctor Barrera and Carlos Hoyos, these categories are conventional means, disruptive means, and violent means.[11]

CONVENTIONAL MEANS

Groups that use conventional means express their nonconformity without temporarily or permanently disrupting the routine functioning of society and without resorting to violence. Examples of conventional means include peaceful marches and rallies. In general, when people organize a peaceful march, the march often involves demonstrators using major roads and routes, making it difficult for land transportation to pass. As a result, many people may arrive late—or not at all—to their daily activities. While this does impact the routine functioning of society, such disruptions typically last only a few hours and are not accompanied by acts of violence that impose significant costs on society.

DISRUPTIVE MEANS

Another way in which social groups express their nonconformity is by temporarily or permanently altering the routine functioning of society, without necessarily resorting to serious acts of violence—although there may be a threat of violence. Occupations of buildings and other structures and invasions are examples of disruptive means. The occupation of a building can last for an indefinite period, during which the routine functioning of the occupied entity is disrupted, although dissenting groups may not engage in acts of violence. For example, if a criminal court is occupied, the execution of sentences would be delayed for the duration of the occupation.

VIOLENT MEANS

This last category encompasses the most harmful means of expression for society as a whole. In these scenarios, social groups express their nonconformity by temporarily or permanently disrupting the routine functioning of society through acts of violence against people or property. Violent marches, riots, and looting are some of the main examples of violent means. In these cases, it is common to witness the destruction of both public and private property, disruptions to services provided by entities such as banks, and intense confrontations between groups expressing widespread discontent and members of security forces, among other undesirable consequences for society. Compared to the tactics employed in conventional and disruptive means, violent and often extralegal actions generally require less organization and coordination for execution—it is often easier to plan destruction and theft (sometimes even spontaneously) than to organize a peaceful and orderly demonstration.

THE IMPACT OF DIGITALIZATION

It is important to highlight that, regardless of the medium of expression, digitalization has played a central role in generating and disseminating social discontent, especially in recent years, because of technological advances that enable any type of information or event to spread almost instantly and on a massive scale. Digitalization has not only facilitated access to information but has also intensified exposure to social issues related to inequality and injustice by providing a platform where anyone can raise their voice, allowing narratives of discontent to reach broad and diverse audiences.[12] Platforms such as X (formerly Twitter), Facebook, and TikTok have become key arenas for amplifying social discontent because they connect individuals facing similar struggles and mobilize them toward collective action. A clear example of this phenomenon is the Yellow Vest movement in France, which began in late 2018 as a protest against a fuel tax. Through social media dissemination, the movement quickly evolved into a broader discourse denouncing economic and social inequality, demonstrating the power and reach of digitalization in articulating and transmitting social discontent.

While digitalization has brought significant benefits to societies—such as making information far more accessible to the general public—it has also had negative effects on democratic systems. Researchers like Ernesto Calvo and Natalia Aruguete argue that the spread of false information on social media can influence individuals' decision-making processes, ultimately harming the functioning of democratic systems.[13] Byung-Chul Han introduces the concept of infocracy to analyze how digitalization has altered the fundamental characteristics of democracy.[14] According to his study, infocracy disregards truth as its foundation, and essential democratic practices such as debate and transparent dialogue are replaced by questionable strategies, including information warfare, political marketing tactics, and algorithmic manipulation (e.g., the use of bots or big data to shape public opinion). In such scenarios, when truth is replaced by media manipulation, the fundamental principles of democracy are severely eroded.

It has been documented that, in practice, social discontent has been rising in recent years across various social groups. These groups demand better living conditions, a more equitable distribution of resources, opportunities for all rather than a privileged few, and greater environmental protection from their governments and leaders. Broadly speaking, it seems that there is a growing demand for a better world for all—a situation that is undoubtedly desirable from the perspective of any policy that is coherent and responsible toward its citizens. The data support this. David Clark and Patrick Regan compiled a database of protests that took place in more than 160 countries (excluding the United States) between 1990 and 2019.[15] The authors define a protest as a gathering of fifty or more people making a demand to the government. For each recorded protest, they indicate whether demonstrators committed acts of violence against the state. Between 1990 and 2019, a total of 11,925 protests against governments were recorded worldwide, with 3,206 of these involving acts of violence by demonstrators—that is, one in four protests included violent actions against the state. The highest number of protests was recorded in 2019, with a total of 813 (figure 2.2).

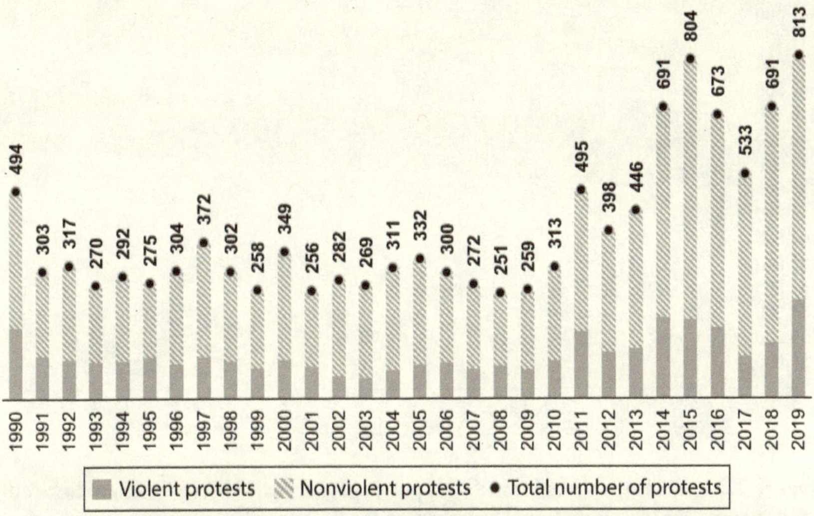

Figure 2.2 Number of antistate protests worldwide, disaggregated by type: violent protests (solid bars), nonviolent protests (patterned bars), and total number of protests (black dots), from 1990 to 2019.

Source: Author's elaboration based on data from David Clark and Patrick Regan, *Mass Mobilization Protest Data* (Harvard Dataverse, 2016).

It is important to determine whether the world we live in today is a better or worse place for everyone in order to identify the factors that have ignited the flames of discontent. Thus, the question to be addressed in the next two sections revolves around the conditions in which societies and individuals find themselves in the modern world.

UNDERSTANDING THE WORLD WE LIVE IN

A MORE NONCONFORMIST BUT BETTER WORLD

A WORLD WITH MORE WEALTH

We have witnessed an increase in the number of various social groups around the world demanding better living conditions. Numerous social movements have emerged in support of this widespread call for change. The father of modern economics, Adam Smith, stated in 1776 that a country becomes wealthier as its population gains access to more goods and services to satisfy their needs.[16] From this perspective, the wealth of

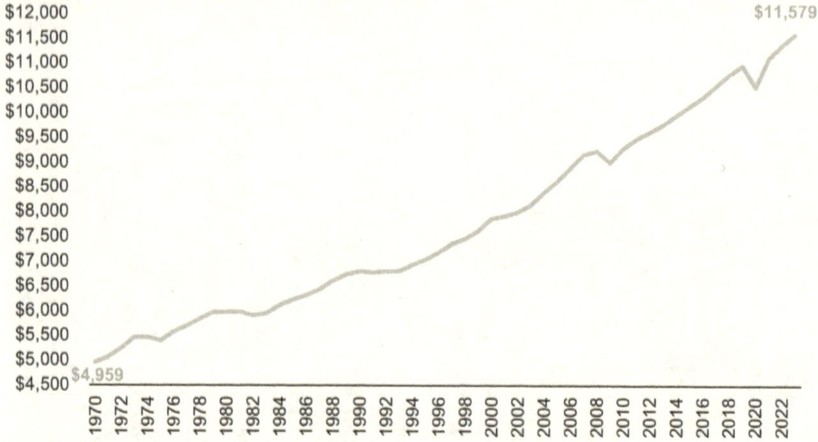

Figure 2.3 Evolution of global GDP per capita from 1970 to 2023, measured in constant 2015 US dollars. Starting at $4,959 in 1970, income per capita increased steadily despite temporary slowdowns in the 1980s and during the 2008 global recession and the 2020 COVID-19 pandemic, reaching $11,579 in 2023.

Source: Author's elaboration based on data from the World Bank, "GDP Per Capita (Constant 2015 US$)," Data360, https://data.worldbank.org/indicator/NY.GDP.PCAP.KD.

a nation is linked to its total output. Based on Smith's criterion, we can assert that, despite widespread discontent, the world has never been a better place to live. Today, the average citizen enjoys better living conditions than those of any past era. This idea is illustrated in figure 2.3.

The world increased its gross domestic product (GDP) per capita by approximately 134 percent from 1970 to 2023. While most regions have seen improvements, some have performed significantly better than others. For example, between 1970 and 2023, Latin America and the Caribbean increased its GDP per capita by 106 percent, Europe and Central Asia by 142 percent, the United States by 161 percent, and East Asia and the Pacific by 559 percent. We say "most regions" because, in certain parts of the world, the increase has been minimal. In sub-Saharan Africa, for instance, GDP per capita was USD 1,360 in 1970 and had risen to only USD 1,581 by 2021—an increase of just 16 percent (figure 2.4).

Clearly, the differences between countries are even more pronounced than those shown in figures 2.3 and 2.4. Some nations have performed significantly better than others, yet the same overall conclusion holds:

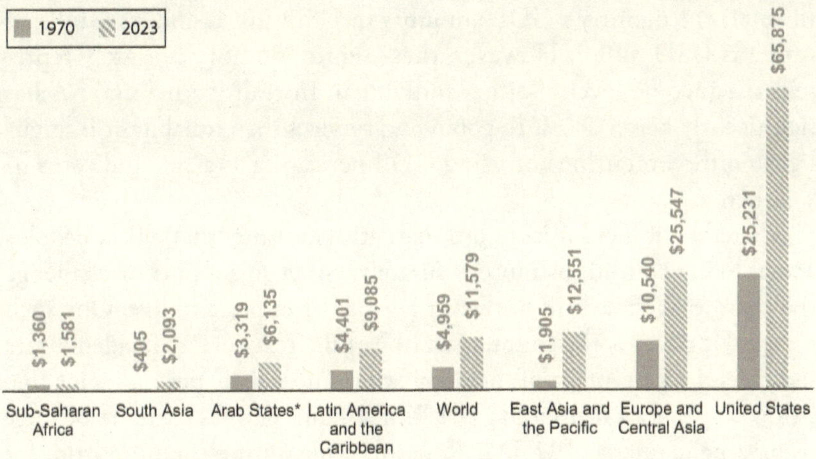

Figure 2.4 Comparison of GDP per capita across world regions in 1970 (solid bars) and 2023 (patterned bars), measured in constant 2015 US dollars. The data show significant disparities in income levels and growth patterns, with the United States recording the highest GDP per capita in both years, increasing from $25,231 to $65,875, while sub-Saharan Africa and South Asia remained at the lowest levels.

Note: * The 1970 data correspond to 1975.

Source: Author's elaboration based on data from the World Bank, "GDP Per Capita (Constant 2015 US$)," Data360, https://data.worldbank.org/indicator/NY.GDP.PCAP.KD.

most countries have improved their economic situation, as reflected in the growth of their GDP per capita. For example, in 1970, Colombia had a higher GDP per capita than South Korea (USD 2,421 versus USD 1,977). Although both countries experienced growth rates exceeding the global average of 134 percent by 2023, Colombia's' GDP per capita grew by 182 percent, reaching USD 6,819, whereas South Korea's soared by 1,626 percent, reaching USD 34,121.

A WORLD WITH FEWER POOR PEOPLE

One of the main weaknesses of GDP per capita as a measure of a country's living conditions is that it does not accurately reflect citizens' actual access to the goods and services produced in the economy. Consider a hypothetical country with only two inhabitants: inhabitant A earns an annual income of USD 1,000, while inhabitant B earns just USD 1.

In total, the country's GDP amounts to USD 1,001, and its GDP per capita is USD 500.5. However, these figures do not accurately represent the income level of either individual. In reality, inhabitant A has significantly better access to goods and services than inhabitant B, highlighting the limitations of using GDP per capita as a sole indicator of well-being.

Therefore, it is essential to use alternative measures that reflect people's actual living conditions more accurately, either to support or challenge the claim that the world has never been a better place to live. One such measure is poverty, the counterpart of wealth. The poverty incidence rate indicates the percentage of the population with a daily per capita income below a specified threshold. The World Bank defines extreme poverty using a benchmark of USD 2.15 per day, measuring the proportion of people living below this level. In 1981, 44.0 percent of the global population lived on less than USD 2.15 per day. By 2022, this figure had dropped significantly, to 9.0 percent (figure 2.5).

One could argue that, although extreme poverty has decreased in relative terms, it may have increased in absolute terms because of the rapid

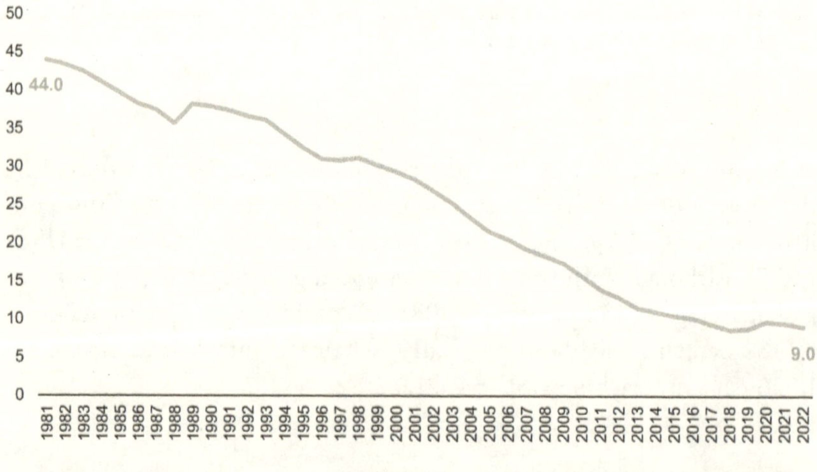

Figure 2.5 Global extreme poverty incidence rate based on $2.15 per day (2017 purchasing power parity), measured as the percentage of the population living below this threshold from 1981 to 2022. The incidence of extreme poverty declined significantly, falling from 44.0 percent in 1981 to 9.0 percent in 2022, reflecting substantial progress in poverty reduction.

Source: Author's elaboration based on data from the World Bank, "Poverty Rate, Percent $2.15," Poverty & Inequality Indicators, https://pip.worldbank.org/poverty-calculator.

population growth of recent decades. However, this is not the case. In 1981, the global population was 4.52 billion, rising to 7.99 billion by 2022. This means that in 1981, approximately 1.99 billion people lived on less than USD 2.15 per day, whereas this number had fallen to 719 million by 2022. In other words, over forty-two years, the absolute number of people living in extreme poverty—based on the incidence rate—declined by 1.27 billion, a figure nearly equivalent to 90 percent of India's total population in 2022. Thus, not only do we live in a world with a greater abundance of goods and services, but it is also a world with significantly fewer people in extreme poverty.

We can also analyze poverty reduction by region. In 1990, the number of people living below the extreme poverty incidence rate was 71 million in Latin America and the Caribbean, 285 million in sub-Saharan Africa, and 1.187 billion in East Asia and the Pacific. Over time, all three regions made progress in reducing poverty, although the extent of improvement varied significantly. By 2022, only 3.5 percent of the population in Latin America and the Caribbean—approximately 23 million people—remained below that poverty line, representing a 68 percent reduction in absolute numbers. East Asia and the Pacific achieved even more remarkable results, with just 1.0 percent of its population living in extreme poverty by 2022. In absolute terms, this equates to around 24 million people, marking a 98 percent reduction over thirty-two years.

However, the situation in sub-Saharan Africa presents a more complex picture. Between 1990 and 2019, the region's extreme poverty incidence rate declined by nearly 18 percentage points. Yet when considering absolute numbers, extreme poverty actually increased. By 2019, 418 million people lived below the poverty line in sub-Saharan Africa—47 percent more than in 1990. This underscores the importance of examining both relative and absolute figures when evaluating progress in poverty reduction (figure 2.6).

A WORLD OF MORE FAVORABLE LIVING CONDITIONS

Life expectancy is a key indicator of a country's well-being because it reflects the population's overall health, quality of life, and access to essential services such as nutrition, health care, and public infrastructure. Generally, higher life expectancy suggests better living conditions, while factors like inadequate medical services, malnutrition, poor sanitation, and the spread of diseases are linked to lower life expectancy.

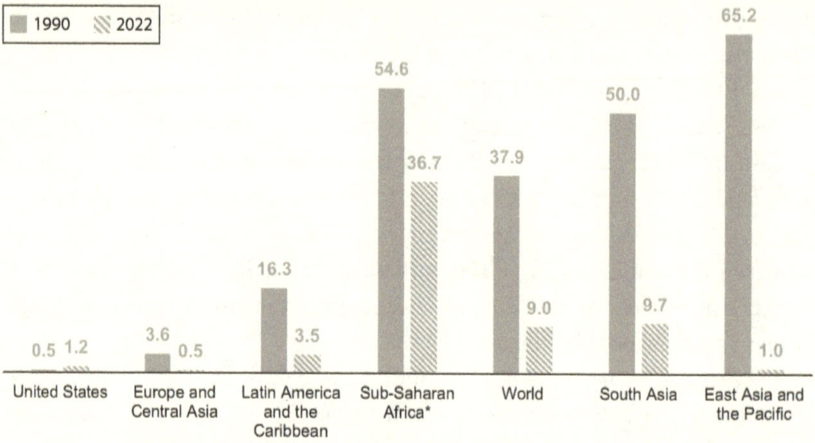

Figure 2.6 Comparison of the percentage of the population living in extreme poverty across world regions in 1990 (solid bars) and 2022 (patterned bars), using the $2.15 per day (2017 purchasing power parity) threshold. Extreme poverty declined across all regions, most notably in East Asia and the Pacific, where it fell from 65.2 percent to 1.0 percent, and in South Asia, where it dropped from 50.0 percent to 9.7 percent.

Note: * The 2022 data correspond to 2019.

Source: Author's elaboration based on data from the World Bank, "Poverty Rate, Percent $2.15," Poverty & Inequality Indicators, https://pip.worldbank.org/poverty-calculator.

From this perspective, life expectancy data suggest that the world has made significant progress in improving health and overall quality of life. From 1960 to 2022, global life expectancy has risen by more than twenty-one years, increasing from 50.9 years in 1960 to 71.9 years in 2022 (figure 2.7). It is important to note that the temporary decline in 2020 was a direct result of the COVID-19 pandemic, but life expectancy has since resumed its upward trend.

Every region in the world has experienced a significant increase in life expectancy from 1960 to 2022. Between 1960 and 2022, Latin America, the Caribbean, and sub-Saharan Africa saw life expectancy rise by approximately nineteen years. Once again, East Asia and the Pacific stand out with the most remarkable improvement, gaining more than thirty-five years over the same period.

Meanwhile, the United States, Europe, and Central Asia already had relatively high life expectancy levels in 1960, averaging around seventy years. As a result, their gains have been smaller compared to other

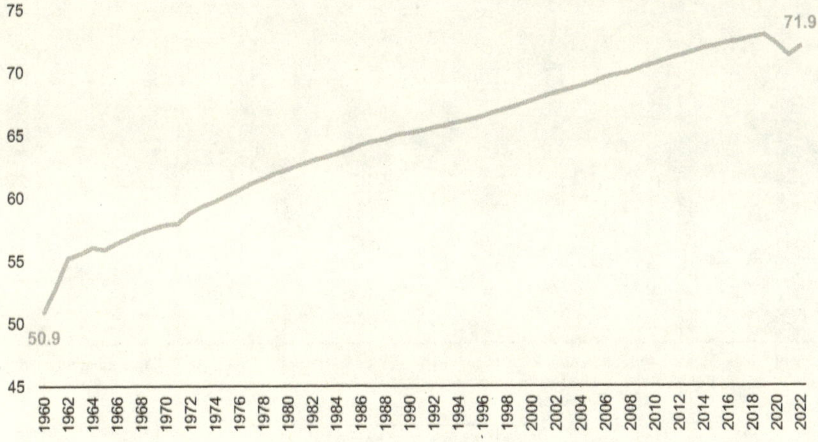

Figure 2.7 Evolution of global life expectancy at birth from 1960 to 2022, measured in years. Life expectancy increased steadily from 50.9 years in 1960 to 71.9 years in 2022, reflecting major improvements in public health, nutrition, and access to medical services.

Source: Author's elaboration based on data from the World Bank, "Life Expectancy at Birth, Total (Years)," Data360, https://data.worldbank.org/indicator/SP.DYN.LE00.IN.

regions. Despite having less room for improvement, both regions (the United States, and Europe and Central Asia) are now approaching an average life expectancy of eighty years (figure 2.8).

A MORE EDUCATED WORLD

More than 2,400 years ago, the vital role of education was already recognized. Plato is attributed with having stated, "If a man neglects education, he walks lame to the end of his life." While his words carry a philosophical perspective, emphasizing personal fulfillment, they also hold profound relevance for modern societies. A society that neglects education is inevitably bound for hardship because education and economic growth share a strong positive correlation, as demonstrated by scholars such as Theodore Schultz and Gary Becker.[17]

While factors like technology and physical capital contribute to economic growth, since the mid-twentieth century the critical role of human capital has been highlighted as a key driver. The transmission mechanism works as follows: greater access to education results in a more skilled workforce composed of individuals with enhanced knowledge and

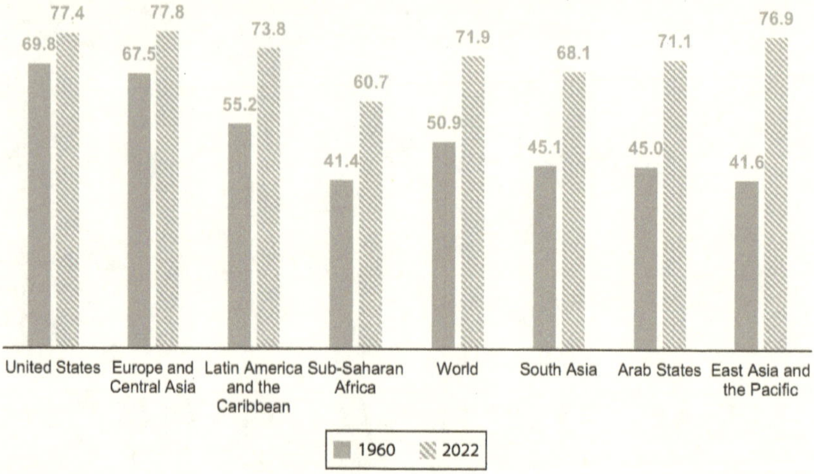

Figure 2.8 Comparison of life expectancy at birth across world regions in 1960 (solid bars) and 2022 (patterned bars). All regions experienced notable increases in life expectancy, with the most dramatic improvements in East Asia and the Pacific, rising from 41.6 to 76.9 years, and in sub-Saharan Africa, from 41.4 to 60.7 years. Europe and Central Asia recorded the highest value in 2022 at 77.8 years.

Source: Author's elaboration based on data from the World Bank, "Life Expectancy at Birth, Total (Years)," Data360, https://data.worldbank.org/indicator/SP.DYN.LE00.IN.

abilities. This in turn leads to a higher level of human capital, making workers significantly more productive. As a result, society experiences an overall increase in economic output.

Given this, there is broad consensus that increasing education levels should be a key policy objective for any society committed to improving its citizens' well-being and achieving higher living standards. More educated individuals tend to be more skilled, leading to better job opportunities, higher salaries, and an overall improved quality of life. This recognition has driven significant global progress in education, with the average number of years of schooling increasing by more than 47 percent from 1990 to 2022—from 5.88 years in 1990 to 8.66 years in 2022 (figure 2.9).

Around the world, societies have recognized the vital role of education in driving economic growth. No region has overlooked this priority; instead, policies have been consistently geared toward increasing

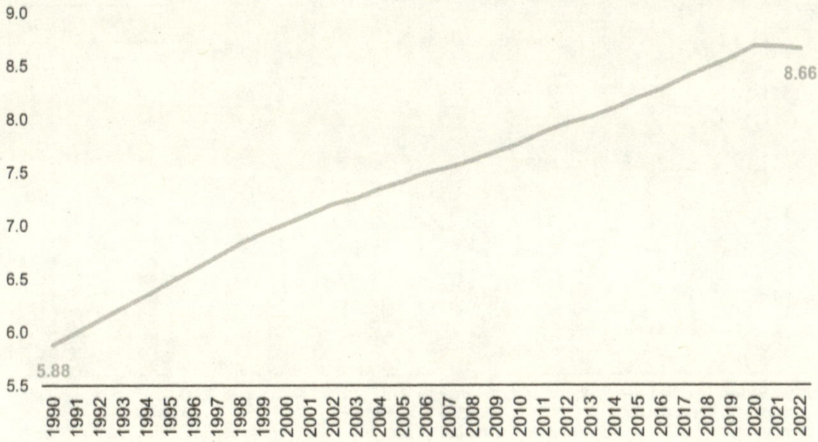

Figure 2.9 Evolution of the global average number of years of schooling from 1990 to 2022. The average increased from 5.88 years in 1990 to 8.66 years in 2022, reflecting sustained progress in educational attainment, with continuous growth and slight stabilization in the most recent years.

Source: Author's elaboration based on data from the United Nations Development Programme, "Mean Years of Schooling (Years)," Human Development Reports, https://hdr.undp.org/data-center/documentation-and-downloads.

educational attainment. While progress has varied, all regions today are significantly more educated than they were in 1990. Europe and Central Asia have increased their average years of schooling by 43.2 percent, while Latin America and the Caribbean, along with sub-Saharan Africa, have seen increases of approximately 64 percent. The most remarkable progress has been in the Arab states, East Asia and the Pacific, and South Asia, where average education levels have surged between 98 percent and 123 percent (figure 2.10).

Beyond its impact on economic growth, education fosters broader societal benefits. More educated individuals tend to be more conscious of their own actions and make informed decisions that enhance their well-being. They are also more likely to demand democratic institutions, inclusive policies, and governments that prioritize the welfare of all citizens. Education nurtures an understanding that prosperity extends beyond wealth—encompassing critical dimensions such as environmental sustainability, which educated populations increasingly advocate for and seek to protect.

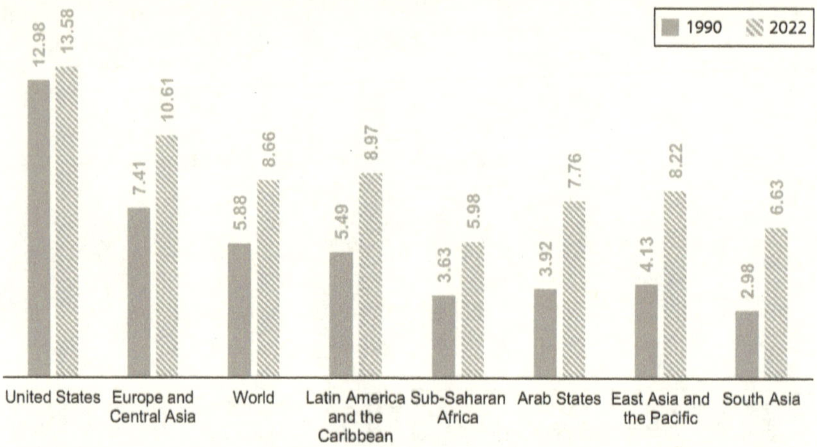

Figure 2.10 Comparison of the average number of years of schooling across world regions in 1990 (solid bars) and 2022 (patterned bars). All regions experienced progress in educational attainment, with particularly strong increases in Latin America and the Caribbean, East Asia and the Pacific, and Europe and Central Asia. In 2022, the United States and Europe and Central Asia recorded the highest averages, while sub-Saharan Africa and South Asia remained at the lowest end of the distribution.

Source: Author's elaboration based on data from the United Nations Development Programme, "Mean Years of Schooling (Years)," Human Development Reports, https://hdr.undp.org/data-center/documentation-and-downloads.

IN SHORT, A WORLD WITH MORE HUMAN DEVELOPMENT

The world has never been a better place to live than it is today. We now enjoy greater wealth, lower poverty rates, improved living conditions, and higher levels of education. The average citizen today has access to far more comforts and opportunities than even the wealthiest individuals of past centuries.

So far, we have examined various indicators that reflect improvements in people's standard of living across multiple dimensions. To summarize these findings, we turn to the Human Development Index (HDI), a comprehensive measure compiled by the United Nations Development Programme (UNDP). Unlike metrics focused solely on income, the HDI evaluates overall development based on three key dimensions: longevity and health, access to education, and a decent standard of living. These dimensions are represented by life expectancy at birth, average number of years of education, and per capita income, respectively.

The HDI ranges from 0 to 1, with higher values indicating greater human development. It also serves as a classification tool, grouping countries into four categories:

1. Low human development (HDI between 0 and 0.550)
2. Medium human development (HDI between 0.550 and 0.699)
3. High human development (HDI between 0.700 and 0.799)
4. Very high human development (HDI between 0.800 and 1)

This index provides a holistic perspective on global progress, reinforcing the notion that human development has significantly improved over time.

In 1990, the global HDI stood at 0.60, placing the world in a state of medium human development—closer to the low human development range than to the high one. Despite this initial gap, however, the HDI surpassed 0.70 by 2010, marking a significant transition from medium to high human development in just two decades (figure 2.11). Apart from the temporary setback caused by the COVID-19 pandemic, the HDI has consistently followed an upward trajectory, reflecting global progress in health, education, and economic well-being. In fact, the 2021/2022

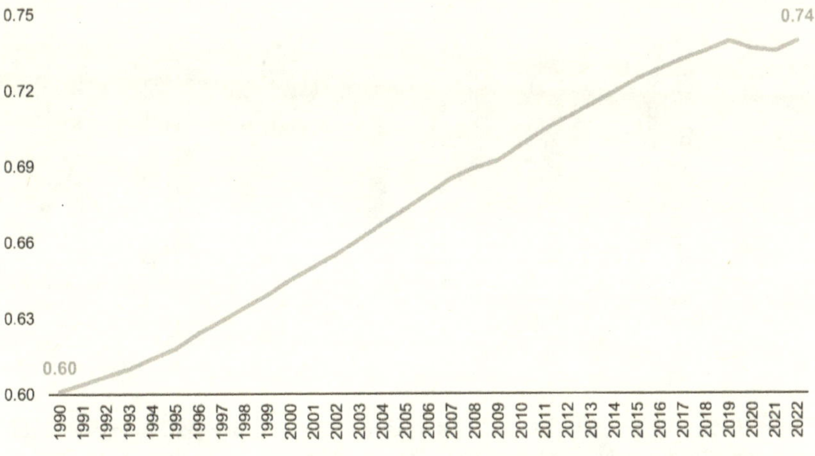

Figure 2.11 Evolution of the global Human Development Index (HDI) from 1990 to 2022. The index increased steadily from 0.60 in 1990 to a peak of 0.74 in 2019, experienced a slight decline during the early 2020s, and recovered in 2022, returning to 0.74.

Source: Author's elaboration based on data from the United Nations Development Programme, "Human Development Index," Human Development Reports, https://hdr.undp.org/data-center/documentation-and-downloads.

UNDP *Human Development Report* projected that, if not for the pandemic, the index would have reached 0.75 in 2021, bringing the world even closer to the threshold of very high human development.[18] The HDI has resumed its upward trend, signaling continued progress.

Certain regions, such as the United States, have consistently maintained a classification of very high human development. Many other regions have made remarkable progress over the past thirty-two years. For instance, South Asia transitioned from low to medium human development, while the Arab states moved from medium to high human development. East Asia and the Pacific made an even more striking leap, advancing from low to high human development. Notable progress has also been seen in Latin America and the Caribbean, which, in just three decades, shifted from medium to high human development. Europe and Central Asia progressed from medium to very high human development, reflecting sustained improvements across multiple regions (figure 2.12).

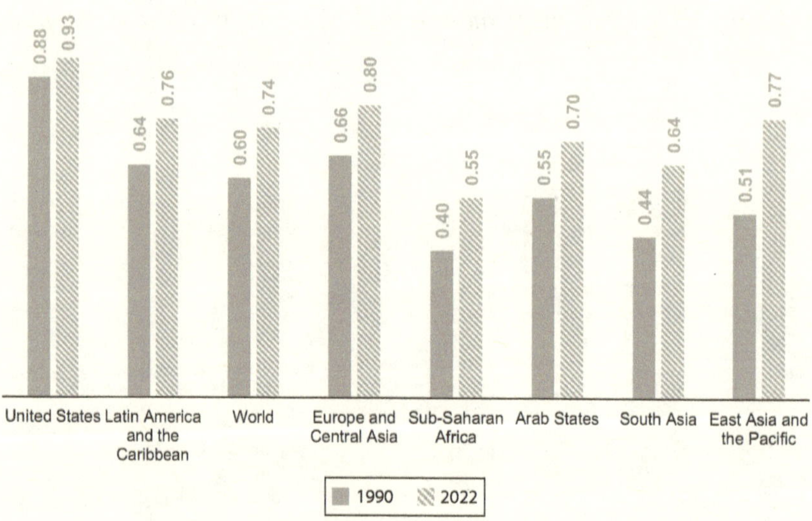

Figure 2.12 Comparison of the Human Development Index (HDI) across world regions in 1990 (solid bars) and 2022 (patterned bars). All regions experienced improvements in HDI over the period, with the most significant gains observed in East Asia and the Pacific, rising from 0.51 to 0.77, and in South Asia, from 0.44 to 0.64. In 2022, the United States recorded the highest HDI at 0.93, while sub-Saharan Africa remained the lowest at 0.55.

Source: Author's elaboration based on data from the United Nations Development Programme, "Human Development Index," Human Development Reports, https://hdr.undp.org/data-center/documentation-and-downloads.

A BETTER WORLD BUT ONE WITH SIGNIFICANT OUTSTANDING ISSUES

Economists like Amartya Sen argue that analyzing a society's well-being requires more than just examining economic variables such as income levels.[19] A society's progress depends on the opportunities and means available for individuals to lead a dignified life—factors that include living conditions and education. This is why, in the previous section, we did not limit our analysis to income alone when concluding that the world has never been a better place to live. In fact, when recalculating the HDI without incorporating per capita income, we observe an even higher rate of progress than in the original index. This reflects significant improvements in health and education, which are key components of human development. As figure 2.13 illustrates, over the years, the HDI values calculated without income have been converging more closely with the original HDI, further underscoring the steady advancements in these critical dimensions.

To gain a deeper understanding of the world we truly live in, we must go beyond the analysis of the previous section. The success of a society

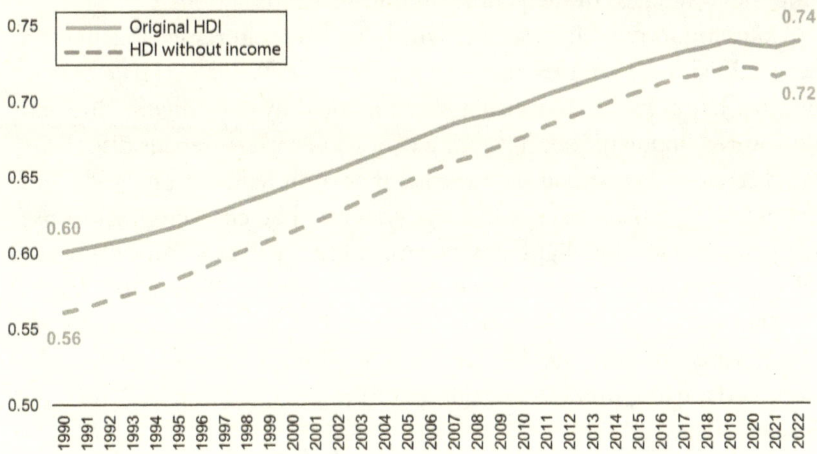

Figure 2.13 Comparison of the original Human Development Index (HDI) (solid line) and the HDI excluding the income component (dashed line) worldwide from 1990 to 2022. Both indicators show steady global improvement over the period. In 2022, the original HDI reached 0.74, while the HDI without income reached 0.72.

Source: Author's elaboration based on data from the United Nations Development Programme, "Human Development Index," Human Development Reports, https://hdr.undp.org/data-center/documentation-and-downloads.

depends on the state of multiple dimensions that shape people's well-being. We have already established that, in areas such as income generation, access to health care, and education, the world has made significant progress toward ensuring a more dignified life for individuals. However, many other crucial dimensions remain to be explored—ones that could help us better understand the root causes of social discontent in various parts of the world.

This argument leads us to an apparent paradox that may seem perplexing to readers: as socioeconomic conditions and opportunities have significantly improved, social frustration has also increased. In political science and sociology, this phenomenon is known as the Tocqueville paradox. In the first half of the nineteenth century, the French political theorist Alexis de Tocqueville analyzed the French and American revolutions and observed that social dissatisfaction tends to grow at a faster rate than socioeconomic progress.[20] One possible explanation for this is that, as societies reach higher levels of well-being, people begin to focus on issues that previously went unnoticed or were not prioritized in favor of more immediate concerns. In other words, progress in general well-being does not always translate into greater collective satisfaction; instead, it often amplifies awareness of inequalities and unmet expectations.

Contemporary social unrest is largely fueled by unresolved issues that have gained increasing relevance in recent years. While it is true that we live in a better world, it is also a world marked by deep income inequality, limited opportunities for young people, persistent gender disparities, rapid economic growth at the expense of environmental degradation, and the alarming erosion of democratic systems. The characterization presented in this section aligns closely with studies such as Isabel Ortiz et al., which examined protests that took place between 2006 and 2020 across 101 countries, covering more than 93 percent of the world's population.[21] The findings are striking: the data show a significant surge in the number of protests, rising from 76 in 2006 to 251 in 2020—an increase of 243.8 percent (figure 2.14).[22]

One of the most significant findings of the Ortiz et al. study is the identification of the main drivers of public outrage that fuel protests. These reasons are closely related to the four key causes of social discontent that we will analyze. According to Ortiz et al., the main motives behind protests include: (1) failure of political representation—issues such as lack of real democracy, corruption, lack of judicial fairness, transparency,

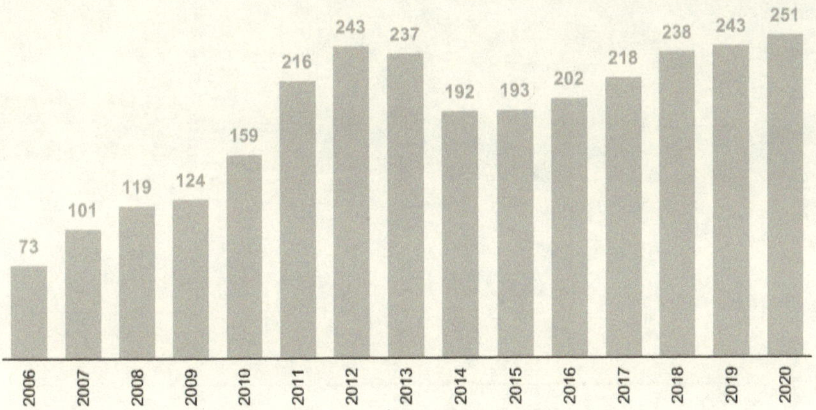

Figure 2.14 Annual number of protests worldwide from 2006 to 2020. Protest activity increased significantly over the period, rising from 73 protests in 2006 to a peak of 251 in 2020, with particularly high levels recorded between 2012 and 2020, suggesting growing global dissatisfaction or mobilization.

Source: Author's elaboration based on data from Isabel Ortiz, Sara Burke, Mohamed Berrada, and Hernán Cortés, *World Protests: A Study of Key Protest Issues in the 21st Century* (Palgrave McMillan, 2022).

accountability, and entrenched oligarchies; (2) economic justice and opposition to austerity—concerns about unemployment, wages, working conditions, inequality, deregulation, privatization, and rising food prices; (3) civil rights—advocacy for ethnic, Indigenous, and racial rights, access to common goods, freedom of expression and the press, women's and girls' rights, and sexual rights; and (4) global justice—protests related to environmental and climate issues, opposition to the International Monetary Fund (IMF) and the World Bank, and resistance to free trade policies (figure 2.15).[23]

A HIGHLY UNEQUAL WORLD

We have already seen that we live in a world with increasing incomes, as reflected in the trend of rising GDP per capita between 1970 and 2023. However, a richer world does not necessarily mean a fairer one. Despite the high levels of income we currently enjoy, it has not been distributed equitably. On the contrary, it has become concentrated in a small group of individuals in the highest income percentiles. In any society, as wealth and income increase, it would be ideal if all individuals have equal access

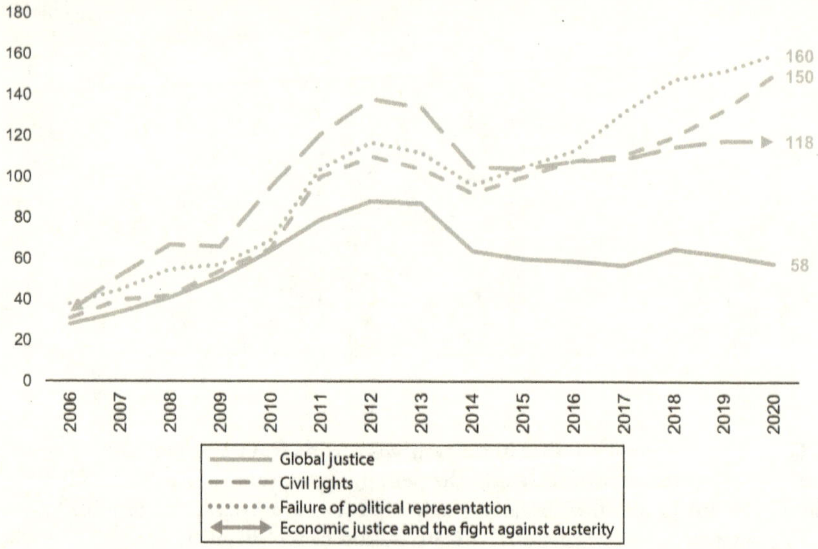

Figure 2.15 Number of protests worldwide by main motivation from 2006 to 2020, disaggregated into four categories: global justice (solid line), civil rights (dashed line), failure of political representation (dotted line), and economic justice and the fight against austerity (dashed line with arrows). Protests related to failures of political representation increased the most, reaching 160 events in 2020, while civil rights protests also grew significantly to 150. Economic justice protests peaked in 2012 and then stabilized, whereas global justice protests remained comparatively lower.

Source: Author's elaboration based on data from Isabel Ortiz, Sara Burke, Mohamed Berrada, and Hernán Cortés, *World Protests: A Study of Key Protest Issues in the 21st Century* (Palgrave McMillan, 2022).

to both, ensuring that no one is left behind. However, the data indicate that people are being left behind.

Figure 2.16 highlights three key facts that illustrate the economic inequality prevailing in our world, a topic explored in chapter 1. First, we present the revenue share held by the top 1 percent of earners. Between 1980 and 2023 this share has consistently exceeded 16 percent. The situation becomes even more concerning when we consider that the bottom 50 percent of the income distribution holds only 8.0 percent. The share of wealth held by the richest 1 percent of the population is also significant. Between 1995 and 2023 this share has consistently exceeded 35 percent, reaching 36.15 percent in 2023. In contrast, the bottom 50 percent held only 2.1 percent in 2023. These data support the conclusion that we

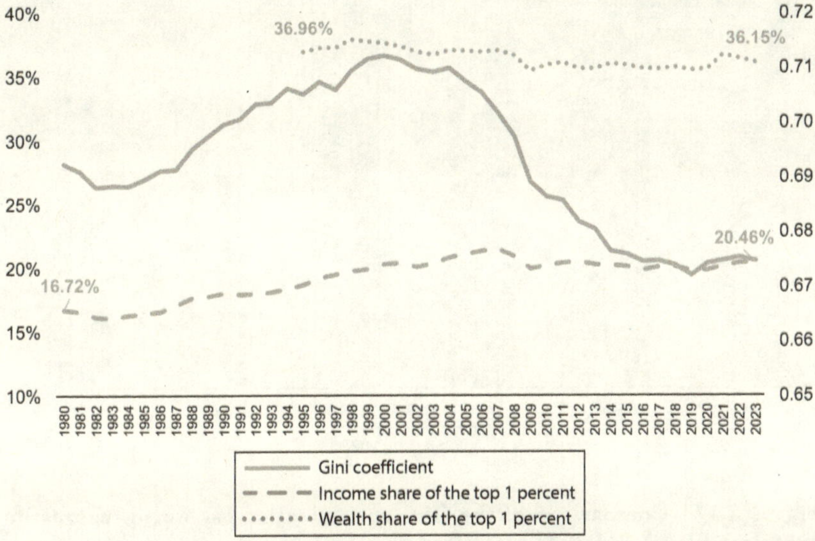

Figure 2.16 Evolution of three global inequality indicators from 1980 to 2023: the Gini coefficient (solid line), the income share of the top 1 percent (dashed line), and the wealth share of the top 1 percent (dotted line), calculated using pretax income. The Gini coefficient peaked in the early 2000s and then declined moderately. The income share of the top 1 percent increased from 16.72 percent in 1980 to 20.46 percent in 2023, while the wealth share of the top 1 percent remained relatively stable, fluctuating around 36 percent.

Source: Author's elaboration based on data from the World Inequality Database, "Gini Coefficient, National Income (Top 1%)" and "Net Personal Wealth (Top 1%)," https://wid.world/data/.

live in a world where income and wealth are distributed unequally: the majority of the population holds a small share of both, while a minority holds most of the resources.

As we indicated in the preface, the Gini coefficient has remained relatively stable between 1980 and 2023, consistently hovering around 0.70—a value associated with a highly unequal world. From this, it can be inferred that, although wealth and income have increased in modern times, they have not been distributed equally among people. This conclusion holds true across almost all regions of the world. Figure 2.17 illustrates that between 1980 and 2023, global inequality has not significantly increased because it was already alarmingly high in 1980. Confirming the data analyzed in chapter 1, the most concerning

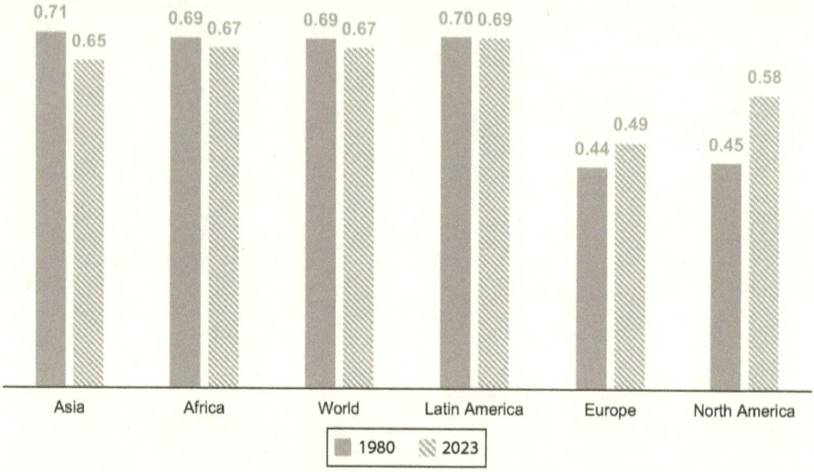

Figure 2.17 Comparison of the Gini coefficient across world regions in 1980 (solid bars) and 2023 (patterned bars), calculated using pretax income. Inequality declined in Asia from 0.71 to 0.65, while Africa and Latin America remained relatively stable. The global average decreased slightly from 0.69 to 0.67. In contrast, inequality increased in Europe from 0.44 to 0.49 and rose more sharply in North America from 0.45 to 0.58.

Source: Author's elaboration based on data from the World Inequality Database, "Gini Coefficient," https://wid.world/data/.

trend is the rising inequality in developed countries, particularly in the United States.

A WORLD WITH INSUFFICIENT JOB OPPORTUNITIES FOR YOUTH

In the labor market, a paradox persists that is particularly harmful to youth seeking employment: to secure a job, they are required to have a certain level of experience, yet they are not hired precisely because they lack that experience. There are not enough opportunities for youth to access jobs where they can be trained, develop their skills, and acquire the experience that the labor market demands. We live in a more educated world, but this education is of little use if we do not provide youth with opportunities to enter the workforce. Figure 2.18 highlights the stark contrast between the unemployment rates of youth (fifteen to twenty-four years old) and adults (twenty-five years and older). The youth

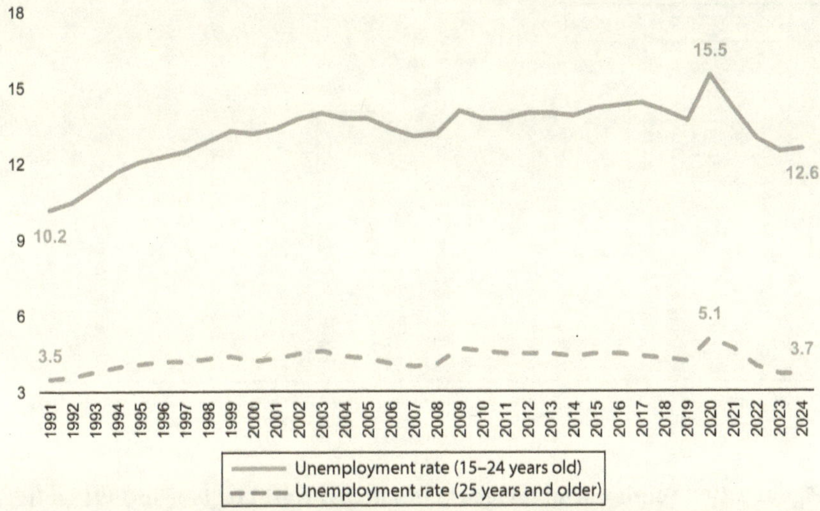

Figure 2.18 Global unemployment rates from 1991 to 2024, disaggregated by age group: ages fifteen to twenty-four (solid line) and ages twenty-five and older (dashed line). Youth unemployment remained consistently higher, peaking at 15.5 percent in 2020 before declining to 12.6 percent in 2024. In contrast, unemployment among individuals aged twenty-five and older remained relatively low and stable, with a slight peak at 5.1 percent in 2020 and a value of 3.7 percent in 2024.

Source: Author's elaboration based on data from the International Labour Organization, "Unemployment Rate (%)," ILOSTAT Data Explorer, https://rshiny.ilo.org/dataexplorer28/?lang=es&segment=indicator&id=SDG_0852_SEX_AGE_RT_A.

unemployment rate has consistently been significantly higher than that of adults. On average, youth unemployment is nearly three times the adult unemployment rate.

In this context, it is not surprising that young people are among the social groups most vocal in expressing their discontent. They have been at the forefront of marches and protests worldwide. This is justified because young people—who often lack equal opportunities or, in many cases, any opportunities at all—feel frustration toward their governments and leaders, who have failed to create a fairer society for them. As shown in figure 2.18, from 1991 to 2024, the youth unemployment rate has shown an upward trend. This presents the worst possible scenario for young people because higher economic growth rates and technological advancements should, in theory, generate opportunities across all social groups. The opposite has occurred, however, and the situation for youth has only worsened over time.

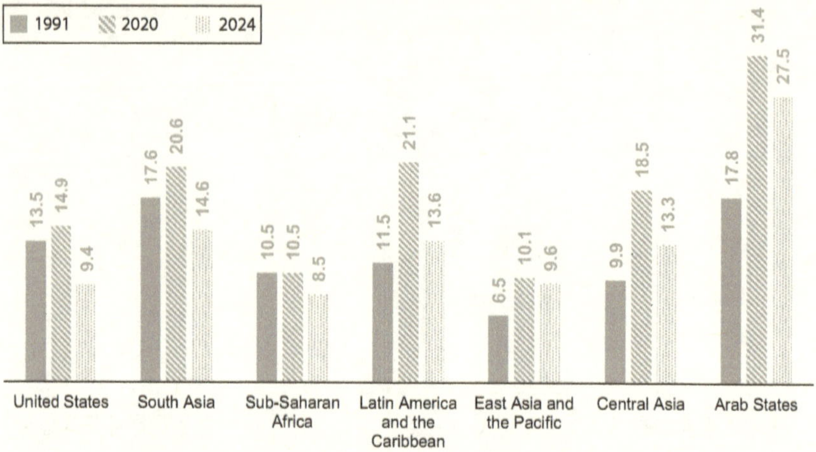

Figure 2.19 Youth unemployment rates across world regions in 1991 (solid bars), 2020 (patterned bars), and 2024 (dotted bars) for individuals aged fifteen to twenty-four. The Arab states consistently recorded the highest rates, reaching 31.4 percent in 2020 and 27.5 percent in 2024, while Central Asia and Latin America also showed relatively high levels. In contrast, East Asia and the Pacific and sub-Saharan Africa maintained comparatively lower rates. Most regions experienced a peak in 2020 followed by a moderate decline in 2024.

Source: Author's elaboration based on data from the International Labour Organization, "Unemployment Rate (%)," ILOSTAT Data Explorer, https://rshiny.ilo.org/dataexplorer28/?lang=es&segment=indicator&id=SDG_0852_SEX_AGE_RT_A.

The COVID-19 pandemic further worsened an already deteriorating situation. With the pandemic, the youth unemployment rate surpassed the 15 percent threshold for the first time, with even more severe impacts in regions such as Central Asia (18.5 percent in 2020), Latin America and the Caribbean (21.1 percent), South Asia (20.6 percent), and the Arab states (31.4 percent). Even without considering the effects of COVID-19, figure 2.19 shows that, except for sub-Saharan Africa, the United States, and South Asia, the youth unemployment rate has increased across most of the world between 1991 and 2024.

A WORLD WITH A MARKED GENDER GAP

Young people are not the only social group that has experienced discrimination. A comparison between the situations of women and men reveals a persistent gender gap throughout history. According to the HDI (discussed in the previous section), men have consistently had a higher HDI

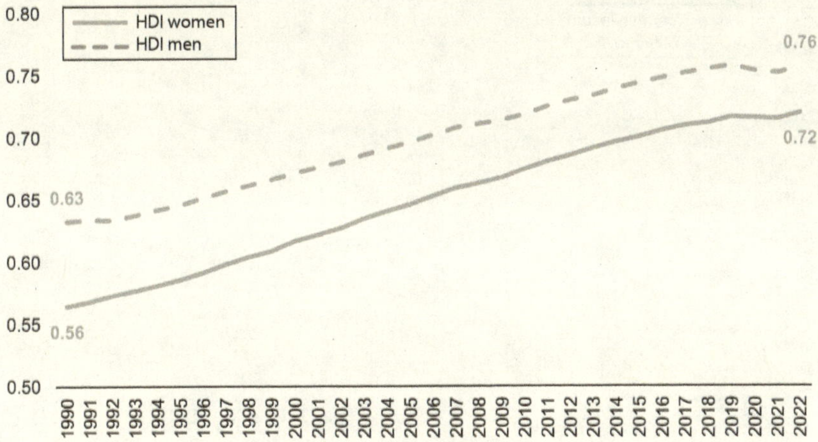

Figure 2.20 Evolution of the Human Development Index (HDI) worldwide by gender from 1990 to 2022, with men represented by the dashed line and women by the solid line. Both indicators show steady improvement over time, although men consistently recorded higher HDI values. In 1990, the HDI was 0.63 for men and 0.56 for women, rising to 0.76 and 0.72 respectively in 2022, indicating a persistent gender gap throughout the period.

Source: Author's elaboration based on data from the United Nations Development Programme, "Human Development Index," Human Development Reports, https://hdr.undp.org/data-center/documentation-and-downloads.

than women. Between 1990 and 2022, women's HDI was approximately 7 percent lower than men's (figure 2.20). These figures indicate that not all people experience the same level of human development: men tend to have higher levels of health, education, and income than women. Given this reality, estimates suggest that at the current rate of progress, achieving full gender equality could take nearly three hundred years.[24]

The gender gap is even more pronounced in terms of income. At the beginning of the previous section, we saw that society's overall income has been increasing steadily, reaching per capita levels that seemed unattainable just a few decades ago. When per capita income is disaggregated by gender, however, it becomes evident that men have fared significantly better than women. On average, between 1990 and 2022, men's per capita income was nearly double that of women's (figure 2.21).

This gap is driven by several factors that contribute to social discontent among women. The first is a labor market that discriminates against them: for the same job, women receive lower wages than men. In addition, companies tend to favor men over women for higher-income

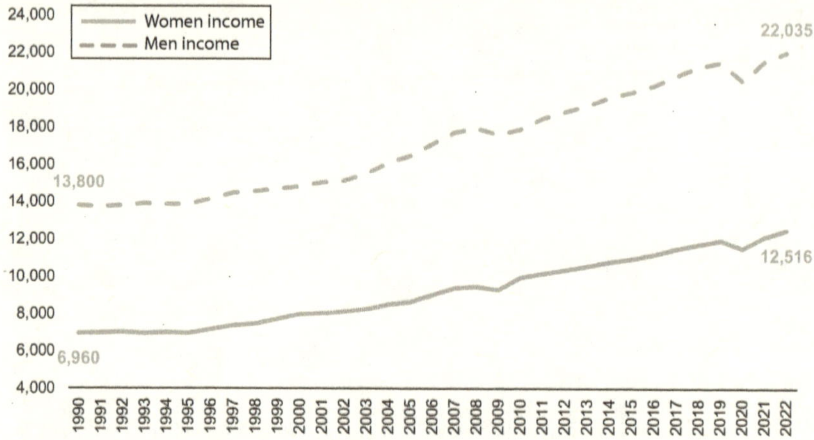

Figure 2.21 Global trends in GDP per capita by gender from 1990 to 2022, measured in 2017 purchasing power parity dollars. Men (dashed line) consistently earned more than women (solid line) throughout the period. In 1990, men's income per capita was $13,800 compared to $6,960 for women. By 2022, men's income had increased to $22,035, while women's income reached $12,516, indicating a persistent gender income gap despite overall growth.

Source: Author's elaboration based on data from the United Nations Development Programme, "Gross National Income Per Capita," Human Development Reports, https://hdr.undp.org/data-center/documentation-and-downloads.

positions, even when both are equally qualified. Traditional gender roles have historically assigned household responsibilities to women—work that unfortunately does not generate any income for them.

When analyzing the HDI gap between men and women, we observe that the least developed regions exhibit the most pronounced disparities. It is important to note however, that this gap has narrowed over time across all regions of the world. Despite this progress, efforts to close the gap must not be relaxed because, as previously mentioned, achieving full gender equality could still take around three centuries. The Arab states and South Asia continue to have a significant HDI gap between men and women, while East Asia and the Pacific, Latin America and the Caribbean, and Europe and Central Asia have made substantial progress in narrowing this gap (figure 2.22).

We noted previously that the gender gap is likely most pronounced in terms of income disparity between men and women. Unlike the HDI gap, however, the income gap has widened in most regions of the world over the years. Figure 2.23 shows that, with the exception of Latin

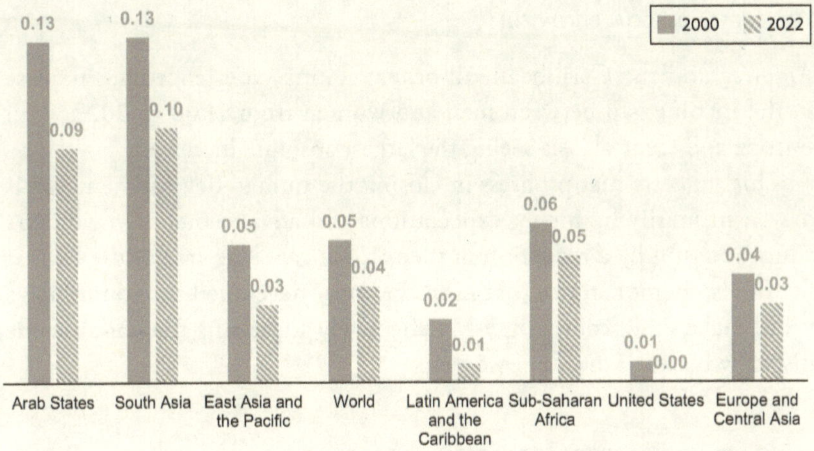

Figure 2.22 Gender gap in the Human Development Index (HDI) across world regions in 2000 (solid bars) and 2022 (patterned bars). All regions experienced a reduction in the gender gap over time, with the most significant declines observed in the Arab states, from 0.13 to 0.09, and in South Asia, from 0.13 to 0.10. In the United States, the gender gap in HDI had disappeared by 2022.

Source: Author's elaboration based on data from the United Nations Development Programme, "Human Development Index," Human Development Reports, https://hdr.undp.org/data-center/documentation-and-downloads.

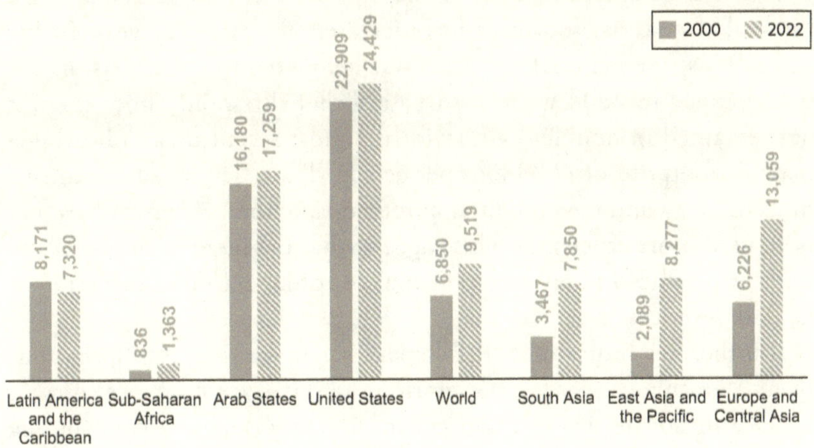

Figure 2.23 Gap in GDP per capita between men and women across world regions in 2000 (solid bars) and 2022 (patterned bars), measured in constant 2017 purchasing power parity dollars. In all regions, men continue to earn significantly more than women. The largest gender income gaps in 2022 are observed in the United States, Europe and Central Asia, and the Arab states. In some regions, such as South Asia and East Asia and the Pacific, the disparity increased over time.

Source: Author's elaboration based on data from the United Nations Development Programme, "Gross National Income Per Capita," Human Development Reports, https://hdr.undp.org/data-center/documentation-and-downloads.

America and the Caribbean, all other regions experienced an increase in the income gap between men and women from 2000 to 2022, with Europe and Central Asia seeing the largest absolute increase.

This suggests that progress in closing the human development gap is driven primarily by higher expectations and advancements in women's education, not by a reduction in the income gap. The case of the United States also demonstrates that even the most developed economies have yet to make significant progress in effectively addressing the stark income disparity between men and women.

A WORLD WITH A THREATENED ENVIRONMENT

With the emergence of new technologies that enable companies to operate more efficiently, one would expect economies to produce more with the same amount of resources or, conversely, to require fewer resources to produce the same quantity of goods and services. An indicator that helps determine whether this expectation has been met in practice is the material footprint. This metric measures the amount of raw materials required to produce the goods and services that satisfy an economy's final demand.

Figure 2.24 shows that, in per capita terms and measured in tons, the global material footprint has increased almost every year. In the early 1990s, the material footprint was below ten tons per person, but this changed in 2004 when it surpassed that threshold. Since then, it has remained in double digits, with the most recent data indicating a material footprint of 12.38 tons per person. Thus, despite advancements in technology and new production methods, natural resources have not been used more efficiently. This suggests that the increase in goods and services produced today comes at the cost of an alarming depletion of natural resources.

Another key indicator of the damage we are causing to the environment is greenhouse gas (GHG) emissions. GHGs are substances present in the atmosphere that can trap radiant heat from the sun, contributing to the greenhouse effect. This effect is essential for maintaining life on Earth because, without it, temperatures would be extremely cold. When GHG concentrations become excessive, however, they lead to a significant rise in the Earth's average temperature—a phenomenon known as global warming. This in turn has severe environmental consequences, including glacier melting, rising sea levels, ecosystem disruptions, and more extreme weather events such as droughts and floods. In just three decades, global

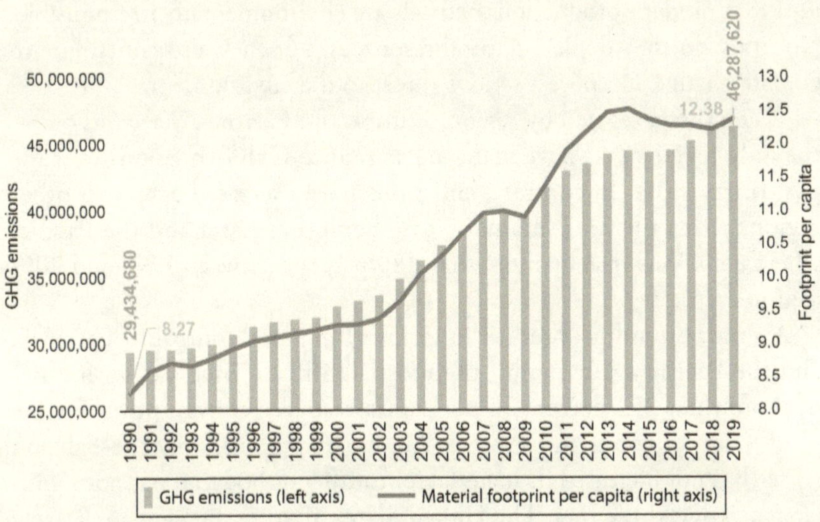

Figure 2.24 Evolution of total greenhouse gas (GHG) emissions worldwide (bars, left axis) and material footprint per capita (line, right axis) from 1990 to 2019. GHG emissions increased from approximately 29.4 million kilotons of CO_2 equivalent in 1990 to 46.3 million kilotons in 2019, while the material footprint per capita rose from 8.27 to 12.38 tons, reflecting the intensification of resource use and environmental pressure associated with economic development.

* "Kt" refers to kilotons, a unit of measurement used to express large quantities of substances, such as GHGs. Carbon dioxide (CO_2) is one of the primary greenhouse gases, but it is not the only one: methane (CH_4) and nitrous oxide (N_2O) are also significant contributors. To compare and add emissions from different GHGs, a common metric called CO_2 equivalent is used. This measurement accounts for the global warming potential of each gas and converts it into an equivalent amount of CO_2. In this way, emissions of gases like CH_4 and N_2O can be expressed in terms of their climate impact relative to CO_2. Therefore, when kt of CO_2 equivalent is mentioned in the context of total GHGs, it refers to the total amount of emissions expressed in kilotons of CO_2 equivalent.

** The material footprint is calculated by adding the total amount of materials extracted and imported and then subtracting the amount exported. This includes four main categories of materials: biomass, fossil fuels, metallic minerals, and nonmetallic minerals. The purpose of this metric is to reflect the quantity of material resources required per person in a given country to meet their needs.

Source: Author's elaboration based on data from the World Bank, "Total Greenhouse Gas Emissions (kt of CO_2 Equivalent)," Data360, https://databank.worldbank.org/metadataglossary/world-development-indicators/series/EN.ATM.GHGT.KT.CE and the United Nations Development Programme, "Material Footprint Per Capita (Tonnes)," Human Development Reports, https://hdr.undp.org/data-center/documentation-and-downloads.

GHG emissions have increased by a factor of 1.6, further supporting the idea that modern production methods are environmentally irresponsible. Not only do they deplete natural resources, but they also contribute to climate change and pose a serious threat to the environment.

When disaggregated by region, Europe and Central Asia stand out as the only regions that have managed to reduce GHG emissions over the past thirty years. In contrast, emissions have increased across all other regions, with the most dramatic case being East Asia and the Pacific, where emissions rose by more than 180 percent between 1990 and 2019 (figure 2.25).

A similar trend is observed in terms of material footprint, East Asia and the Pacific again exhibit the most significant increase, with a rise of more than 252 percent in per capita resource consumption for the production of goods and services. Among all regions, only sub-Saharan Africa has not increased its material footprint—although it has not significantly reduced it either. The United States, despite showing a relatively

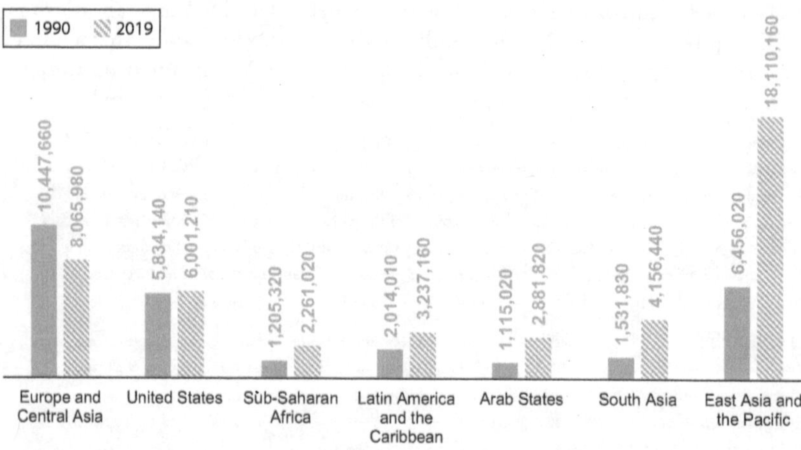

Figure 2.25 Total greenhouse gas emissions across world regions in 1990 (solid bars) and 2019 (patterned bars), measured in kilotons of CO_2 equivalent. Emissions increased in most regions, particularly in East Asia and the Pacific, where they rose from 6.5 to 18.1 million kilotons. Notable increases also occurred in South Asia and sub-Saharan Africa, while Europe and Central Asia reduced their emissions over the same period.

Source: Author's elaboration based on data from the World Bank, "Total Greenhouse Gas Emissions (kt of CO_2 Equivalent)," Data360, https://databank.worldbank.org/metadataglossary/world-development-indicators/series/EN.ATM.GHGT.KT.CE.

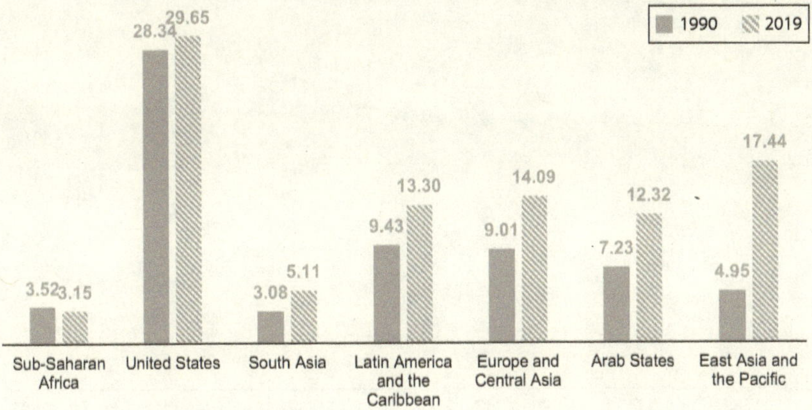

Figure 2.26 Material footprint per capita across world regions in 1990 (solid bars) and 2019 (patterned bars), measured in tons. While the United States maintained the highest footprint, increasing slightly from 28.34 to 29.65 tons, substantial increases occurred in East Asia and the Pacific, from 4.95 to 17.44 tons, and in Europe and Central Asia, from 9.01 to 14.09 tons. Sub-Saharan Africa was the only region where the material footprint per capita declined.

Source: Author's elaboration based on data from the United Nations Development Programme, "Material Footprint Per Capita (Tonnes)," Human Development Reports, https://hdr.undp.org/data-center/documentation-and-downloads.

modest increase of 4.6 percent, has the highest material footprint in absolute terms, reaching nearly thirty tons per capita, the largest among all regions in the sample (figure 2.26).

A WORLD WITH WEAK DEMOCRACIES

We conclude this section with an analysis of recent trends in democracy. For this, we refer to the Liberal Democracy Index (LDI), developed by Varieties of Democracy (V-Dem) in Sweden. The LDI measures both the electoral and liberal aspects of democracy, with values ranging from 0 to 1. An increase in the index indicates a strengthening of democracy in a given country.

Regarding electoral aspects, the index assesses the presence of key elements such as the quality of elections, individual rights, media independence, and freedom of association. On the liberal democracy side, it captures the extent to which checks and balances on the executive, respect for civil liberties, the rule of law, and the independence of the legislature

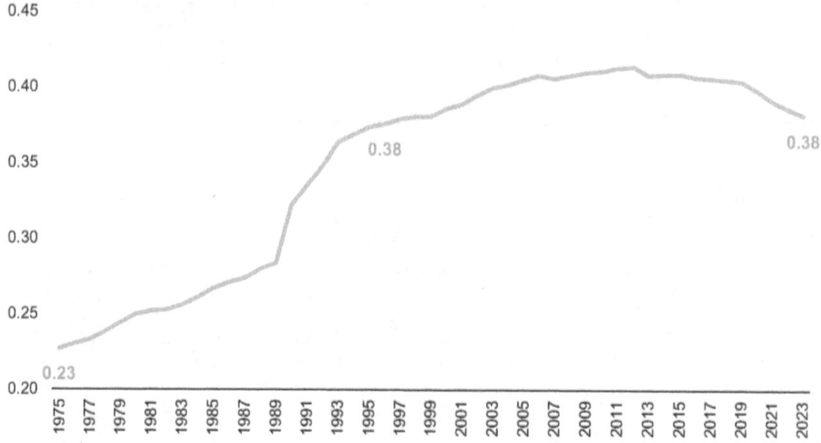

Figure 2.27 Evolution of the global Liberal Democracy Index (LDI) from 1975 to 2023. The index increased steadily from 0.23 in 1975 to a peak of around 0.40 in the early 2000s, indicating a global strengthening of democratic institutions. After 2012, the trend reversed, and by 2023 the index had declined to 0.38.

Source: Author's elaboration based on data from the V-Dem Institute, "Liberal Democracy Index," the V-Dem Dataset, https://www.v-dem.net/data/the-v-dem-dataset/.

and judiciary are upheld. In line with this, figure 2.27 presents the average LDI worldwide.

We highlight three key findings in this regard, which indicate that we are living in a world where democracy is weakening. These findings were analyzed in greater detail in the V-Dem Institute's *Democracy Report 2024*.[25] First, global democratic progress has suffered a significant decline over the past decade. The 2023 LDI recorded a value of 0.38, the same level observed in 1998. It is important to note that figure 2.27 presents the simple average of the countries included in the analysis. However, when the index is weighted by population, as done in the report, the findings are even more concerning, indicating that democracy in 2023 regressed to levels last seen in 1985. Since 2022, and for the first time in more than twenty years, the number of closed autocracies worldwide has surpassed the number of liberal democracies, indicating a global trend toward autocracy.

To reach this conclusion, the V-Dem Institute classifies political regimes into four categories: closed autocracy, electoral autocracy, electoral democracy, and liberal democracy. Overall, there were ninety-one democracies and eighty-eight autocracies worldwide in 2023. However, when broken down by category, the number of liberal democracies stood at thirty-two, while the number of closed autocracies reached thirty-three. A deeper analysis based on population size reveals that most of the world's population now live under autocratic regimes. Although the number of democracies and autocracies is nearly equal, 71 percent of the global population—approximately 5.7 billion people—resides in countries classified under one of the two autocracy categories.

Moreover, as indicated by figure 2.28, the weakening of democracy is a phenomenon present in all regions of the world. Even though most countries are, in terms of democracy, in a better situation than in 1975, many have experienced significant setbacks in democratic levels over the past decade. However, there are notable regional differences. According

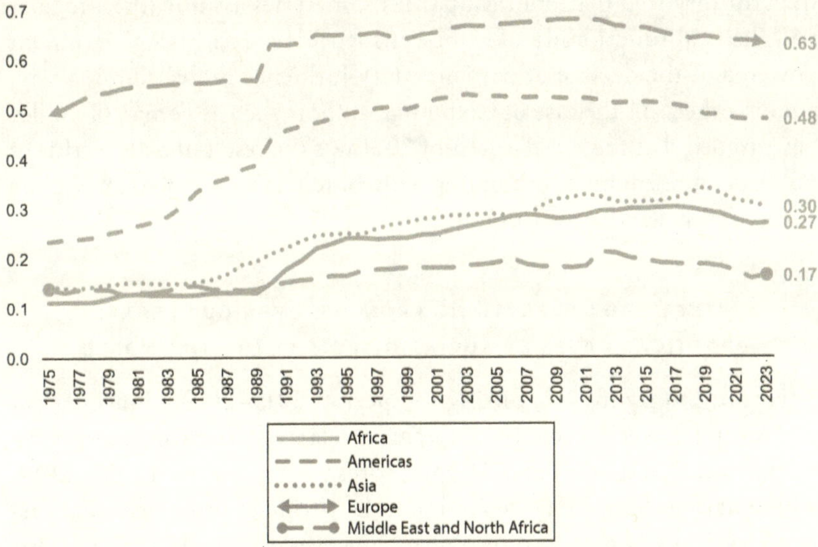

Figure 2.28 Liberal Democracy Index (LDI) by region from 1975 to 2023. Europe (dashed line with arrows) consistently recorded the highest levels, peaking around 0.70 in the early 2000s and reaching 0.63 in 2023. The Americas (dashed line) increased until the early 2000s and then declined slightly to 0.48. Asia (dotted line) and Africa (solid line) showed gradual improvements, reaching 0.30 and 0.27 respectively in 2023, while the Middle East and North Africa (dashed line with circles) remained the lowest at 0.17.

Source: Author's elaboration based on data from the V-Dem Institute, "Liberal Democracy Index," the V-Dem Dataset, https://www.v-dem.net/data/the-v-dem-dataset/.

to the V-Dem Institute, most of the population in the Middle East and North Africa, sub-Saharan Africa, East Asia and the Pacific, and Eastern Europe live under autocratic regimes—98 percent, 82 percent, 78 percent, and 66 percent of the population, respectively. In contrast, the majority of people in Western Europe and North America reside in democracies, with 96 percent of the population in each region, while in Latin America the figure is 86 percent, living under democratic governance.

It is important to highlight that the weakening of democracy is further exacerbated by what has been termed the crisis of representation in democracies. This phenomenon affects both developed and developing countries and has been identified in some studies as a growing disconnect between citizens and the political power of traditional parties.[26] Alfredo Ramírez points out that several factors have fueled the crisis of representation and thus have weakened democratic systems.[27] These factors include the arbitrary role that political parties sometimes assume, the irregular and disloyal functioning of public institutions, excessive government power, and the decline of parliamentary influence in decision making, among others. In the case of Colombia, authors such as Fernán González have argued that the social unrest of 2021 was the result of a deep crisis of political representation, prompting a discontented citizenry to take to the streets and make their voices heard.[28]

"THEY TOOK EVERYTHING FROM US, EVEN OUR FEAR": PRACTICAL CASES OF SOCIAL DISCONTENT IN THE WORLD

According to figure 2.2, during the period 2015–2019, an average of 703 protests were recorded per year, a relatively high number compared to the annual average of 336 protests for the period 1990–2014. These data indicate that we are living in a time of growing social discontent. It is important to recognize, however, that large-scale protests demanding change are not exclusive to recent years. They have been a recurring phenomenon throughout history. For example, nearly two centuries ago, in 1830, the period of liberal revolutions began across much of Europe, driven by factors such as hunger, the absence of press freedom, the lack of political and civil rights, the low representation of the poor in government, and widespread dissatisfaction among the working class. Just over a century ago, the Russian Revolution of 1917 emerged as a result of prolonged social unrest. A combination of war, political disenfranchisement, and famine contributed to a wave of protests that ultimately led to the fall of the tsarist regime, the collapse of the provisional government, and the rise of the Bolsheviks. The fundamental causes of social discontent remain largely unchanged over the decades.

David Clark and Patrick Regan's database not only compiles the number of protests that occurred each year but also identifies the primary demands made by protesters.[29] Of the nearly twelve thousand protests recorded between 1990 and 2019, more than 60 percent were driven by demands for changes in political processes. Approximately 11 percent focused on calls for better working conditions or wages (figure 2.29).

As we will explore in the following case studies, poor political and labor conditions appear to be the primary causes of social discontent in today's world. Events such as the Arab Spring and the social uprisings in Chile and much of Latin America further support this claim. As we will see in the case of Latin America, however, demands for change extend beyond political and labor issues to other critical areas as well.

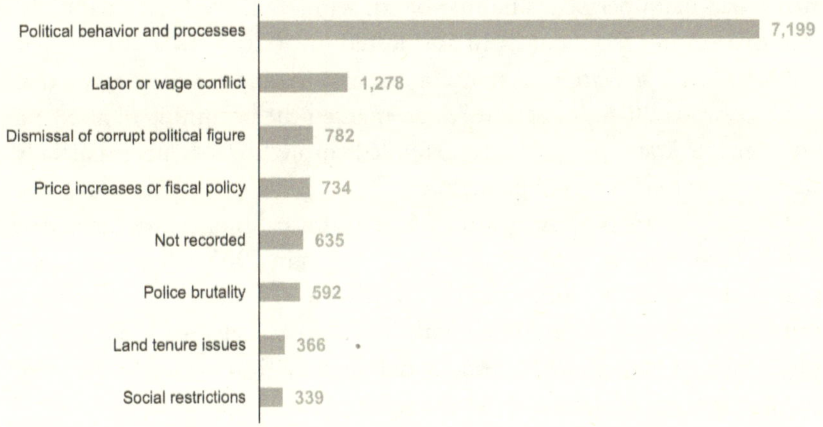

Figure 2.29 Antistate protests worldwide by type of demand. Political behavior and processes constitute the most frequent cause, with 7,199 protests, followed by labor or wage conflicts (1,278) and the dismissal of corrupt political figures (782). Other notable categories include price increases or fiscal policy, police brutality, land tenure issues, and social restrictions.

Source: Author's elaboration based on data from David Clark and Patrick Regan, *Mass Mobilization Protest Data* (Harvard Dataverse, 2016).

THE ARAB SPRING: THE DISCONTENT OF YOUTH IN THE MIDDLE EAST

Mohamed Bouazizi was born in March 1984 in Sidi Bouzid, a town in central Tunisia. At the age of three, he lost his father, forcing him to take on various jobs from a young age to help support his family. As a result, he had to abandon his studies before completing high school in order to provide for his mother and siblings. On December 17, 2010, twenty-six-year-old Bouazizi was working at his fruit and vegetable stall when he was stopped by police; he was fined and had his goods confiscated. In addition to this, the officers slapped and humiliated him. Seeking justice, Bouazizi went to the municipal authorities to file a complaint and recover his confiscated goods, but his pleas were ignored. In response to this injustice, Bouazizi made the drastic decision to set himself on fire in front of the Government Palace, shouting: "How do you expect me to make a living?"[30] His goal had been to expand his business by upgrading his cart to a truck, but instead his tragic act of self-immolation became the catalyst for what is now known as the Arab Spring.

The Arab Spring refers to a series of protests and demonstrations across the Arab world. It was driven by demands for more democratic societies and the protection of social rights. The Arab Spring can be divided into two broad main periods. The first began with Mohamed Bouazizi's self-immolation in December 2010 and lasted until 2013. In a 2019 article published in *The Nation*, Tesbih Habbal and Muzna Hasnawi argue that the December 2018 protests in Sudan marked the beginning of a second wave of the Arab Spring, which extended through 2024, albeit partially slowed by the COVID-19 pandemic.[31]

Other scholars propose a three-phase historical framework instead of two.[32] According to them, the first phase began in 2005, when Iraqis participated in elections following the overthrow of Saddam Hussein, with other key events such as Syria's withdrawal from Lebanon. The second phase started with Bouazizi's act of defiance in Tunisia, while the third phase began with Sudan's 2018 protests.

The protests erupted in countries governed by authoritarian regimes, which were characterized by corrupt political elites, electoral fraud, and widespread political and social repression. High unemployment—especially among young people—stagnant economic growth, and extreme wealth concentration further fueled public discontent.

What began in Tunisia quickly spread across the region, sparking uprisings in Egypt, Libya, Yemen, Morocco, Syria, Sudan, and Bahrain. Despite the differences in each country, the common thread among these revolts was a society deeply frustrated by poverty, exclusion, and oppression under authoritarian rule. Young people were at the forefront of the protests, leading demonstrations and demanding societal rights. Social media played a crucial role—at least in the early stages—by mobilizing people and coordinating mass gatherings. Its influence was so significant that, in countries like Egypt, authorities resorted to blocking internet access to curb the movement.[33] The prominent role of youth in these uprisings is closely linked to the demographic reality of the Arab world at the time. The average age across Arab League member countries was just twenty-three years old,[34] with half of the region's population under that age.[35]

As documented by Zidane Zeraoui,[36] by mid-2012, the Arab Spring had led to the overthrow of four long-standing rulers: Zine El Abidine Ben Ali (Tunisia), who was ousted on January 14, 2011, after twenty-four years in power; Hosni Mubarak (Egypt), who resigned on February 11, 2011, after thirty years in power; Muammar Gaddafi (Libya), who was killed on October 20, 2011, after forty-two years in power; and Ali Abdullah Saleh (Yemen), who stepped down on February 27, 2012, after twenty-one years in power. While the social uprisings succeeded in toppling long-standing authoritarian leaders, true democratization in the Arab world remained elusive. In many cases, the fall of these rulers was followed by military takeovers or the rise of Islamist movements through elections. In the worst scenarios, countries descended into prolonged civil wars. As a result, democratic consolidation never materialized—leaders changed, but the underlying political and economic structures remained intact. After 2010, societies across the Arab world continued to be controlled by entrenched political elites, while economies faced worsening inequality and particularly dire conditions for young people.

The Arab Spring of 2018 saw the emergence of new protagonists, primarily countries that had not participated in the 2011 protests. The initial wave of demonstrations took place in Sudan, Lebanon, and Algeria. In Sudan, street protests began in December 2018 in response to rising bread prices, eventually leading to the overthrow of President Omar Al Bashir on April 11, 2019, after thirty years in power. In Lebanon, mass demonstrations erupted in October 2019, sparked by the government's controversial decision to impose taxes on WhatsApp and Skype calls. The protests quickly evolved into a broader demand for systemic political change, culminating in the resignation of Prime Minister Saad Hariri. In Algeria, protests began on February 16, 2019, following President Abdelaziz Bouteflika's announcement of his candidacy for a fifth presidential term. Although Bouteflika resigned on April 2, 2019, the demonstrations persisted because

Algerians demanded a complete overhaul of the ruling elite, a political transition, and a government chosen through national consensus.

Given all the above, the Arab Spring can be understood as a prolonged process, during which public discontent—primarily driven by young people—was expressed in the streets through 2024. While these movements successfully removed long-standing authoritarian leaders from power, they did not achieve a full transition toward more democratic societies. The exception to this trend was Tunisia, which managed to transition to a more democratic political system by adopting a constitution that upheld the fundamental rights of its citizens.[37]

SOCIAL DISCONTENT IN LATIN AMERICA

Starting in the mid-2010s, social protests surged across Latin America (figure 2.30), coinciding with a regional political shift toward right-wing governments. Social protest has been the primary means of expressing

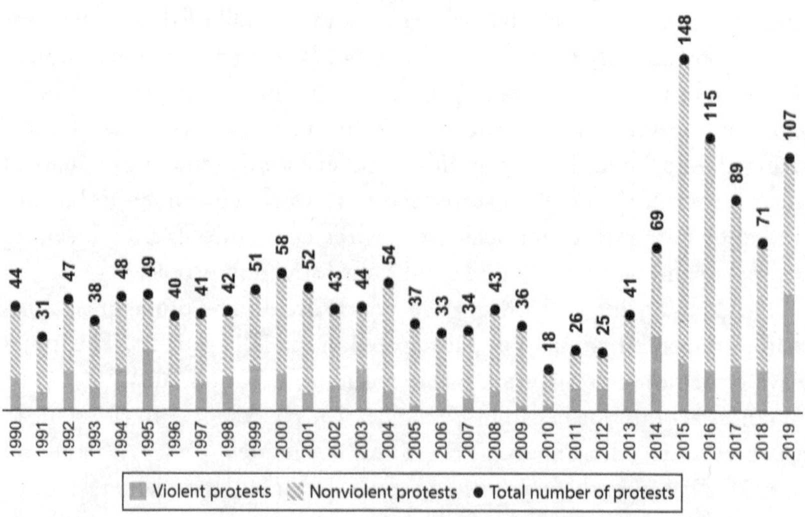

Figure 2.30 Number of antistate protests in Latin America from 1990 to 2019, distinguishing between violent protests (solid bars) and nonviolent protests (patterned bars). The total number of protests (black dots) increased significantly after 2012, peaking at 148 events in 2015. Throughout the period, nonviolent protests consistently outnumbered violent ones.

Source: Author's elaboration based on data from David Clark and Patrick Regan, *Mass Mobilization Protest Data* (Harvard Dataverse, 2016).

public discontent in most Latin American countries, so it is essential to explore this concept further. According to María Quiroga and Ana Magrini, social protests "constitute a valid resource of community life in democracy, and, more importantly, a guarantee of the right to freedom of expression. Through them, various groups, movements, citizens, and collective identities struggle to make their demands, their repertoires, and their aesthetics visible."[38] To the extent that social protest is understood as a guarantee of the right to freedom of expression, Quiroga and Magrini emphasize that protests are not the antithesis of democracy but rather a necessary condition for its proper functioning.[39]

Latin America is a region that meets the five criteria for social discontent analyzed in the previous section. The region faces severe economic inequality, a lack of opportunities for young people, pronounced gender gaps that put women at a disadvantage, productive processes that harm the environment (and consequently people's health and lives), and increasingly weak democratic systems.

HISTORICALLY HIGH ECONOMIC INEQUALITY

With the Gini coefficient as a measure, Latin America is the most unequal region in the world.[40] This trend has been recorded from 1980 to 2023, as shown in figure 2.17. The twenty-first century not only brought the rise of progressive governments in the region but also a surge in raw material prices. This boom ended in 2014, leading to a reversal of the progress made in reducing poverty and inequality. In response, social discontent was reflected at the ballot box: regardless of voters' ideological leanings, they chose to vote against the ruling parties, as demonstrated by the 2019 presidential elections in Uruguay and Argentina. In Uruguay, the left lost power, leading to a shift to the right with the election of Luis Lacalle Pou. In Argentina, the right was defeated, resulting in a swing to the left with the victory of Alberto Fernández. It is worth noting that in 2024, the left regained power in Uruguay with Yamandú Orsi, while the right did the same in Argentina in 2023 with Javier Milei.

YOUTH: PROTAGONISTS OF THE SOCIAL OUTBURST

A series of situations that have generated widespread discontent in the region are related to policy decisions made in various countries that have been considered antipopulist. The most striking and recent example of this is the so-called Chilean October. In October 2019, the government of Sebastián Piñera announced an increase in metro fares, raising the cost from 800 to 830 Chilean pesos (approximately 1.17 dollars) as a result of adverse macroeconomic factors such as fluctuations in diesel oil prices and rising labor costs, among others. The discontent was initially felt among young people but soon spread to a large portion of the population. On October 14, 2019, young protesters organized a mass fare evasion in Santiago de Chile's subway system.

On October 19, the Chilean president suspended the fare increase, but this was not enough because discontent had already spread. On October 25, 2019, the largest march in Chile's history took place, gathering more than 1.2 million people in Santiago alone.[41] What began as a protest against a metro fare increase evolved into broader demands for an improved quality of life.[42] Under previous governments, these demands had not been addressed. More than ever, people were calling for improvements in health care, education, and political management, among other areas.[43] By the end of 2019, social protests in Chile led to efforts to approve a new constitution to replace the existing one, which was a legacy of the Pinochet dictatorship and considered an obstacle to the demanded reforms.[44]

It became clear that young Chileans were demanding a change of course—one that rejected traditional institutions and politics, with new leaders different from those who had governed throughout their lives.[45] This proposed constitution was ultimately rejected by the majority, however, as was a subsequent political charter developed with significant support from the right.

PRONOUNCED GENDER GAPS: UN DÍA SIN NOSOTRAS (A DAY WITHOUT US)

At the beginning of 2020, Mexico recorded alarming numbers of murdered women. In January alone, 320 women were killed—an average of more than ten per day. Social discontent among women over this issue grew with each passing day, but tensions escalated following the femicides of Ingrid Escamilla and Fátima Aldrighett. Escamilla, a twenty-five-year-old woman from Mexico City, was stabbed, skinned, and eviscerated, with her remains discovered on February 9, 2020. Aldrighett, a seven-year-old girl, disappeared on February 11 and was found dead in a garbage bag on the outskirts of Mexico City on February 15.

In response to this wave of femicides, the feminist collective Brujas del Mar from Veracruz shared on social media an initiative for a national social demonstration called A Day Without Us. International Women's Day, celebrated on March 8, is dedicated to the fight for equality and the empowerment of women in all areas of society. A Day Without Us was scheduled for the day after International Women's Day, with the aim of highlighting and denouncing gender-based violence, inequality, and discrimination faced by women in various spheres of society.

By adopting the slogan "The best way to make the invisible visible is to remove it," Un Día Sin Nosotras (A Day Without Us) was a nationwide call for all women not only to stop working but also to refrain from any type of activity, including paid labor, studies, and domestic chores. The goal was to highlight the impact of women's absence on society. In this sense, A Day Without Us sought to make visible the fundamental role of women in all spheres of human activity: in the workplace, in traditionally assigned domestic tasks, in the care of infants and the elderly, among others. But it was also a day to raise voices against the persistent discrimination and violence women face and to demand strong measures to address these issues.

It should be clarified that Un Día Sin Nosotras (A Day Without Us) is not an isolated initiative. In fact, this form of social protest dates back many decades. For example, in 1975, women in Iceland staged a work stoppage to demand equality and greater representation in public office. In October 2016, Argentina became the first country in Latin America to carry out a work stoppage after a week in which a series of femicides sparked outrage among women across the country. In October 2017, feminists in the United States joined the strike movement under the slogan A Day Without Women.

By 2023, Un Día Sin Nosotras had now been held in Mexico for four consecutive years. Despite such initiatives, however, the root cause of women's discontent in Mexico remains unresolved. In 2022 alone, Mexico recorded 3,754 murders of women, maintaining the alarming average of ten femicides per day.[46]

RESOURCE EXTRACTION AS A DESTRUCTIVE ENVIRONMENTAL FACTOR

For Argentine environmentalist Maristella Svampa, social protests related to environmental protection can be understood in two ways: (1), as "the empowerment of ancestral struggles for land, hand in hand with indigenous and peasant movements" and (2) as "the emergence of new forms of citizen mobilization and participation, focused on the defense of natural resources, biodiversity, and the environment."[47] Latin America is the most dangerous region for environmental leaders and defenders.[48] This is further confirmed by Alejandro Alvarado, who reports that between 2014 and 2018, at least 536 people defending land and the environment in Latin America were murdered (table 2.1).[49]

Latin America has been characterized as a region whose economic growth model is largely based on extraction—that is, large-scale exploitation of natural resources and environmental degradation. Many actors in the region have expressed their discontent with this extractive model. Such is the case of the organization Mothers of Ituzaingó, which has been fighting for environmental protection for more than twenty years in the Ituzaingó Annex neighborhood of Córdoba, Argentina. In 2001, a group of mothers from this neighborhood grew concerned about a rise in cases of leukemia, cancer, respiratory diseases, and other illnesses, as well as an increase in congenital malformations. They attributed these health issues initially to the poor condition of the neighborhood's aqueduct and sewer systems.

Table 2.1 Number of murders of land and environmental defenders in Latin America between 2014 and 2018, by country

Country	2014	2015	2016	2017	2018	Total
Argentina	0	0	0	2	0	**2**
Brazil	29	50	49	57	20	**205**
Chile	0	0	0	0	2	**2**
Colombia	25	26	37	24	24	**136**
Costa Rica	1	0	0	0	0	**1**
Dominican Republic	0	0	0	2	0	**2**
Ecuador	1	0	0	0	0	**1**
Guatemala	5	10	6	3	16	**40**
Honduras	12	8	14	5	4	**43**
Mexico	3	4	3	15	14	**39**
Nicaragua	0	12	11	4	0	**27**
Paraguay	3	0	0	0	0	**3**
Peru	9	12	2	8	0	**31**
Venezuela	0	0	0	1	3	**4**
Total	**88**	**122**	**122**	**121**	**83**	**536**

Note: Brazil registered the highest number of murders, with 205, followed by Colombia, with 136, and Honduras, with 43. The total number of murders in the region during this five-year period is 536.

Source: Alejandro Alvarado, "La criminalización de la protesta social: Un estado de la cuestión," *Revista Rupturas* 10, no. 1 (2020): 27.

In February 2002, the mothers reported the situation to the provincial Ministry of Health, seeking assistance in determining the causes of the illnesses. However, their concerns were ignored. In response, the women organized and took to the streets in protest. Amid these social demonstrations, the group came to identify themselves as the Mothers of Ituzaingó.[50]

In 2002, the causes of the illnesses were identified thanks to the intervention of Raúl Montenegro, an Argentine biologist and founder of the Foundation for the Defense of the Environment. It was determined that the Ituzaingó Annex neighborhood, surrounded by soy plantations, was exposed to high concentrations of pesticides and herbicides used in soybean cultivation.

Street demonstrations continued as the mothers protested in defense of the environment, demanding an end to fumigation around the neighborhood. In response, health authorities declared a health emergency in the neighborhood in 2002. A decade later, in 2012, a court ruling in favor of the Mothers of Ituzaingó recognized fumigation as a crime.

A FRAGILE INSTITUTIONAL FRAMEWORK

Democracy entails civil and political liberties for all members of society, without any form of discrimination. Based on this principle, there is a growing demand in Latin America for freedom of expression, the right to mobilization and protest, and the right to elect and be elected in a transparent context, among others. Discontent in Latin America has arisen from various issues, including constant ideological persecution, alleged fraud in presidential elections, state repression during protests, the killing of demonstrators exercising their right to protest, and even the systematic murder of social leaders.

Diego Escobari and Gary Hoover conducted an experiment to identify and quantify fraud in Bolivia's 2019 presidential elections.[51] The results of their study provide evidence that fraud was committed, increasing votes for the ruling party, Movement Towards Socialism, while reducing votes for the opposition party, Comunidad Ciudadana. According to the authors, this fraud was sufficient to alter the final results. In November of that same year, public discontent erupted in the streets. People were outraged by the electoral fraud and the prospect of Evo Morales remaining in power indefinitely. Widespread social protests against his government ultimately led to his resignation on November 10.

Venezuela presents another significant case. Although the country's leaders have been accused of concealing information about the true extent of social protests, the Observatorio Venezolano de Conflictividad Social (OVCS, Venezuelan Observatory of Social Conflict) has compiled key statistics on social demonstrations throughout Nicolás Maduro's regime—and even before, dating back to 2011. According to OVCS data, between 2011 and 2021, approximately 93,000 social protests took place in Venezuela, with the peak occurring in 2019, when 16,739 protests were recorded (figure 2.31).[52]

The OVCS classifies protests in Venezuela into two major categories. The first group includes protests demanding economic, social, cultural, and environmental rights (ESCER); the second group consists of protests related to civil and political rights (CPR). Of the 6,560 protests recorded in 2021, 4,853 (74 percent of the total) fell under the ESCER category; 1,707 (26 percent) were classified as CPR protests. That year, social protests in Venezuela were expressed primarily through rallies, although

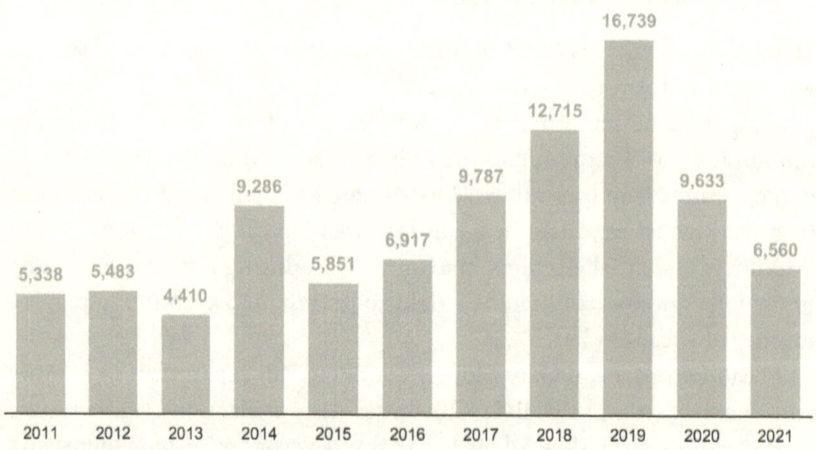

Figure 2.31 Number of social protests in Venezuela from 2011 to 2021. Protest activity increased markedly during the period, reaching a peak of 16,739 protests in 2019 amid severe political, economic, and humanitarian crises. Although the number declined in subsequent years, it remained substantially higher than in the early 2010s.

Source: Author's elaboration based on data from the Observatorio Venezolano de Conflictividad Social, "Protestas en Venezuela," Conflictividad Social en Venezuela 2021, https://www.observatoriodeconflictos.org.ve/tendencias-de-la-conflictividad/conflictividad-social-en-venezuela-en-2021.

street and avenue blockades, strikes, and marches were also significant forms of demonstration.

In more detailed terms, Venezuela's discontent in 2021 stemmed from society's demands for both political and human rights. According to OVCS, the protests were distributed as follows:

1. 2,066 protests were related to basic services, including access to drinking water (980 protests), opposition to electricity cuts (587 protests), and demands for domestic gas (499 protests).
2. 2,015 protests focused on labor rights, primarily driven by workers' demands for salary dollarization because the Venezuelan minimum wage was less than two dollars.
3. 1,240 protests were centered on the right to health care.
4. 1,051 protests addressed the right to political participation, with one of the main triggers being discontent over alleged irregularities in the 2021 mayoral and gubernatorial elections.
5. 578 protests demanded justice.
6. 270 protests focused on the right to food.
7. 218 protests were related to the right to life.
8. 213 protests called for improved citizen security.

CHAPTER 3

Social Discontent and Politics

During the 2010s, we witnessed a rise in social discontent worldwide, reflected in a significant increase in protests. In chapter 2, we explored some of the reasons behind this discontent as people take to the streets in search of better living conditions. Despite the socioeconomic progress humanity has made throughout history, significant challenges remain, including high economic inequality, a lack of opportunities for young people, pronounced gender gaps that put women at a disadvantage, the climate crisis, and the severe weakening of democracies. In this chapter, we take a step further. After documenting a world that has achieved great progress yet remains largely mired in social discontent, we now explore and analyze, based on data, the consequences this discontent can have on the political configuration of societies.

At the outset, we want to make one point clear: social discontent can have both positive and negative effects on political structures. It would be a mistake to view social discontent in a simplistic way, as inherently good or bad. In reality, the relationship between social discontent and political configuration is complex and ambiguous. Its impact depends largely on various factors, such as the nature and objectives of the protests, the response of political leaders, and the context in which they take place.

We dedicate the first section of this chapter to exploring the many positive effects of social discontent, classifying them into three proposed categories: greater political awareness, a new political reality, and radical change in the power structure. In the second section, we examine the negative effects. Social discontent can give rise to opportunistic practices that threaten society's well-being, which we categorize as either political opportunism or interest group opportunism. In the third section, we analyze the political and economic consequences of power exercised by a political opportunist.

POSITIVE EFFECTS OF SOCIAL DISCONTENT

Social protests have become a defining feature of democratic societies. True democracy ensures that citizens have the right and ability to organize protests as a means of political participation and freedom of expression. In modern societies, protests serve as one of the most important mechanisms for citizens to voice their concerns, demands, and opinions on political and social issues.

Social protest is a fundamental right of every citizen in a democracy. However, this right is subject to legal restrictions aimed at maintaining public order and security. The general rule is that protests must be peaceful and must not infringe on the rights of others. Protests should not endanger the lives of demonstrators, nondemonstrators, and security forces, nor should they result in damage to public or private property. This means that individuals exercising their right to protest must do so responsibly and respectfully.

The right to protest has been widely studied and discussed in numerous works that recognize its crucial role in the political and social dynamics. For instance, Sidney Tarrow provides a detailed analysis of various social movements, concluding that protests have a significant impact on policies and institutions.[1] According to Tarrow, collective action can influence policy decisions by pressuring policymakers to address the issues raised by protesters. Tarrow argues that social protests can also drive institutional changes, such as reforms in the electoral system or the creation of new mechanisms for citizen participation.

In a similar research agenda, Doug McAdam, Sidney Tarrow, and Charles Tilly examine how and why protests have occurred throughout history.[2] Their book explores the evolution of collective action, from popular revolts to modern demonstrations. The authors argue that protests have been a fundamental component of societies and have often led to transformations in power structures. This occurs for several reasons, including the direct challenge that protests pose to established elites—a challenge that has, in many cases, led to the overthrow of dominant groups. Protests can also empower historically marginalized and disadvantaged communities, potentially leading to a redistribution of political power in their favor.

It is also worth mentioning Alberto Melucci's book, which encapsulates the core ideas of the theory of new social movements.[3] Developed between the 1970s and 1980s, this theory emerged in response to shifts in the nature and dynamics of social movements at the time. It challenges the traditional view that social movements are solely driven by class struggle or economic concerns, instead highlighting the role of cultural identities and social issues in political mobilization. Building on these premises, Melucci argues that social protests serve as expressions of identity and forms of citizen participation in politics.[4] According to him, protests have the power to unite people around issues they consider fundamental to their identity and enable citizens to influence political decision making and voice their concerns on public matters.

We can also build on other previous works, such as that developed by Doug McAdam, which examines how protests emerge in response to societal tensions and challenges, and that of Frances Piven and Richard Cloward, who argue that protests serve as a means of pressuring for social and political change.[5] Based on this literature review, we classify the positive effects of social discontent into three categories: increased political awareness, a new political reality, and radical change in the power structure. Through these categories, we aim to show that social discontent not only drives changes in policies or power structures, as is commonly believed, but also significantly shapes how people engage with society and influences their attitudes toward political performance and development.

INCREASED POLITICAL AWARENESS

When faith in the institutions and political framework that govern a society is lost, several outcomes can arise. One possibility is that citizens adopt an attitude of complete disengagement, believing that no matter what they do, nothing will change. This scenario is particularly damaging to democratic societies and is often reflected in low voter turnout. The alternative—and the one most conducive to strengthening democracy—is for citizens to channel their discontent into a genuine concern for societal issues, translating this concern into political action aimed at improvement.

By "political awareness," we refer to an individual's understanding of and concern for political issues. This entails not only grasping the political dynamics of their context—such as the governing system, key leaders, and significant political processes—but also actively participating in political decision making in an informed manner.

Three positive effects of social discontent fall under this first category of political awareness. The first relates to social and political mobilization. When people's discontent grows and they refuse to remain passive, choosing instead to take action, social discontent drives greater political participation. In such cases, discontent heightens public awareness of political and social issues that might otherwise be overlooked. For example, when communities become frustrated with the pollution caused by companies in their environment and organize to demand action from their leaders—such as the case of the Mothers of Ituzaingó in Argentina—social discontent transforms into collective activism. When social discontent leads to increased social and political mobilization, it also creates a favorable environment for public debate and discussion. This in turn fosters a more democratic society by encouraging the expression of diverse perspectives and addressing a wider range of societal needs.

The second effect relates to the oversight of public resources. A discontented citizenry is more likely to monitor and scrutinize the actions of political leaders. While proper oversight of public resources should always be in place in any political system, this scrutiny tends to intensify when citizens lose faith in existing oversight mechanisms and feel a greater need to hold their leaders accountable. The advantage of increased public oversight is that when citizens actively question government actions and demand accountability, they help reduce opportunities for corruption and promote greater transparency in governance.

The third effect concerns electoral participation. Dissatisfaction with the status quo can motivate people to become more informed and engaged in politics. Social discontent, in this sense, can drive greater voter interest during elections when citizens see voting as a means to influence policy direction. During elections, people tend to seek candidates who promise solutions to the sources of their frustration. A key example of this effect was the 2020 US presidential election, which saw the highest voter turnout since 1904.[6] In that election, Joe Biden (Democratic Party) faced then president Donald Trump (Republican Party), who was seeking reelection. One interpretation is that growing public discontent with Trump's policies and controversial statements led to heightened voter turnout and Biden's victory. In the 2024 US presidential election, however, the electorate shifted course, returning to Trump's political program. As a result, he was inaugurated once again as president of the United States in January 2025.

A NEW POLITICAL REALITY

Social discontent, expressed through protests, is not only a way for dissatisfied individuals to raise their voices. It is also a powerful mechanism for pressuring authorities to enact change. Marginalized groups, disadvantaged communities, or any collectives that perceive a particular situation as harmful to their interests often see protests and social mobilization as opportunities to demand political change from those in power and to alleviate their grievances.

In this second category, which we refer to as "new political reality," we group three positive effects that contribute, broadly speaking, to changes in the political landscape. These changes extend beyond the specific policies implemented at a given time and place, sometimes also influencing the individuals responsible for shaping and enforcing those policies.

The first positive effect is increased political competition. When people are dissatisfied with the state of their society, it is natural for new leaders or political parties to emerge in response, seeking to gain power and address public demands. Competition is beneficial, particularly in politics, because it fosters democratic debate and encourages both established and alternative groups to refine their policies and proposals. This dynamic ultimately benefits society as political actors strive to develop agendas with policies that appeal to the widest possible support base in order to win at the polls.

The second positive effect is changes in policy decisions. Achieving this does not always require a change in leadership; if social movements exert enough pressure on the existing political structure, their demands can be addressed without the need for a turnover in power. In this sense, social discontent pushes policymakers to respond to public concerns, compelling them to adapt and modify policies to address the root causes of dissatisfaction. This pressure can lead to significant policy shifts aimed at improving societal conditions and meeting citizens' demands.

The third positive effect, closely related to the second, is political reform. Here, we make the following distinction: policy changes can vary in scope. When a change addresses a specific issue with a temporary or localized policy response, we refer to it as a "change in policy decisions," as discussed in the previous section. For example, if a company is polluting the environment, policymakers may intervene to regulate that particular company or introduce broader measures, such as stricter regulations or a pollution tax.

However, when a change seeks to resolve a more fundamental issue with long-term implications, we refer to it as "political reform." This involves modifying the rules and structures of governance, typically through constitutional amendments or changes to fundamental laws. Political reforms are larger in scale but remain achievable in democratic societies, often driven by the sustained pressure of social discontent.

Social discontent can lead to positive political shifts within a society. One of the most notable examples of this is the case of Franklin D. Roosevelt, who was president of the United States from 1933 to 1945. The Great Depression caused a severe economic crisis, which in turn fueled widespread discontent and distrust toward the US government, led at the time by President Herbert Hoover. Social protests, including marches by the unemployed and demands for government intervention, became frequent during this period.

Against this backdrop, Roosevelt ran for president in 1932 as the Democratic Party nominee. His campaign centered on the promise of a New Deal—a series of policies aimed at addressing the economic crisis and improving the socioeconomic conditions of the American people. With this message, Roosevelt won the election and became the thirty-second president of the United States.

As president, Roosevelt implemented a series of programs and reforms under the New Deal. They were aimed primarily at alleviating poverty, improving working conditions, and revitalizing the economy. His policies focused on increasing public spending and expanding state intervention to establish a pension system, create an unemployment subsidy program, protect workers' rights, and finance infrastructure projects. The New Deal is widely regarded as the foundation of the modern welfare state in the United States.[7]

RADICAL CHANGE IN THE POWER STRUCTURE

When social discontent is significant and persistent, it can lead to profound and lasting changes in the composition and dynamics of the power structure. In this third and final category, we focus on the deep and enduring transformations that social discontent can bring about in societies. History has documented several instances where widespread discontent has reshaped power structures, ultimately paving the way for a more favorable social, economic, and political environment for the population.

One of the most emblematic examples of this effect is the French Revolution (1789–1799). Widespread dissatisfaction with the monarchy, deep economic and social inequality, and a heavy tax burden fueled a popular revolt that ultimately led to the overthrow of the monarchy and the establishment of the First French Republic. Another illustrative example is the Russian Revolution (1917–1923), where discontent with the tsar's autocratic rule, among other factors, sparked both the February Revolution and the October Revolution. These events culminated in the fall of the tsarist monarchy and the rise of a Bolshevik-led communist regime.

Although the revolutions led to social reforms in both cases, they did not necessarily result in the political changes desired by those who participated in the protests. In France, this was evident in the subsequent rise of the empire under Napoleon and the eventual resurgence of the monarchy. In Russia, the revolution led to the consolidation of a nondemocratic political structure, which persisted for decades. Much later, in the 1990s, significant political transformations took place—also driven by successive social mobilizations across several Eastern European countries.

A similar phenomenon has occurred more recently with the Arab Spring, which we analyzed in chapter 2 and will revisit later in this chapter in relation to Egypt. In many cases, demands for greater democracy did not result in the lasting political changes that protesters had hoped for, highlighting the complex and often unpredictable nature of social mobilizations.

In figure 3.1, we summarize the arguments presented in this section regarding the positive effects of social discontent.

NEGATIVE EFFECTS OF SOCIAL DISCONTENT

Social discontent can also have serious negative effects on societies, including weakening the performance of democracies and economies. In this section, we analyze two negative effects of social discontent: political opportunism and opportunism of interest groups, with the former having more significant repercussions.

POLITICAL OPPORTUNISM

Social discontent is potentially dangerous because it can serve as an effective tool for individuals to gain political power and advance

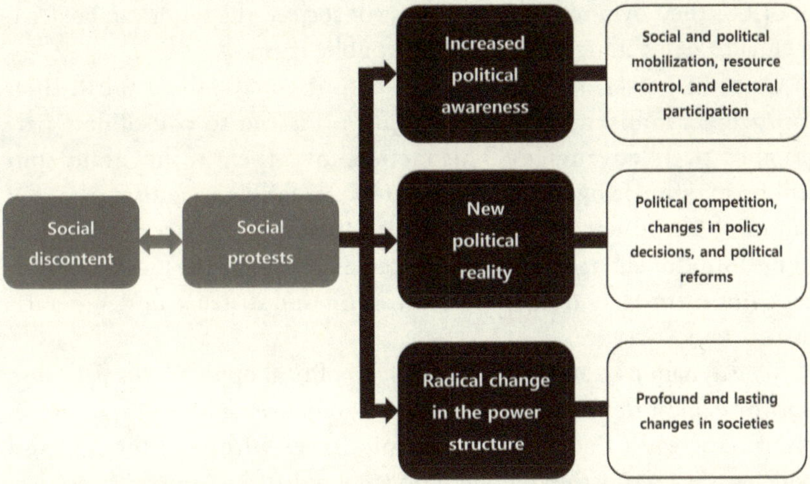

Figure 3.1 Dynamic relationship between social discontent and social protests and their potential positive effects. Social mobilization can increase political awareness, contribute to the emergence of a new political reality through greater competition and policy reforms, and lead to deeper changes in power structures that produce lasting transformations in society.

Source: Author's elaboration.

personal interests at the expense of collective well-being. The key mechanism through which social discontent is converted into political power is political opportunism, which involves manipulating the emotions and frustrations of the dissatisfied and thus turning their grievances into votes that enable opportunistic politicians to attain power. Once in power, however, these leaders do not necessarily address the problems affecting those who elected them. In concrete terms, political opportunism refers to the ability of politicians to convert public indignation into electoral support.

An opportunistic politician is someone who prioritizes maximizing their own position and power, regardless of the consequences of the means they use to achieve their goals. This idea has been explored extensively in political science, particularly within the framework of public choice theory. Pioneering works were instrumental in highlighting that not all politicians act in the public interest—some seek to maximize their personal gain, often leveraging their positions of power and access to resources at the expense of the general welfare.[8] When political leaders prioritize their own interests over those of society, the result can be detrimental to democratic institutions and public trust.

Once in power, the political opportunist may fail to fulfill their campaign promises, using their position instead to consolidate personal or party advantages. This tactic allows them to maintain control by manipulating public sentiment while failing to address the root causes of discontent. In this way, social discontent, rather than leading to meaningful change, can be exploited as a tool for personal or political gain, ultimately deepening frustration and distrust in democratic institutions.

This dynamic creates a cycle in which political opportunists gain support by exploiting dissatisfaction but fail to deliver substantive improvements. Instead of addressing systemic issues with well-thought-out policies, they resort to symbolic actions, populist rhetoric, or short-term measures that do little to resolve underlying problems. Over time, this not only erodes trust in political institutions but also fuels further discontent, making societies more vulnerable to future waves of opportunism.

When discussing political opportunism, we must also address what we call political moral hazard. "Moral hazard" is an economic term used to describe opportunistic behavior by an agent who, possessing information that others do not, has incentives to take risky actions, knowing that the consequences will not be borne by themselves but by a third party. Moral hazard is one of the many situations that can arise in the presence of information asymmetries (where some agents have knowledge that others lack). It is a concept extensively studied within the field of information economics, one of the most important branches of economic neo-institutionalism.[9]

In times of social discontent, if a political opportunist comes to power, they will likely fail to fulfill the policy promises that helped them rise to the top. Even if they implement measures to improve people's living conditions, these measures often prove unsustainable in the medium and long term, ultimately worsening those conditions. This represents a situation of moral hazard—specifically, political moral hazard—because the political opportunist possesses information that their followers do not (they cannot know whether the opportunistic politician will fulfill their campaign promises once in power; only they do). And the consequences of their actions are not borne by the politician but by society. If the measures implemented by the opportunist fail and instead harm society, that does not necessarily mean the opportunistic politician loses. The benefits and privileges of power ensure that their personal interests are met. While the opportunist ultimately benefits, society bears the consequences of the politician's reckless actions.

Political opportunism can manifest in multiple ways, and they have been well documented from both theoretical and empirical perspectives. It is important to clarify that these manifestations are not mutually exclusive and often overlap in practice. We will examine three ways in which politicians can capitalize on social discontent: populism, resource mobilization, and political polarization.

POPULISM

Populism is a political practice that seeks to capitalize on the frustrations and demands of the population. It relies on a strong communication strategy that appeals directly to nonconformists and the grievances of the people. This strategy is based on simplified rhetoric designed to create an emotional connection with dissatisfied individuals. These speeches prioritize popular sentiment over reason, aiming to stir emotions rather than foster critical analysis. By delivering emotional and oversimplified messages, opportunists gain people's trust.

Populist politicians exploit social discontent to attract more followers by constructing a narrative of heroes and antagonists. In this narrative, antagonists represent politicians and elites who have failed the people while in power, while heroes embody those who aspire to take power and address the grievances of the discontented. Populists present themselves as the voice of the dissatisfied. This antagonistic struggle is crucial to populist discourse because it elevates the hero's image—without a villain to fight, there is no hero to exalt.

Despite this negative outlook on populism, it is important to note that many argue it is an essential component of democracy[10] because "it is the way in which excluded sectors have accessed political participation."[11] The emergence of populism is not merely the result of chance or the malice of a few; rather, it can be attributed to the shortcomings of the political system. When mechanisms for participation and communication are lacking, leaving excluded groups without a means to address their grievances through the political system, populism emerges as an avenue to capitalize on social discontent.

Latin America has been the birthplace of several prominent populist leaders, perhaps the most emblematic being Hugo Chávez in Venezuela.

Elected president in 1998, Chávez remained in power until his death in 2013. He skillfully capitalized on the deep social discontent of Venezuelans, who were frustrated by a lack of opportunities, corruption, and inequality. Through charismatic and emotional speeches aimed at connecting with the most disadvantaged and excluded, Chávez quickly became the voice of the people. His promises consistently focused on reducing poverty and social inequality, but over time, the country's situation deteriorated, with widespread corruption, a severe economic crisis, periods of high inflation, and human rights violations.[12] These problems have only worsened under his successor, Nicolás Maduro.

Populism has been traditionally associated with left-wing political leaders. However, this approach has been widely employed by both left- and right-wing leaders. Regarding the latter, it is worth briefly mentioning the populist strategies used by the leaders of Hungary and the United States. Viktor Orbán is Hungary's ultraconservative prime minister since 2010 (he also held the position from 1998 to 2002). Donald Trump is the current president of the United States from the Republican Party, who previously served from 2017 to 2021.

The common denominator between these two right-wing leaders is that, in their populist rhetoric and in an effort to secure greater support, they have identified certain social groups as enemies that their respective countries must overcome. In Hungary, it has been documented that Orbán employs a specific othering strategy that involves framing certain social groups as harmful to society. According to Marton Gera, Orbán utilizes an us-versus-them discourse where the "them" includes the LGBTQIA+ community, which is portrayed as a severe threat to Hungarian society.[13] He links this community to other external groups that have also been labeled as dangerous to the nation's interests.

In the United States, one of the key campaign promises that secured Trump's presidency on both occasions was his anti-immigration rhetoric. Trump's primary populist tool is the promotion of a narrative that fuels xenophobia among Americans. According to Daniel Béland, Trump has depicted immigrants as a source of rising insecurity and unemployment, framing them as one of the most urgent threats the United States must confront.[14] Once again, an us-versus-them narrative is constructed—this time, the "them" consists of immigrants arriving in the United States, generally in search of better socioeconomic opportunities for themselves and their families.

RESOURCE MOBILIZATION

Politicians exploit social discontent to mobilize various types of resources in their favor, securing the support and power needed to achieve their personal goals. The resources mobilized can be categorized broadly as material and human. Consider, for example, the business sector of a given country that is highly dissatisfied with current tax policies, believing that it faces an excessively high tax burden. A politician could capitalize on this discontent by promising to lower taxes once in power. With this promise in mind, the business sector might inject funds into the politician's electoral campaign or provide other forms of support, such as physical venues for meetings or favorable media coverage.

POLITICAL POLARIZATION

In situations of social discontent, a confrontation inevitably arises between groups dissatisfied with a particular situation and those responsible for maintaining that situation. A politician who views social discontent as an opportunity for personal gain may resort to political polarization, which involves creating or intensifying conflicts between different groups in society. The political opportunist aligns with the dissatisfied, framing the situation as a battle between the others' interests and our own well-being to further fuel hostility and division.

Without a villain to fight, there is no hero to exalt. Through polarizing tactics, the image of the villain can be deliberately magnified. Rhetorical manipulation, exaggerated accusations, and misinformation are some of the strategies used to inflate the negative image of the antagonist. The greater the villain, the more support the so-called hero demands—leading to increased protests at their direction, more followers of their ideology, and ultimately more votes in their favor.

In Latin America, many leaders have used polarization to position themselves and strengthen their political power. One prominent example is Rafael Correa in Ecuador. Correa served as Ecuador's president from January 2007 to May 2017. In a 2021 article, Paolo Moncagatta and Ana Poveda analyzed the political polarization Ecuador experienced during Correa's decade in office.[15] Using data from the Americas Barometer and the Latin American Public Opinion Project, the authors propose an indicator of political polarization based on the idea that polarization involves a shift from the ideological center toward the extremes. One of their key findings is that Ecuador underwent a gradual increase in political polarization between 2006 (a year before Correa took office) and 2014.

This trend is explained quantitatively by the steady rise in the number of citizens identifying as leftist during that period. Correa consistently maintained a confrontational leftist discourse, which helps explain the growth of leftist supporters in Ecuador. His rhetoric framed the political landscape as a battle between himself, the defender of the people and the most vulnerable, and Ecuador's political and economic elites.

A recent example of polarization resulting in the victory of a right-wing candidate is the case of Argentina, where Javier Milei triumphed at the end of 2023 against the variant of Peronism that was in power. His victory was driven by a severe economic crisis and the inability of centrist parties to present a viable alternative. The most striking aspects of the crisis included rising poverty despite substantial public service subsidies, persistently high and increasing inflation, distorted relative prices, high public debt, depleted international reserves, and significant distortions in the foreign exchange market. This crisis is part of a decades-long pattern of slow economic growth, largely attributed to the recurring frequency of economic downturns. The failure of policies to reverse this trend, coupled with the severity of the recent crisis, led to an unexpected surge in support for a more extreme political position.

The agenda proposed by the new president is arguably the most neoliberal in Latin American history, surpassing even the policies introduced by Augusto Pinochet's dictatorship in Chile at the beginning of his rule. Upon taking office, Milei upheld his objectives with a mix of pragmatism and boldness, despite facing significant challenges to governability. The decisions implemented have sparked strong confrontations, including intense legal debates over the extent of executive authority; reactions from various sectors affected by the repeal of favorable legislation; and social mobilizations against the government, particularly from labor unions.

STATE CAPTURE

Populism, resource mobilization, and political polarization are ways in which political opportunism manifests itself. These forms often intertwine in practice. For example, in a typical populist speech, the speaker not only makes grand promises to the audience but also encourages them to take to the streets in protest while fueling their struggle against the established elite through sentiment and exaggeration. These three forms of political opportunism can be highly effective in positioning politicians in power. However, gaining power is not the only way to exploit social discontent; politicians can also use public indignation to maintain their hold on power. Once opportunistic politicians assume office, they can continue employing populism, resource mobilization, or political polarization. However, they now have access to a fourth mechanism, which we refer to here as state capture.

Here, we define state capture as the inappropriate practice by political leaders of manipulating norms and institutions to serve their personal interests and priorities—often to the detriment of the general public.[16] State capture takes multiple forms, including the appointment of loyal individuals to key positions in state entities, the use of clientelism or nepotism to serve personal interests, the awarding of public contracts under prearranged conditions, and the restriction of political competition to secure a prolonged hold on power.

Politicians may once again exploit the discontent that brought them to office—this time to justify policies and measures that consolidate and expand their dominance. The power and influence they now wield enables them to control and manipulate state institutions, branches of government, and public resources, as well as regulatory and oversight bodies.

In chapter 2, we examined the Arab Spring, a historical period marked by widespread protests against authoritarian regimes across the Arab world. Egypt was a key part of this movement. Demonstrations in February 2011 led to the resignation of President Hosni Mubarak after nearly thirty years in power—a rule characterized by corruption and upheld by a military regime. The protests continued, however, driven by the people's demand for a transition to democracy. As a result, elections were held in July 2011, leading to the victory of Mohamed Morsi, the candidate from the Islamist Muslim Brotherhood party. Morsi would go down in history as Egypt's first democratically elected president.

Democracy was short-lived, however, because Morsi's government employed state capture to consolidate the Muslim Brotherhood's hold on power and prevent Egyptians from replacing them in future elections. To achieve this, Morsi captured the state by, for instance, granting members of the Muslim Brotherhood disproportionate control over the judiciary and the media, issuing presidential decrees to expand his powers, restricting the courts' ability to review his decisions, and strengthening his control over the military with the appointment of members of the Muslim Brotherhood to key positions within the armed forces.

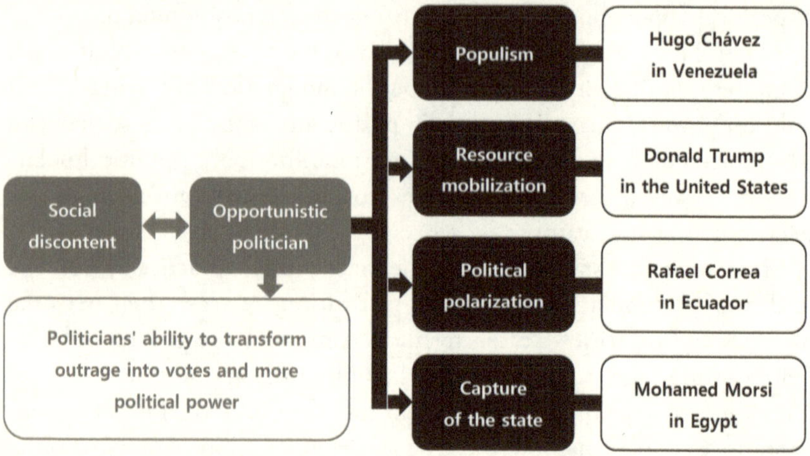

Figure 3.2 Political actors exploiting social discontent to gain political advantage. Social discontent can be transformed into political capital through opportunistic strategies such as populism, resource mobilization, political polarization, and the capture of the state, illustrated by cases including Hugo Chávez in Venezuela, Donald Trump in the United States, Rafael Correa in Ecuador, and Mohamed Morsi in Egypt.

Source: Author's elaboration.

Morsi's state capture was always intended to grant him dictatorial powers, making it evident that he and the Muslim Brotherhood aimed to entrench their rule rather than serve the general welfare of Egypt's' population. It is not surprising that his government lasted only about a year. The same social discontent that had brought him to power ultimately became the force that overthrew him because of his excessive and abusive use of state capture.

In figure 3.2, we summarize the arguments presented in this section regarding political opportunism in times of social discontent.

OPPORTUNISM OF INTEREST GROUPS

In every country, interest groups seek to influence political leaders to promote decisions that align with their objectives. Mancur Olson studied the consequences of these dynamics and pointed out that they often lead to protectionist policies that hinder technological innovation and restrict economic growth. A particularly concerning aspect, according to Olson, is the lack of significant opposition to such policies.[17] This absence of resistance may stem from the fact that the benefits of these policies are largely concentrated within lobbying groups, while the costs are distributed across a broader segment of society. Because these costs are so widely dispersed, they become difficult for individuals to identify, reducing the general population's ability to perceive them and take action.

Social discontent is often used as a bargaining tool to increase the leverage of interest groups in negotiations. While the agendas of interest groups may be legitimate, they are often advanced coercively by instrumentalizing social discontent. This results in negotiations that are not truly balanced because the objectives and interests of opposing parties are significantly weakened. In most cases, the party most affected by the opportunism of interest groups is the government.

How can social discontent be used to promote the interests of a particular group? To answer this question, it is useful to examine some of the most common cases of opportunism by interest groups. For instance, widespread public discontent can serve as leverage for unions seeking higher wages in negotiations with the government and businesses. It can also benefit business groups that demand tax exemptions or subsidies from the government.

Suppose a social protest erupts because of a decline in the quality of higher education. In response, it is expected that young people will take to the streets to demand improvements in the education system. This situation could be leveraged by unions to advance their own agenda. A common strategy in such cases involves first publicly expressing solidarity with the students' demand for a better education system. Then, amid the protests, unions introduce their own call for higher wages. In this way, what initially began as a movement focused on a specific issue (better education) becomes intertwined with the broader objectives of a particular interest group (union members seeking higher wages).

Interests pursued by business groups, such as advocating for tax breaks and subsidies, can significantly influence government policies. An example is the case of gasoline subsidies. Cars and gasoline are complementary goods—meaning that both are needed for proper use; a sharp increase in gasoline prices discourages car purchases. Thus, businesses involved in car sales are not only focused on selling vehicles but also on ensuring that gasoline prices remain low enough to encourage demand. One of the most favored mechanisms by the business community to achieve this is government subsidies for gasoline. When these subsidies are removed, widespread social protests are likely to emerge among car owners. The public transport sector would protest because their operational costs increase. Everyday commuters would protest because of the higher cost of transportation. At first glance, these protests may seem solely about public grievances, but they often serve the commercial interests of car sellers, who leverage the unrest as a means to pressure the government into maintaining gasoline subsidies to protect their profits.

CONSEQUENCES OF POLITICAL OPPORTUNISM

POLITICAL CONSEQUENCES

Democracy is a political system that enables citizens to choose their leaders through participation mechanisms, primarily elections. Voting represents a citizen's trust in a particular government program, making it crucial for aspiring political leaders to gain public confidence. Political opportunists excel in this regard because they are skillful about connecting with the electorate to secure power through democratic means. Unlike revolutionaries or coercive actors, opportunistic politicians do not need force to attain leadership; instead, they leverage democracy itself to rise to power.

Once such politicians are in power, however, political opportunism can have serious consequences that undermine the very system that enabled it. While not an exhaustive list, three key negative political outcomes of opportunism include (1) the destruction of democracy, (2) the suppression of citizen diversity, and (3) an increase in social discontent. These consequences should be carefully considered by all members of a democratic society when electing their leaders.

DESTRUCTION OF DEMOCRACY

For readers, it may seem paradoxical that if democracy is the means by which a political opportunist seizes power, it is also what is destroyed once the opportunist clings to power. This paradox is rooted in the system of checks and balances that should exist in any well-constituted democracy. Once in power, the political opportunist inevitably clashes with the same democratic institutions that enabled their rise. The system of checks and balances, also known as the separation of powers, is a fundamental element of any democratic system, and it is designed to prevent the excessive concentration of power in a single figure (such as the political opportunist). This is achieved by distributing power among different branches of government, which should be able to check and balance each other. A system of checks and balances typically distributes political power among three branches: the executive branch, responsible for public administration and the formulation and implementation of public policies; the legislative branch, tasked with making laws, approving budgets, and overseeing the actions of the executive; and the judicial branch, responsible for administering justice, interpreting laws, and ensuring their fair application, with the authority to review the legality of actions taken by the other two branches.

When political opportunists win elections in a democracy, they are rarely satisfied with this alone; their ambitions drive them to seek additional means to impose their will and extend their hold on power. Imposing their will and perpetuating themselves in power are actions in fundamental opposition to democracy. To achieve these goals, it becomes necessary to tip the balance of power in favor of the executive branch, thereby dismantling the system of checks and balances and ultimately undermining democracy itself. To consolidate their authority, political opportunists must eliminate constraints on their power, leading them to attack and weaken the democratic institutions that serve as counterweights, such as the judiciary and the legislative branch, and also the media.

SUPPRESSION OF CITIZEN DIVERSITY

At election time, political opportunists present themselves as the voice and representative of the population groups that have long been excluded from government policies. For example, in much of Latin America, political opportunists have emerged, promising to vindicate the political rights and civil liberties of marginalized groups such as Indigenous people, descendants of Africans, peasants, youth, women, the working class, and the poor. Political opportunists rise to power with the support and votes of multiple social groups, but once in power, they simplify the political landscape into an us-versus-them battle, where the elite have traditionally governed in favor of a few in opposition to the multiple social groups convinced by the political opportunists' promises. This simplification benefits opportunists because it allows them to present their crusade in favor of citizens, providing them with legitimacy for the decisions they want to implement to advance their government programs.

However, the problem lies in the fact that societies are inherently complex and diverse, making it extremely difficult to reduce political confrontation to a simple us-versus-them dynamic. Such simplification contradicts the reality of citizen diversity: not everyone has the same needs, not everyone thinks the same way, and not everyone demands the same solutions. Given this heterogeneity, grouping all the discontented under a single label effectively denies their unique identities and silences their voices. Political opportunists, now in power, disregard the distinct demands of each population group, opting instead for a broad, homogenized narrative that fails to truly address their concerns.

INCREASE IN SOCIAL DISCONTENT

Political opportunists have the ability to transform public discontent into votes. Social discontent fuels the opportunist's rise and serves as the driving force behind their election campaigns. Once in power, leaders should address the needs of the discontented who elected them, as well as those of all citizens because a democratically elected government is meant to serve society as a whole. This ideal scenario rarely materializes, however, because political opportunists almost never fulfill their promises of improvement. Their campaign rhetoric offers simplistic solutions to highly complex problems. Once in office, they confront the difficulties of implementing their proposed policies, often finding them unfeasible. When citizens realize that their elected leaders will not deliver on their promises, social discontent resurfaces—sometimes even more intensely than before—leading to further protests, destruction of public and private property, loss of lives, and growing distrust in political institutions. Yet broken promises are not the only factor fueling discontent. The destruction of democracy and the denial of citizen diversity further exacerbate societal frustration. Figure 3.3 summarizes the political consequences that political opportunism could bring about, which we have analyzed in this section.

ECONOMIC CONSEQUENCES

Politicians who assume power have two alternatives: to fulfill or not to fulfill their campaign promises. In the case of political opportunists,

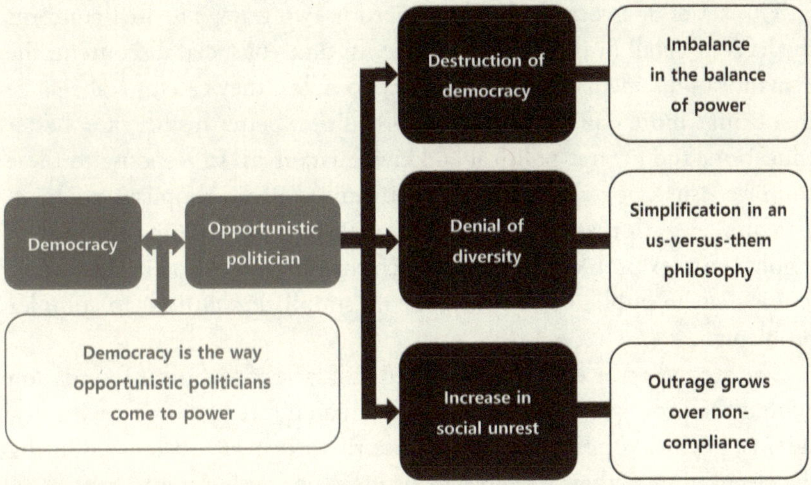

Figure 3.3 Political consequences of political opportunism. Opportunistic politicians, empowered through democratic processes, can generate negative political outcomes such as the erosion of democratic institutions, the denial of social diversity, and increased social unrest. These dynamics are associated with effects including power imbalances, oversimplified us-versus-them narratives, and rising public outrage.

Source: Author's elaboration.

either choice almost inevitably leads to a problem of political moral hazard. If they choose not to fulfill their promises and instead prioritize their personal interests from the outset, the consequences of their actions are not borne by them but by society. The result could be increased inequality, fewer opportunities for young people, and a widening gap in well-being between men and women. Meanwhile, political opportunists benefit from the privileges and favors that come with power and successfully advance their own objectives at the expense of the majority.

The other alternative for political opportunists is to fulfill their campaign promises. Even with the genuine intention to do so, however, this fulfillment often remains superficial because many of these promises are simply unachievable. Why? Because during election campaigns, the political opportunist frequently makes a series of mistakes—whether intentional or not—from the perspective of sound public policy design.

This series of errors can be categorized in two ways. The first concerns the level of detail in the promises made. In times of social discontent, the demands of dissidents are generally very complex: they call for real change that brings more equality, more opportunities, better health care, better education, and greater political and civil guarantees. In response to these complex issues, however, political opportunists offer a simplistic promise. To connect with dissatisfied citizens, they propose simple solutions to highly complex problems—an approach that appeals to voters. The problem is that, in public policy, there are no simplistic solutions to complex problems.

The second error can be categorized as a lack of technical foundation behind the promises made. Once again, in an effort to connect with dissidents, political opportunists prioritize rhetoric over substance. During the electoral race, their speeches focus more on stirring public sentiment and igniting popular fervor than on providing concrete, well-founded policy proposals. The technical aspects of their promises are either pushed to the background or omitted entirely. What matters most is crafting a speech that resonates emotionally with the people, turning their indignation into votes. Without a solid technical foundation, however, these simplistic promises become impossible to fulfill after political opportunists assume power.

What can be done? Between the two alternatives every politician faces there exists a gray area in which they attempt to fulfill their promises, at least to some extent. When politicians realize that their promises are unachievable but they do not want to outright abandon them, they often resort to implementing public policies that yield short-term results, regardless of their long-term sustainability. In particular, they adopt measures aimed at increasing equity in the short term, seeking to partially appease the indignation of those who placed their trust in them. This short-term approach to equity often neglects long-term sustainability and, more specifically, can pose a threat to economic growth. This scenario still constitutes a form of political moral hazard because society bears the consequences of declining economic growth, while the political opportunists have likely already secured their own interests. (The reasons why pro–equity policies may be linked to lower economic growth rates will be explored in chapter 4.)

The data are conclusive in quantifying the economic damage caused by political opportunism. Manuel Funke, Moritz Schularick, and Christoph Trebesch compiled a global database identifying fifty-one populist

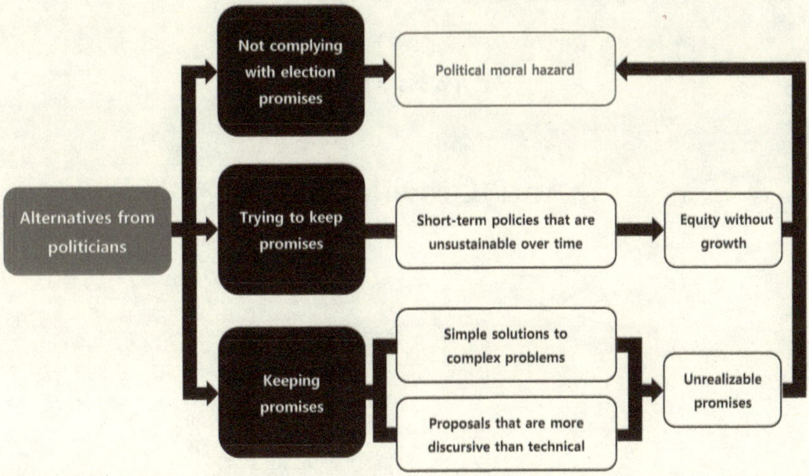

Figure 3.4 Economic consequences of political opportunism. Political leaders facing electoral commitments may follow three main strategies: failing to comply with election promises, attempting to keep promises through short-term and unsustainable policies, or implementing simplified solutions to complex problems. Each path generates different outcomes, including political moral hazard, equity without growth, and unrealistic policy commitments.

Source: Author's elaboration.

presidents and prime ministers elected to office between 1900 and 2020.[18] The authors estimated that the economic costs of populism include a 10 percent lower gross domestic product (GDP) per capita compared to a nonpopulist counterfactual scenario. They attributed this loss to the deterioration of the economic system, a decline in macroeconomic stability, and the weakening of institutions—conditions that typically arise under populist governments. Figure 3.4 summarizes the economic consequences that political opportunism could bring about, which we have analyzed in this section.

CHAPTER 4

Anti–Growth Equity

In chapter 3, we examined how political opportunism can emerge in response to growing social discontent. To capitalize on widespread dissatisfaction, it is common to promise citizens swift solutions to the issues causing their unrest. While these quick solutions may temporarily alleviate problems, they can also have significant repercussions on economic growth.

In this chapter, we shift from the political sphere to the economic sphere and explore the implications of social discontent for economic growth. Political opportunism, while potentially generating higher levels of equity in the short term, also carries the risk of reducing economic growth. This inverse relationship between equity and growth, arising in a context of social discontent, can be explained through several channels: the investment channel, the ill-timed welfare state channel, and the market interference channel, which will be discussed in the following pages.

Our task is to examine the research that has explored situations where greater equity comes at the cost of lower growth. Therefore, before delving into the three channels we just mentioned, we first review what the literature says about these scenarios of equity without growth.

As we will see, traditional economic theory generally treats growth as an end in itself, often overlooking other dimensions that are equally or even more important than the economic one, such as the environment. In response to this gap in traditional economic theory, alternative approaches have been proposed in which degrowth is considered an objective, with the potential for better environmental outcomes.

POLICIES OF ECONOMIC GROWTH AND DEGROWTH

THEORIES OF ECONOMIC GROWTH

Economists often define economic growth as the quantitative expansion, from one year to the next, of the income and value of final goods and services produced within a given economic system. This concept is typically measured by the gross domestic product (GDP) growth rate adjusted for inflation. For economists, this variable is crucial because the prevailing idea is that the higher the GDP growth rate, the more goods and services society can access to meet its needs, ultimately leading to higher levels of well-being.

For this reason, from the moment economics was recognized as an independent science—marked by the publication of Adam Smith's *Wealth of Nations*—economic growth has been and remains a central theme in economic research.[1] Smith himself dedicated much of his work to identifying and understanding the factors that make one country wealthier than another, using the criterion of a greater quantity of goods and services. Since then, a myriad of theories on economic growth have been proposed. Those that have gained the most traction more recently in economic, social, and political spheres are those that use mathematical tools extensively to formulate models that help us understand growth dynamics.

Among the most prominent models is Robert Solow's growth model, a seminal work on the subject.[2] Solow's model concluded that economic growth is driven primarily by increases in the factors of production—namely, capital accumulation and labor force growth. The first of these factors highlights the importance of investment and savings for growth because savings finance investment, which in turn leads to capital accumulation. According to Solow, technological progress plays a fundamental role because it enables economies to grow even when production factors remain constant. For this reason, Solow's model is classified as an exogenous growth model because long-run growth is explained by factors that are not determined within the model itself but are instead taken as given.

A few years before the publication of Solow's seminal work, Keynesian economists Roy F. Harrod and Evsey Domar developed a highly influential growth model. Harrod and Domar emphasized the importance of investment and its multiplier effect on growth.[3] They also highlighted the inherent instability of the economy, arguing that, because growth depends on investment, any decline in investment could lead to decreases in both employment and growth.

Not all growth models are exogenous. Unlike exogenous models, which assume that key variables such as savings and investment are given, endogenous growth models explain economic growth based on internal factors—factors that are themselves determined within the model. One of the most prominent models in this field is the Ramsey model, originally proposed by Frank Ramsey in 1928.[4] In Ramsey's model, saving is an intertemporal decision influenced by factors such as the interest rate and individuals' preference for present consumption over future consumption. This model allows for the calculation of an optimal savings rate that maximizes the well-being of both present and future generations.

The key recommendation derived from the optimal savings rate is that an economy should save enough to sustain an investment rate that enables sustainable economic growth—without the consumption of present generations coming at the expense of the consumption of future generations.

In the mid-1960s, Ramsey's proposal was taken up and further refined by David Cass and Tjalling Koopmans, who adapted Solow's model by introducing two key elements: the incorporation of a utility function and the derivation of the optimal level of savings.[5]

It is important to clarify that not all endogenous growth models focus on the savings rate. Some models explain growth based on factors such as investment in research and development (R&D) or the accumulation of human capital. Paul Romer argues that knowledge and technology can function as nonrival goods, meaning their use by one person or company does not prevent their use by others.[6] In this model, investment in education and R&D serves as a key driver of growth because greater investment in these areas leads to the creation of more knowledge and new technologies. Knowledge is not only a nonrival good; it is also one that accumulates and spreads over time, generating a virtuous cycle of sustained economic growth.

Two years prior to Romer's proposal, Robert Lucas developed a model that focused on the accumulation of human capital as a source of growth.[7] According to Lucas, human capital encompasses the knowledge, education, experience, and technical skills that individuals possess, all of which influence their labor productivity. As more people acquire skills and knowledge, human capital increases, leading to higher economic growth. Therefore, investment in education and workforce training is essential for any economic system seeking to maintain sustained growth rates over time.

In addition to classifying a model as either exogenous or endogenous, another significant distinction is between orthodox and heterodox growth models.[8] The orthodox approach includes models that attribute economic growth primarily to supply-side factors, placing less emphasis on issues related to demand and income distribution. In contrast, the heterodox approach views aggregate demand as the main driver of economic growth, prioritizing aspects of income distribution in its research agenda. This approach is associated, although not exclusively, with post-Keynesian schools of thought. Based on this classification, the contributions of Harrod and Domar are recognized as foundational for multiple post-Keynesian perspectives because they were the first to incorporate John Maynard Keynes's ideas into an economic growth model.[9]

From a heterodox perspective, the contributions of the Hungarian-British economist Nicholas Kaldor are also of great importance. His work is synthesized in what is now known as Kaldor's development law whose central argument is that the industrial sector is the main driver of economic growth.[10] Since this thesis was also proposed by the Dutch economist Petrus Verdoorn, it is commonly referred to as the Kaldor-Verdoorn law.[11]

The core idea of the Kaldor-Verdoorn law is that there is a positive causal relationship between industrial sector growth and overall GDP growth. One reason for this, according to the law, is the positive relationship between productivity growth in the industrial sector and productivity growth in the economy as a whole, which in turn drives GDP growth. As industrial production expands, workers shift from other economic sectors into industry, leading to an increase in the economy's overall productivity. Thus, the law suggests that total productivity growth is positively linked to industrial output and employment growth but negatively correlated with the growth of nonindustrial employment.

Kaldor's contributions are part of work by a broader group of authors who make up the post-Keynesian school. In addition to Kaldor, this school includes Michal Kalecki, Hyman Minsky, Joan Robinson, Lance Taylor, and many others. Some of the key contributions of this school were compiled in a work edited by José Antonio Ocampo.[12] An essential element of this school is its emphasis on price formation under conditions of imperfect competition.

Regarding economic growth, and in line with Keynesian principles, the post-Keynesian school challenges the neoclassical assumption that economies operate under full employment. It highlights instead the crucial role of aggregate demand in driving growth. This includes the effects of investment dynamics and its financing, as well as income distribution—particularly between workers and capital owners. Workers tend to have a higher propensity to consume, so an unequal distribution of income can influence economic growth. If the savings of capital owners do not translate into higher investment, the result may be negative effects on growth.

But what do the previous models have in common? They have all enjoyed significant popularity and acceptance. Regardless of whether they fall under endogenous or exogenous growth models, or whether they align with orthodox or heterodox theory, their common denominator is their focus on economic growth. The problem, however, is that in everyday life, not everything revolves around economic growth—nor should it. For this reason, there is now an urgent call to shift the paradigm: economic growth can no longer be seen as an end in itself; at most, it must be understood as a means to broader objectives.

Although these models primarily seek to explain the overall economic growth of a given economy, in practice, the growth of individual sectors must also be considered. This leads to various types of growth regimes and a debate over which regime should be implemented. A central controversy in classical economic development debates is the distinction between balanced and unbalanced growth.

The balanced growth regime implies uniform expansion across all sectors of the economy, aiming for proportional increases in productivity and economic activity to prevent extreme imbalances. In contrast, the unbalanced growth regime suggests that some sectors must grow faster than others. Implementing a truly balanced growth model is highly challenging, which is why authors such as Albert Hirschman advocate for unbalanced growth.[13] Hirschman introduces the concept of a sequence of investments triggered by an initial investment. If an initial investment in one sector sets off a chain reaction of further investments in related sectors, then a balanced growth strategy would be inefficient. Instead, unbalanced growth makes more sense because prioritizing investment in a strategic sector can eventually ignite a broader chain reaction, thereby promoting greater economic growth.

Another essential topic, closely related to the central theme of this book, is the need to integrate economic growth with social objectives. As discussed in chapter 2, the Human Development Index (HDI), developed by the United Nations Development Programme (UNDP), goes beyond mere production metrics by incorporating life expectancy and education—both of which, we should add, are strongly linked to environmental conditions. The Inclusive Development Index (IDI), created by the World Economic Forum (WEF), evaluates countries based on twelve indicators that extend beyond GDP, capturing factors such as poverty, life expectancy, and environmental sustainability.

When Jigme Singye Wangchuck was crowned king of Bhutan in 1972, he famously stated that Gross National Happiness (GNH) was more important than GDP. The four pillars of GNH include economic self-sufficiency, environmental conservation, the preservation and promotion of Bhutanese culture, and good governance through democracy. Although happiness may seem difficult to measure, the UN World Happiness Report attempts to quantify it by incorporating not only GDP but also factors such as generosity, perceived corruption, and the expected number of healthy life years, among others.

AN UNUSUAL ALTERNATIVE: ECONOMIC DEGROWTH TO PROTECT THE ENVIRONMENT

In chapter 1, we introduced several applications of the Kuznets curve, including the environmental Kuznets curve. This model examines the relationship between economic growth and environmental degradation, demonstrating that, in the early stages of development, economic growth leads to greater environmental degradation. Beyond a certain threshold, however, further growth is associated with improved environmental conditions.

One of the main reasons for the current call for a paradigm shift is precisely the concerns outlined by the environmental Kuznets curve: the pursuit of continuous economic growth can have severe consequences for the environment. For example, economic expansion can lead to increased air pollution; higher production levels generate more industrial and domestic waste, which often contaminates water bodies; and the ongoing growth of both the population and the economy intensifies the demand for natural resources, frequently resulting in their overexploitation, sometimes to the point of irreversible depletion.

Two key implications of these environmental effects are the need both to modify energy demand and sources of energy generation and to implement mechanisms for managing waste from consumption and production. The most radical approaches advocate for a deliberate reduction in production to protect the environment—a shift represented by the move from X to Y at the top of figure 4.1. This approach is known as deliberate degrowth.

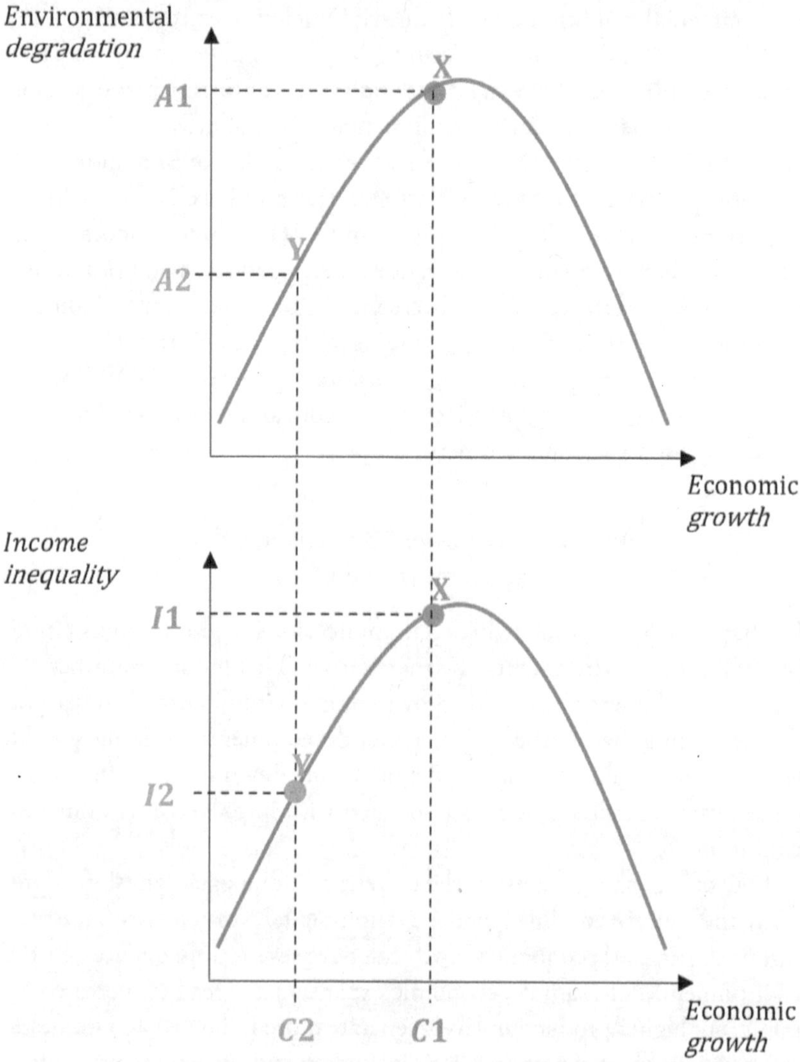

Figure 4.1 Environmental and traditional Kuznets curves in a situation of economic decline. The figure illustrates two nonlinear relationships with economic growth (one for environmental degradation and another for income inequality). The shift from point X to point Y represents a contraction in economic activity (from *C1* to *C2*), which is associated with environmental improvement (from *A1* to *A2*) and a reduction in inequality (from *I1* to *I2*), highlighting that economic decline can under certain conditions produce positive environmental and social outcomes.

Source: Author's elaboration.

Deliberate degrowth has been widely criticized, primarily because economic growth is intrinsically linked to employment. A reduction in economic activity could lead to job losses and thus a decline in overall well-being. The implementation of deliberate degrowth cannot be uniform across developed and developing countries. Developed nations, having historically contributed more to environmental degradation, bear greater responsibility for environmental protection. Meanwhile, imposing overly strict environmental protections on developing countries could hinder their economic progress.

The priority of preserving the environment can be traced back to the Club of Rome, a nongovernmental organization founded in 1968 and composed of politicians and scientists concerned about the planet's future. Seeking solutions to global environmental challenges, the Club of Rome commissioned a team of researchers from the Massachusetts Institute of Technology to conduct an in-depth analysis. The result of this initiative was the 1972 report *The Limits to Growth*, the first major study to highlight the negative consequences of unchecked economic growth on the environment. Using data on population and natural resources, the report concluded: "If the current trends of growth in the world's population, industrialization, pollution, food production, and resource exploitation continue unchanged, the limits of growth on this planet will be reached sometime within the next hundred years."[14]

The Entropy Law and the Economic Process was published in 1971 by the Romanian economist and mathematician Nicholas Georgescu-Roegen, widely regarded as the father of degrowth theory.[15] Georgescu-Roegen starts from the premise that resources are finite and, based on this, applies the second law of thermodynamics to the economy. He argues that every economic system is subject to the same physical limitations as any natural system: the production of goods leads to an increase in entropy, resulting in the depletion of natural resources and environmental degradation.[16]

Herman Daly, a disciple of Georgescu-Roegen, later proposed that economies should reach what he termed a "steady state," in which economic production remains at a constant level within the planet's ecological limits.[17] Georgescu-Roegen himself criticized Daly's proposal, contending that even in a steady-state economy, entropy and resource depletion would persist because of the finite nature of natural resources and the continuous generation of waste.

In 1987, the report *Our Common Future* (also known as the Brundtland Report) was published by the UN World Commission on Environment and Development (WCED), chaired by the former Norwegian prime minister Gro Harlem Brundtland. The report is widely recognized for introducing the concept of sustainable development into the global debate and highlighting the interconnection between economic development and environmental conservation. "Sustainable development" was defined as development that meets the needs of the present without compromising the ability of future generations to meet their own needs.[18]

In the early twenty-first century, the contributions of the French economist Serge Latouche further developed the theory of degrowth. Latouche stresses that degrowth seeks primarily to underline the need to abandon the pursuit of growth for its own sake.[19] Latouche argues that infinite economic growth on a planet with finite resources is unsustainable and calls for a fundamental challenge to the dogma of unlimited growth. He also advocates for a redefinition of prosperity, asserting that GDP alone is insufficient for measuring well-being. Instead, he proposes understanding prosperity in terms of quality of life, personal satisfaction, and collective well-being. Latouche recommends selectively reducing activities that excessively consume nonrenewable resources or that generate massive waste while encouraging research in renewable energy and sustainable agriculture.

Despite these proposals, no government has adopted a policy of deliberate degrowth—that is, intentionally plunging its economy into a state of degrowth to protect the environment. The common approach, which we consider correct, is to pursue economic growth policies with environmental sustainability, one of the core principles behind the UN Sustainable Development Goals (SDGs) adopted in 2015. Indeed, among the seventeen SDGs, several directly address the balance between economic growth and environmental sustainability.

On the economic growth side, SDG number eight (decent work and economic growth) aims to promote sustained, inclusive, and sustainable economic growth, along with full and productive employment and decent work for all. SDG number nine (industry, innovation, and infrastructure) seeks to foster sustainable industrialization that benefits everyone. SDGs number seven (affordable and clean energy), eleven (sustainable cities and communities), twelve (responsible consumption and production), thirteen (climate action), fourteen (life below water), and fifteen (life on land) emphasize the need to implement strategies that support both economic growth and environmental conservation. Achieving these SDGs is also the most effective way to fulfill the Brundtland Report's principle of meeting the needs of the present generation without compromising those of future generations.

BEYOND THE ENVIRONMENT: DEGROWTH AS A PATH TO EQUITY

Although degrowth theory does not explicitly focus on income equality as a goal, it is sometimes promoted not only to protect the environment but also to improve equity. In this view, degrowth can simultaneously contribute to a healthier environment and a more equitable society. This aligns with the models presented in chapter 1 because it corresponds to positioning within the initial section of both the traditional Kuznets curve and the environmental Kuznets curve, selecting relatively low levels of growth associated with a lower Gini coefficient (see figure 4.1).

Deliberate degrowth can lead to lower levels of inequality in several ways, including the following three. First, it can reduce inequality in access to natural resources. By decreasing production, a more equitable distribution of natural resources can be achieved, benefiting populations that have historically been marginalized, disadvantaged, or exploited. Second, it can be implemented through social welfare policies. In a context of deliberate degrowth, governments may be inclined to introduce social welfare measures to mitigate the potential negative social consequences of reduced economic activity, focusing primarily on the poorest citizens. Third, degrowth policies can specifically target sectors that have generated wealth at the expense of environmental degradation. This aligns with Latouche's concept of selective degrowth, as previously mentioned.[20] By reducing production in sectors that have concentrated wealth among a few while significantly harming the environment, society would benefit in two ways: lower inequality and an improved environmental state. A practical example of such a policy would be imposing higher taxes on unsustainable profits.

Given the above discussion, it is evident that deliberate economic decline can be one of the causes of higher levels of equity. In practice, however, higher equity levels are not primarily the result of intentional economic degrowth because it is rare for a government to choose to push its economy into a state of decline. Instead, governments directly implement pro–equity policies, with the causal relationship running from equity to growth rather than the reverse, as suggested in the degrowth scenario.

In the next section, we explore situations in which greater equity is associated with lower economic growth.

UNINTENTIONAL DEGROWTH: AN EFFECT OF SOCIAL DISCONTENT

Social discontent exacerbates social conflict by motivating dissidents to protest in pursuit of, for example, better living conditions. When social conflict reaches its peak, one of two scenarios—both of which we discussed in chapter 3—tends to unfold, each with significant implications for economic growth. In the first scenario, political leaders genuinely seek to improve the situation of those protesting by implementing well-designed and sustainable pro–equity policies. These policies can create synergy with economic growth strategies, ensuring that equity and growth progress together. Chapter 5 focuses on examining these types of pro–equity policies in detail. The second scenario involves political opportunism—when leaders exploit general discontent for their own gain. This strategy consists of offering grandiose solutions to the problems presented by dissidents, securing enough votes to seize power. The issue with these grandiose solutions is that they rarely provide a genuine resolution. If they do, it is often only superficial because the higher levels of equity achieved through the political opportunist's pro–equity policies would come at the expense of lower economic growth.

An additional scenario could complement either of the previous two while also directly influencing economic growth. In a context where social conflict intensifies, economic growth is highly likely to decline because of factors such as the destruction of capital, resource waste, and loss of business confidence, which in turn lead to a drop in investment and other unfavorable conditions that threaten growth. Thus, social conflict can have a significant impact on economic growth—either indirectly, by prompting pro–equity policies that may stimulate or hinder growth, or directly, through the undesirable consequences mentioned above (figure 4.2).

DIRECT EFFECTS OF SOCIAL DISCONTENT

A body of research has explored the various ways in which an increase in social conflict can directly and negatively affect economic growth. Negative impacts on the economy are not always the case, however, because social conflict does not necessarily lead to negative outcomes. As discussed earlier in this chapter and in chapter 3, social conflict arising from social discontent can have certain virtues, such as fostering political debate and promoting democratic arrangements. When protests and

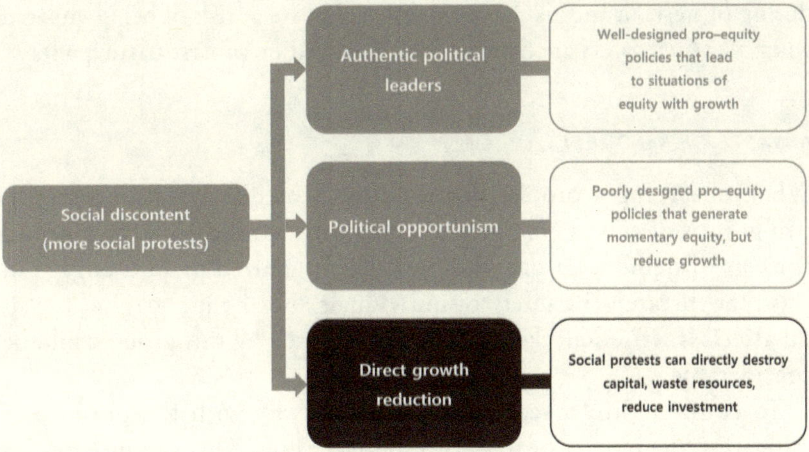

Figure 4.2 Three potential pathways through which increased social discontent, reflected in more frequent protests, can influence economic growth. Responses by authentic political leaders may generate well-designed pro–equity policies that promote equity alongside growth, whereas political opportunism may lead to poorly designed policies that provide short-term equity gains while reducing growth. A third pathway shows how social unrest may directly reduce growth by destroying capital, wasting resources, and discouraging investment.

Source: Author's elaboration.

demonstrations escalate into violence, however, social conflict can give rise to the situations we will describe below.

THE THREAT TO PROPERTY RIGHTS

Based on the compilation by Verónica Amarante and Gioia de Melo of studies that analyze the relationships between inequality and growth, we can affirm that social conflict, in the form of protests and violent riots, can pose a threat to capital.[21] Physical assets, such as machinery and production plants, may be damaged or destroyed during such events. The impact on these assets results in significant repair or replacement costs, which undoubtedly affects companies' ability to carry out their economic activities effectively.

Social conflict as a threat to capital also implies a broader threat to property rights. If the integrity of physical assets cannot be ensured during protests, it means that property rights are at risk of being violated whenever such assets are damaged or destroyed by protest participants.

A WASTE OF RESOURCES

When observing a protest that employs violence to gain attention, two groups of actors emerge and come into conflict. The first group consists of demonstrators who, whether organized or not, engage in acts that threaten the safety of individuals and the integrity of physical assets. If left unchecked, the damage caused by this group could be considerable.

To counter this, a second group must exist with the purpose of mitigating the impact of the first group's actions. This second group is responsible for defensive efforts while the protests take place. As Robert Barro points out, social conflict can lead to a waste of resources because individuals participating in the protests—whether as aggressors or defenders—are dedicating time and energy to nonproductive activities.[22] The efforts expended during a protest could be better utilized in productive activities that contribute to economic growth.

A DISINCENTIVE TO INVESTMENT

One of the main determinants of economic growth is investment, and social conflict can have a significant impact on this crucial factor. Based on the studies of Alberto Alesina and Robert Perotti and Philip Keefer and Stephen Knack, we can identify at least three ways in which social conflict can reduce investment levels.[23] The first relates to the threat to property rights. In a country where property rights are violated because of social conflict, an environment of business distrust is likely to emerge, hindering the creation of new companies and the expansion of existing ones. The second highlights that, beyond fostering distrust, social conflict can also create uncertainty for investors. In an uncertain environment, investment projects are more likely to be postponed or even relocated to other countries. The third factor concerns the political sphere. Social conflict shortens politicians' time horizons, leading them to impose significantly higher taxes on capital to generate greater public revenue—an approach that ultimately discourages investment.

Let's delve a little deeper into the above, into how social discontent can be a disincentive to investment. Let's start from the following, and that is that the level of investment I is determined by the following functional form:[24]

$$I(i) = I_0 + bi$$

This means that investment depends on two components: I_0 and i, where I_0 is the level of investment that does not depend on the interest rate, and i is the real (i.e., inflation-adjusted) interest rate.

Investment that does not depend on the interest rate fundamentally reflects a country's stability. This component includes, on the negative side, factors such as violence, transaction costs, and the state of the institutional framework responsible for protecting capital, among others. For example, consider two countries: Country A, where the government respects property rights and facilitates private enterprise development, and Country B, where property rights are constantly violated, and private enterprise lacks sufficient guarantees for growth. An investor deciding where to invest will feel more confident choosing Country A over Country B.

A country's stability depends on many factors, but in relation to our subject of study—social discontent—we can argue that investment, and consequently production, collapses in situations of severe social protests. Protests involving violence and destruction often lead to increased investor distrust, resulting in a decline in the resources available for investment plans. When deciding where to invest, investors first assess a country's risk. The lower the political and social risk, the more confident investors will be in allocating their resources. Because violence and destruction during protests are seen as indicators of political and social instability—and therefore higher risk—such protests undermine the component of investment that is independent of the interest rate.

For international investors, this effect is reflected in foreign direct investment (FDI). FDI measures the money that an individual, company, or government from one country invests directly in businesses or assets of another country. Unlike buying stocks or bonds, FDI involves acquiring a significant stake in a company or ownership of physical assets, such as factories or real estate, in another country. As shown in table 4.1, the reduction in FDI as a result of social protests is significant in practice in both developed and developing countries. For a sample of protests involving acts of violence, table 4.1 illustrates how FDI responded in such contexts. The results suggest that FDI experienced significant reductions following social

Table 4.1 Social protests and investment that does not depend on the interest rate (FDI as a percentage of GDP)

Country	Event	Start of the protest	FDI year of reference	FDI one year after the reference	FDI variation
Chile	Social outburst	October 2019	4.9% (2019)	4.5% (2020)	-8.2%
Colombia*	Civic strike in Buenaventura	May 2017	4.9% (2016)	4.4% (2017) and 3.4% (2018)	-10.2% (2017) and -30.6% (2018)
United States	Multiple protests against President Donald Trump	January 2017	2.5% (2016)	2.0% (2017)	-25.0%
France	Yellow Vest Movement	November 2018	2.8% (2018)	2.0% (2019)	-28.6%
Spain*	15-M Movement	May 2011	2.6% (2010)	1.8% (2011) and 1.6% (2012)	-30.8% (2011) and -38.5% (2012)
Hong Kong	Protests against the law mandating extradition to China	March 2019	26.8% (2018)	16.1% (2019)	-39.9%
Germany	Fridays for Future Movement	December 2018	4.2% (2018)	1.9% (2019)	-54.8%
South Africa	Demonstrations during the World Cup games	January 2010	2.3% (2009)	0.9% (2010)	-60.9%
Tunisia	Mohamed Bouazizi's immolation	December 2010	2.9% (2010)	0.9% (2011)	-69.0%
Egypt	White Revolution	January 2011	2.9% (2010)	-0.2% (2011)	-106.9%

* For Colombia and Spain, where the protest begins around the middle of the year, the year prior to the protest is taken as the reference for FDI, and the two subsequent years to this reference year are also reported.

Note: Data on foreign direct investment (FDI) as a percentage of GDP before and after major social protests in ten countries. The analysis uses the FDI value from the year prior to the protest as a reference and compares it with the FDI values one and two years later. In almost all cases, there is a noticeable decline in FDI following the protests, regardless of the country's economic context or the nature of the protest. The results suggest that social instability discourages international investment. The most dramatic drop is observed in Egypt, where FDI fell by over 100 percent relative to its reference value.

Source: Author's elaboration based on data from the World Bank, "Foreign Direct Investment, Net Inflows (% of GDP)," Data360, https://data.worldbank.org/indicator/BX.KLT.DINV.WD.GD.ZS.

protests. For example, France's Yellow Vest Movement began in November 2018, with FDI at 2.8 percent of GDP that year, dropping to 2.0 percent in 2019. In South Africa, some groups used the global attention on the World Cup as a platform to protest local issues such as economic inequality, homelessness, and other social concerns, leading to an FDI decline of more than 60 percent. The sample also indicates that the countries experiencing the largest decreases in FDI because of social protests were those affected by the Arab Spring—specifically Tunisia, the birthplace of the movement, and Egypt, where President Hosni Mubarak resigned.

One of the key differences between developed and developing countries is that the former developed countries have stronger institutional frameworks to protect foreign resources and stimulate local economic activity. One might then expect that, in the presence of nonpeaceful social protests, developing countries would experience a greater reduction in FDI than developed countries. The data in table 4.1 show that this is not necessarily the case.

Although the impact on FDI depends on many factors beyond social protest—including the nature and manner in which each protest unfolds—we can conclude that the effect of social protests on investment (independent of interest rates) is not necessarily more severe in developing countries than in developed ones; it can be significant in any country. This is evident when comparing the impacts observed in Chile and Colombia with those in France, Spain, and Germany.

Let us now examine the component of investment that depends on the interest rate, which in the investment equation is expressed as *bi*. From the perspective of those who borrow money for investment projects, the interest rate represents the cost of borrowing. Thus, the higher the interest rate, the lower the investment because launching investment projects becomes more expensive. In this sense, there is a negative relationship between the interest rate and investment, meaning that in the *bi* expression, *b* is a negative number.[25] This raises the question of the relationship between social discontent and the interest rate. If social discontent intensifies social protests, it can have significant economic and financial implications that may drive interest rates higher.

What mechanisms underlie this relationship? Let's start with the fact that nonpeaceful social protests can have a severe impact on a country's economic and political stability. In such a scenario, two key economic agents would react as follows. First, amid economic instability, foreign investors would demand higher rates of return to compensate for the increased risk, making the coefficient *b* more negative. Second, social protests could influence monetary policy decisions because central banks might raise interest rates to stabilize the economy.

In practice, we must recognize the existence of multiple interest rates: the central bank intervention rate, the interest rate on government bonds, and the interest rates that banks offer to savers and charge to debtors, among others. All of them have an impact on investment, typically in the direction we have discussed.

A key factor is the behavior of credit to the private sector granted by banks (as a percentage of GDP) because this credit is highly influenced by movements in the various interest rates present in the market. Figure 4.3 illustrates the behavior of credit granted by banks to the private sector in countries and regions that were the epicenter of major social protest events. For each country or region, credit levels are presented for two different years: the baseline year and the final year. The baseline year refers to the year before the social protests began, while the final year represents the point when credit reached its lowest level following the protests. The graph includes social protests that occurred during Donald Trump's administration in the United States (2017–2021), which contributed in part to the rise of a new wave of progressive governments in Latin America and the Caribbean (2020–2022). It also covers social protests in sub-Saharan Africa during 2010 (coinciding with the World Cup games, with protests spanning 2010–2014), those of the Arab Spring (2010–2012), and protests that contributed partly to the emergence of the pink tide in Latin America (1998–2003).

For these sample protests, comparing the credit level in the reference year with that in the final year reveals a decline in all regions and countries. These decreases range from 3.6 percent in the United States to 31.0 percent during the pink tide in Latin America and the Caribbean. An important caveat must be noted, however: figure 4.3 does not imply that the declines in credit are exclusively the result of social protests. Social protests are often triggered by underlying issues that can lead to credit reductions on their own. For example, the protests in South Africa in 2010 were driven by severe economic, political, and social challenges, such as extreme inequality—an issue that, by itself, could contribute to lower credit levels. Therefore, the results in figure 4.3 should be interpreted with caution, considering that the observed declines in credit are not solely attributable to social discontent.

To summarize, investment consists of two components: one that is independent of the interest rate and linked to a country's political and social stability, and another that depends inversely on the interest rate. When social discontent, expressed through protests, turns violent, it generates instability in the affected country, leading to a decline in investment that does not depend on the interest rate. It raises the cost of borrowing,

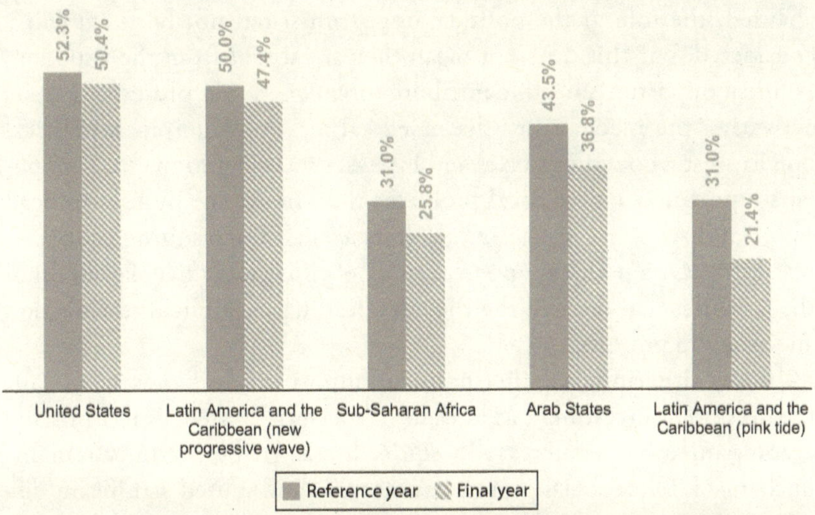

Figure 4.3 Comparison of domestic credit to the private sector (as a percentage of GDP) between a reference year (solid bars) and a final year (patterned bars) across selected regions and political-economic contexts. In all cases (ranging from the United States to regions in Latin America and the Caribbean, sub-Saharan Africa, and the Arab states), the data show a decline in domestic credit following periods of increased social unrest. These trends suggest that investments that depend on interest rates are also sensitive to sociopolitical instability and protests, potentially because of tightened credit conditions or decreased investor confidence.

Source: Author's elaboration based on data from the World Bank, "Domestic Credit to Private Sector by Banks (% of GDP)," Data360, https://data.worldbank.org/indicator/FD.AST.PRVT.GD.ZS.

increasing interest rates and reducing the component of investment that depends on the interest rate. Thus, in both cases, greater social discontent is associated with lower investment and, as a consequence, a decline in economic growth. This entire situation can be understood as a direct market-driven penalty for countries that fail to manage the potential economic consequences of social unrest effectively and promptly. The punishment is slower economic growth.

SIDE EFFECTS OF SOCIAL DISCONTENT

The investment channel we have just explored illustrates how social discontent can have a direct impact on economic growth. Within this channel, the role of the political opportunist has not been explicitly considered, but this does not mean they are absent from the situation. Political opportunism can contribute to violent social protests, thereby activating the mechanisms discussed earlier. For example, a political opportunist who reduces taxes and increases spending to maintain popular support may create fiscal problems that, in the medium term, lead to social discontent, triggering protests against the resulting economic instability. Or a political opportunist who gains power may fail to fulfill the promises that secured their victory, leading to public dissatisfaction and renewed protests.

In any situation, whether political opportunism is present or not, the decline in investment as a result of social discontent is not initially accompanied by an increase in equity levels. At best, equity remains unchanged. Once social protest has matured and caused significant disruption in society, however, the political opportunist may fully emerge, offering solutions that may temporarily mitigate unrest but rarely provide definitive resolutions to the underlying problems.

Pro–equity policies, which may seem to resolve these issues, can improve equity in the short term but may prove unsustainable over time and pose a threat to economic growth. Studies by Alberto Alesina and Dani Rodrik and Torsten Persson and Guido Tabellini construct models based on median-voter theory to examine the links between equity and growth.[26] These works conclude that in countries characterized by distributive conflicts, politicians, in an effort to win votes, tend to propose and implement transfer-based redistribution policies. These policies can reduce incentives for capital accumulation. As a result, equity is achieved without economic growth because the adopted measures, while improving distribution, are not designed to foster sustainable economic development.

In line with the above, we now introduce two additional channels through which social discontent can reduce economic growth. Unlike the direct effects on investment, these channels can initially increase equity levels and fully involve political opportunism. The two channels are untimely welfare states and market disincentives.

UNTIMELY WELFARE STATES

The welfare state refers to a political and economic model in which the state assumes responsibility for ensuring the well-being and quality of life of its citizens. This model involves providing various social services and benefits, covering areas such as education, health care, housing, social security, and other essential aspects of public welfare.

Discussions about the welfare state date back to the nineteenth century (and possibly even earlier), but today its origins are primarily associated with the post–World War II period. After the war, many European countries were devastated and needed to rebuild their economies and societies. In this bleak postwar context, proposals emerged advocating for greater state involvement in protecting and promoting citizens' well-being.

The welfare state flourished primarily in developed countries. Nordic nations such as Sweden, Denmark, Norway, and Finland implemented policies aimed at reducing social inequalities and providing a strong social safety net. France, Germany, and the United Kingdom adopted similar policies, though with variations.

Today, the welfare state is characterized by key features such as free (or at least easily accessible) education, social security systems—including universal health care—and housing subsidies, among other measures. It is no coincidence that developed countries provide the natural setting for the emergence of welfare states because this model depends on the economic development that generates the fiscal resources needed to sustain it. Financing measures such as free education or universal health care requires substantial resources, which are obtained primarily through taxation.

Therefore, for a welfare state to be implemented, a country's citizens must have a certain average income level because the taxes levied on them will fund welfare programs. In a low-income country, establishing a welfare state should be a long-term goal, but tax revenues would not be sufficient to finance a system comparable to those in developed nations. As we will see in chapter 5, however, there are elements that can gradually lead toward that objective.

In any case, it is important to recognize that income is not the only determining factor in the emergence of welfare states. Factors such as society's willingness to accept state intervention through higher taxation and the presence of efficient, transparent institutions are also essential. When analyzing the data, it is evident that public expenditure per capita is higher in countries with higher income levels, as shown in figure 4.4.

In an effort to win the votes of a dissatisfied electorate or to maintain power and credibility, political opportunists can implement welfare states at the wrong time. This occurs when the state enacts welfare policies that

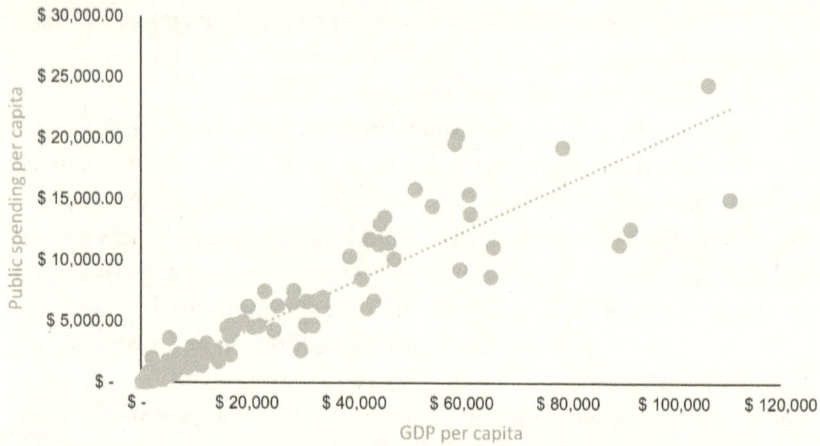

Figure 4.4 Scatterplot showing the positive relationship between GDP per capita and public expenditure per capita across 149 countries in 2023 (GDP in USD at constant 2015 prices). Countries with higher GDP per capita tend to allocate more public resources per person, illustrating how national income levels are strongly correlated with government spending capacity. The trend line emphasizes this positive association, although some outliers exist, indicating variability in fiscal effort among nations with similar income levels.

Source: Author's elaboration based on data from the World Bank, "General Government Final Consumption Expenditure (Constant 2015 US$)," Data360, https://data.worldbank.org/indicator/NE.CON.GOVT.KD.

do not align with the economy's income level but are perceived by dissidents as promising solutions to their grievances. While such measures may improve equity in the short term, they are fiscally unsustainable in the medium and long term. They create the illusion that everything is improving, but at some point, the fiscal outlook will deteriorate, affecting key variables such as investment, economic growth, public spending, and consequently social spending.

THE COLOMBIAN CASE

These considerations are particularly relevant to the Colombian case. When comparing Colombia to Organisation for Economic Co-operation and Development (OECD) member countries, we see that the country's tax revenue has historically been much lower. According to data from the OECD, between 1990 and 2022, the average tax revenue of

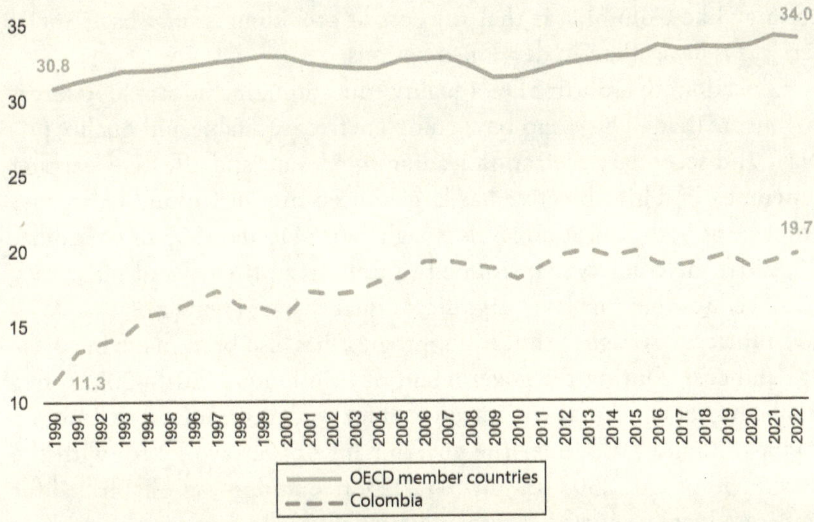

Figure 4.5 Comparison of the evolution of total tax revenues as a percentage of GDP between OECD member countries (solid line) and Colombia (dashed line) from 1990 to 2022. While OECD countries show a relatively stable upward trend, increasing from 30.8 percent in 1990 to 34.0 percent in 2022, Colombia exhibits a slower and more fluctuating rise, from 11.3 percent in 1990 to 19.7 percent in 2022. The persistent gap illustrates Colombia's lower fiscal capacity relative to OECD standards and highlights the challenges associated with tax collection and revenue mobilization.

Source: Author's elaboration based on data from the OECD, "Revenue Statistics in OECD Member Countries - Comparative Tax Revenues," OECD Data Explorer, https://data-explorer.oecd.org/vis?lc=en&fs[0]=Topic%2C1%7CTaxation%23TAX%23%7CGlobal%20tax%20revenues%23TAX_GTR%23&pg=0&fc=Topic&bp=true&snb=150&df[ds]=dsDisseminateFinalDMZ&df[id]=DSD_REV_COMP_OECD%40DF_RSOECD&df[ag]=OECD.CTP.TPS&dq=..S13._T..PT_B1GQ.A&lom=LASTNPERIODS&lo=10&to[TIME_PERIOD]=false.

OECD member countries and Colombia, as a percentage of GDP was 32.5 percent for OECD member countries and 17.7 percent for Colombia (figure 4.5).[27] In other words, OECD countries collect taxes at a rate proportionally 1.8 times higher than Colombia. However, this gap has narrowed because of a series of tax reforms implemented since the last decade of the twentieth century to uphold the social rights established in the 1991 constitution.

The transition to a well-developed welfare state requires both higher tax revenues and a clear redistributive approach, with social policies designed in accordance with the country's level of development and specifically aimed at benefiting low-income sectors. One advantage for a country like Colombia is that the cost of providing several basic social services is lower than in developed nations.

Education, the fourth SDG (quality education), includes a 2030 target to "ensure that all girls and boys complete free, equitable and quality primary and secondary education leading to relevant and effective learning outcomes."[28] This objective has largely been met in Colombia because coverage at both education levels is high. With Decree 4807 of December 20, 2011, the country transitioned to fully free primary and secondary public education. However, significant quality issues remain.

In the case of higher education, progress has also been made in coverage and cost. During the government of Iván Duque (2018–2022), free public higher education was introduced for students from socioeconomic strata 1, 2, and 3.[29] Under the government of Gustavo Petro, with the enactment of Law 2307 on July 31, 2023, free tuition was established for undergraduate programs at public higher education institutions, including universities as well as technical and technological institutions. Private universities enroll a significant proportion of students, and no subsidy mechanism exists for them—only loans through the Colombian Institute of Educational Credit and Technical Studies Abroad (ICETEX, Instituto Colombiano de Crédito Educativo y Estudios Técnicos en el Exterior). It is also likely that the greatest expansion of enrollments in the coming years will occur in these private universities.

At the Latin American level, Colombia stands out for the universalization of its health system, with coverage exceeding 99.6 percent. This is one of the achievements of Law 100 of 1993, which aimed to guarantee the right to health care. Approximately half of the population is covered under the contributory regime (where health financing is the responsibility of affiliates), while the other half is under the subsidized regime (where health financing is the responsibility of the state). Despite achieving universal health-care coverage, certain areas still require improvement.

The first issue is limited effective coverage, particularly in municipalities and remote rural areas, which highlights the need to improve primary care for the populations in these regions. The second concern relates to the target population of the subsidized regime because the country lacks an adequate identification process to ensure subsidies reach those who truly need them. The absence of a proper mechanism to assess and validate the socioeconomic conditions of potential beneficiaries results in an unequal distribution of health-care services, with many individuals who do not require subsidies still benefiting from them. This in turn can lead to inefficient allocation of health sector resources.

The third issue concerns expensive treatments funded by the state. The Colombian health system lacks a cost-effectiveness analysis to guide decisions on the provision of medications or the authorization of medical treatments, making it difficult to assess their viability. In several high-income countries, certain medical treatments are approved only for patients who meet specific quality-of-life criteria (for example, having a sufficiently high life expectancy to justify funding their treatment). In contrast, Colombia has no such mechanism, nor does it conduct thorough evaluations for the allocation of medications. In general, the expansion of education and health-care services has been adequate but still faces several challenges.

In other areas, particularly pensions, coverage remains limited, and subsidies are often granted to relatively high-income sectors; to overcome this problem, at least partly, the 2024 pension reform introduced a guaranteed minimum pension for the poor elderly individuals with no access to the contributory system. Therefore, it cannot be said that the country has developed a welfare state prematurely. Instead, it must continue building a broader social policy—one that aligns with its level of development. Achieving this will require higher public revenues, including adequate social security contributions.

MARKET INTERFERENCE

For a specific good or service, the market consists of aggregate supply and demand. The interaction between these two forces determines the quantity to be traded and the corresponding price. According to orthodox economic theory (also known as neoclassical theory), any form of subsidy introduced into a market disrupts its efficiency, preventing the optimal allocation of resources. As a result, society as a whole experiences a decline in overall well-being.

What does this have to do with the previous discussion? Why should market prices remain unchanged? Although widely criticized, the work of Milton Friedman and Rose D. Friedman—one of the most conservative in this field—attempts to justify the existence of economic systems free from market interference.[30] According to these authors, prices serve as signals in a market economy, indicating to market agents the relative scarcity of goods and services. Changes in prices influence the decisions of both consumers and producers. For example, when a price rises, it signals that the associated good or service is scarce, prompting producers to increase supply. Conversely, a price decrease may indicate lower demand or greater availability of the good or service, which may lead to a reduction in supply. Within this framework, when prices are determined by market forces (the interaction of supply and demand), they serve as an efficient mechanism for coordinating economic activity and allocating resources effectively.

A subsidy is a form of financial support provided by the state to certain industries, enterprises, or groups in society to encourage specific behaviors, activities, or outcomes deemed beneficial to society as a whole. This economic support can take various forms, such as direct payments, loans at reduced interest rates, or lower prices, among others. Recipients of subsidies generally welcome such policies because they provide financial support or specific economic advantages. However, this creates a clear dilemma: some argue that subsidies distort the market and lead to inefficient resource allocation; others defend them as a necessary tool for achieving specific social or economic objectives.

The proposal by the Friedmans can be quite extreme because some subsidies are necessary and do not have a significant impact on market efficiency. Examples include subsidies for education, health care, or housing for the most economically vulnerable populations. However, their argument holds merit in cases where subsidies are poorly designed. A poorly designed subsidy may result from political opportunism, for example, when it is introduced to appease social protests rather than address a fundamental issue. In such cases, subsidies serve as quick and easily implemented solutions, which dissidents are likely to welcome because direct cash transfers or price reductions are measures few would reject.

In this scenario, subsidies function as a short-term, politically motivated solution that secures approval from those who initially protested. However, when subsidies are implemented this way—rather than as a means to solve a genuine problem—they can distort prices to the point that the market no longer functions properly, leading to inefficient resource allocation. When this happens, incorrect signals are sent to market agents, resulting in wasted resources. In Colombia, several cases could be mentioned, but we will focus on two that affect employment and transportation: transfers that generate disengagement from the labor market and cases when social pressure threatens even the environment.

TRANSFERS THAT GENERATE DISENGAGEMENT FROM THE LABOR MARKET

When designing public policies for subsidies or cash transfers to households or individuals, one of the main aspects to consider is their impact on the labor supply of beneficiaries. Problems may arise when state economic support is conditional on the low income of the beneficiaries.

According to Robert Moffitt, a beneficiary may choose not to work or to work fewer hours to avoid exceeding the income threshold that would disqualify them from receiving state support.[31] Several empirical studies have examined this phenomenon. For example, Rafael Ribas and Fábio Soares and Alan de Brauw et al. found that Brazil's Bolsa Família program, which provides cash transfers to the poorest families, led to a shift of workers from the formal to the informal sector.[32] In Europe, Johannes Koettl and Michael Weber observed that informality increased in six Eastern European countries (Bulgaria, Czech Republic, Estonia, Latvia, Poland, and Slovakia) in response to the rising opportunity cost of formal employment.[33]

For Colombia, the studies by Stefano Farné, David Rodríguez, and Paola Ríos and Carlos Castañeda and Lorena Trujillo identify two reasons why subsidies can lead to detachment from the labor market, or at least from the formal sector.[34] The first is that subsidies increase the opportunity cost of entering the labor market. If state economic support is conditional on an income threshold, Moffitt's mechanism may come into play, leading to a reduction in employment levels.[35] The second reason is that formal employment involves income monitoring. As a result, labor informality becomes an attractive option for subsidy recipients who do not want to lose public support because informal labor makes it more difficult to track their true earnings. Whether a person chooses to work fewer hours (underemployment), not work at all (voluntary unemployment), or move to the informal sector, each scenario can have a negative impact on a country's economic growth by preventing the full utilization of its labor force.

WHEN SOCIAL PRESSURE THREATENS EVEN THE ENVIRONMENT

Since 2007, Colombia has had the Fuel Price Stabilization Fund (FEPC, Fondo de Estabilización de Precios de los Combustibles), which aims to mitigate fluctuations in international oil prices, preventing them from being immediately passed on to the prices of liquid fuels (gasoline and diesel). The FEPC was structured to operate autonomously as follows: it would subsidize part of fuel prices when oil prices were high and accumulate savings when oil prices declined. In other words, it was designed as a mechanism to stabilize domestic prices without generating a permanent deficit that the national government would need to cover. As figure 4.6 illustrates, one instance in which the FEPC deficit increased significantly was because of the decision of the Duque administration not to raise domestic fuel prices despite a sharp rise in international prices following Russia's invasion of Ukraine in February 2022. The economic support provided by the FEPC caused a significant distortion in liquid fuel prices. This effect was so pronounced that, by the end of May 2022, the prices per gallon of gasoline and diesel in Colombia were 44 percent and 39 percent lower, respectively, than the continental average (figure 4.7).

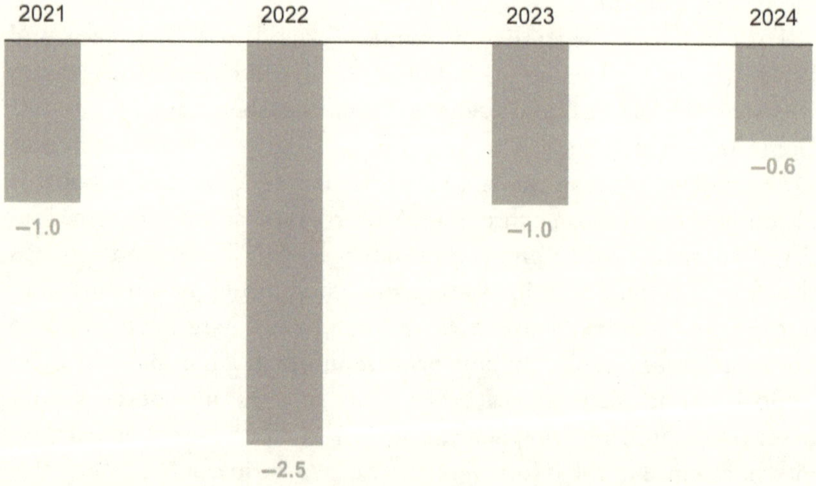

Figure 4.6 Net deficit of the Fuel Price Stabilization Fund (FEPC, Fondo de Estabilización de Precios de los Combustibles) in Colombia as a percentage of GDP from 2021 to 2024. The data reveal a sharp increase in the deficit in 2022, reaching −2.5 percent of GDP compared to −1.0 percent in 2021. This spike reflects the rising fiscal cost of maintaining fuel subsidies amid global price volatility. The deficit declined in subsequent years, falling to −1.0 percent in 2023 and −0.6 percent in 2024.

Source: Author's elaboration based on data from the Ministry of Finance and Public Credit of Colombia, "Marco Fiscal de Mediano Plazo 2023," https://www.minhacienda.gov.co/w/boletin-n.-25-minhacienda-presenta-el-marco-fiscal-de-mediano-plazo-2023.

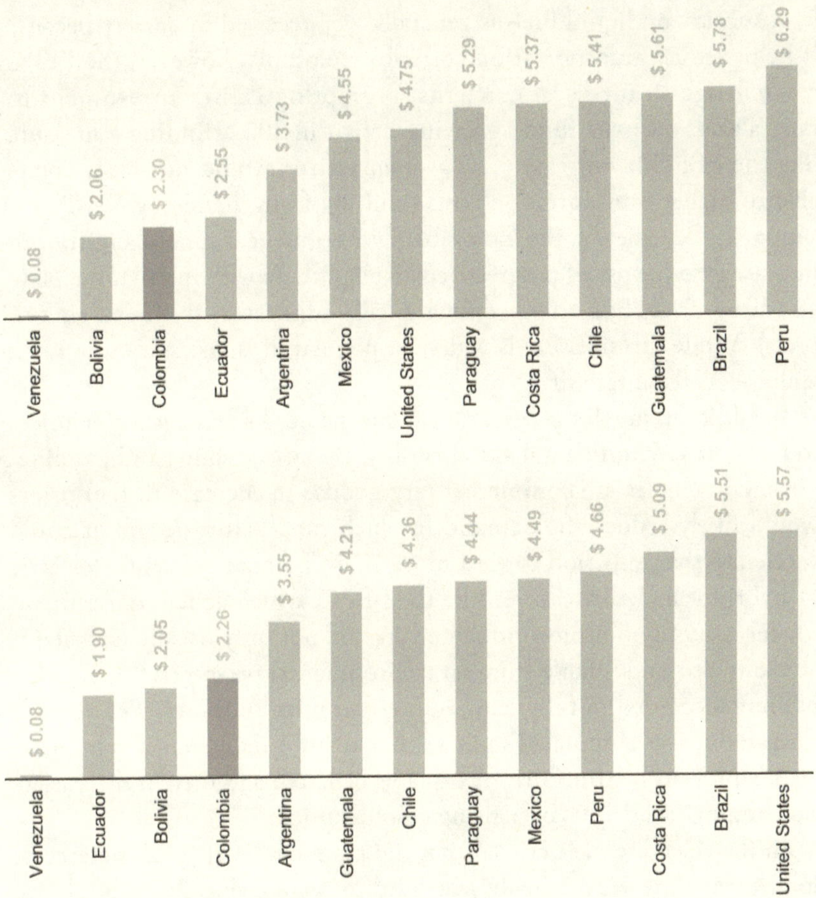

Figure 4.7 Comparison of the retail prices of liquid fuels per gallon in selected countries of the Americas as of May 30, 2022 (USD). The figure presents gasoline (*top*) and diesel (*bottom*) prices across countries in the region. Venezuela reported the lowest fuel prices ($0.08 per gallon), while the United States had the highest diesel prices ($5.57) and Peru the highest gasoline prices ($6.29). Colombia appears among the countries with relatively low fuel prices ($2.30 for gasoline and $2.26 for diesel), reflecting the impact of the Fuel Price Stabilization Fund (FEPC).

Source: Author's elaboration based on data from the Ministry of Finance and Public Credit of Colombia, "Marco Fiscal de Mediano Plazo 2022," https://www.irc.gov.co/conoce-colombia/informacion-fiscal/marco-fiscal-mediano-plazo/-/document_library/rvji/view_file/263624?_com_liferay_document_library_web_portlet_DLPortlet_INSTANCE_rvji_redirect=https%3A%2F%2Fwww.irc.gov.co%3A443%2Fconoce-colombia%2Finformacion-fiscal%2Fmarco-fiscal-mediano-plazo%3Fp_p_id%3Dcom_liferay_document_library_web_portlet_DLPortlet_INSTANCE_rvji%26p_p_lifecycle%3D0%26p_p_state%3Dnormal%26p_p_mode%3Dview&_com_liferay_document_library_web_portlet_DLPortlet_INSTANCE_rvji_fileEntryId=263624.

A subsidy on liquid fuels is generally well received by society because it helps reduce transportation costs. In Colombia, however, the FEPC created significant fiscal concerns, prompting Petro's government to raise alarms over the fund's growing deficit in 2022. Ending a measure like the FEPC is not easy. The average citizen would not react favorably to higher transportation costs resulting from the removal of FEPC support. Nevertheless, the Colombian government had no choice but to increase gasoline prices progressively to align them with international levels (diesel prices had only been marginally adjusted as this book goes to press). While this measure is widely unpopular, it is necessary to protect Colombia's fiscal stability.

In addition, much has been said about the need to raise gasoline prices to promote environmental sustainability. Because gasoline and gasoline-powered vehicles are complementary goods, an increase in fuel prices would likely reduce the demand for such cars. If this occurs, it could accelerate the transition toward more environmentally friendly electric or hybrid vehicles. Measures like the FEPC, which generate incentives for the use of pollution-producing cars, are not only fiscally unsustainable but also undesirable from an environmental perspective. Colombia has not succeeded in fully eliminating fuel price subsidies. The subsidy for gasoline was eliminated in 2023, but that for diesel remains in place. Strong protests by truck drivers explain the latter, and there is dissatisfaction among taxi drivers over rising gasoline prices.

In the first case, it is crucial that the planned diesel price increase be implemented. It was originally scheduled to begin in July 2023, but it was postponed multiple times, with only minimal increases having been decreed so far. The government has considered a possible gasoline subsidy exclusively for taxi drivers, but no steps have been taken in that regard. According to economic analysis institutions such as the National Association of Financial Institutions, this new subsidy would be unjustified because higher-income individuals are the primary users of taxis and could absorb a fare increase to offset rising fuel costs.[36] Subsidizing gasoline for taxis would be an expense borne by all Colombians. A subsidy for taxi drivers, like the FEPC, would be both fiscally and environmentally unjustifiable.

A SYNTHESIS

In summary, we can identify at least three channels through which greater equity—often unsustainable over time—comes at the expense of lower economic growth rates. The first is the investment channel, where social protests involving violence have a negative impact on investment, a key macroeconomic variable. The second is the ill-timed welfare state channel, which refers to cases where a government implements equity policies that exceed its capacity for income generation and tax collection. The third is the market interference channel, which encompasses situations where seemingly pro–equity policies disrupt market functioning to the extent that resources are no longer allocated efficiently.

We also outline how each of these three channels operates in the context of social discontent. The investment channel is directly triggered by violent social protests, whereas the ill-timed welfare state and market interference channels come into play when political opportunists seek to capitalize on social unrest. Figure 4.8 summarizes the discussion.

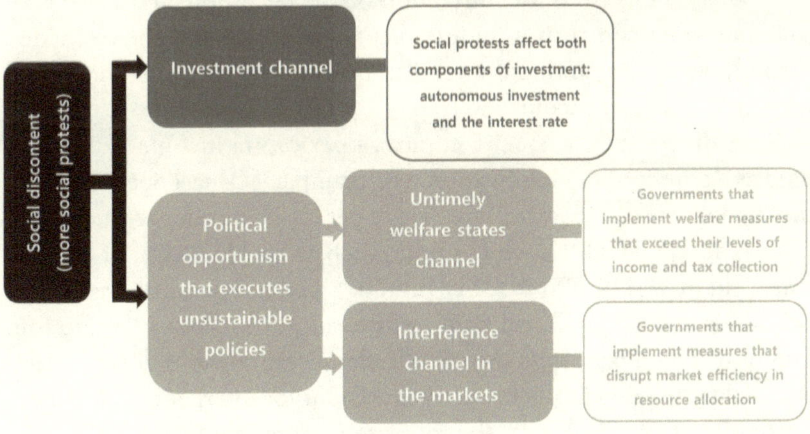

Figure 4.8 Channels through which social discontent, reflected in an increase in social protests, can generate negative effects on economic growth. The investment channel highlights how protests can reduce both autonomous investment and investment influenced by interest rates. Political opportunism includes two additional mechanisms: the untimely welfare states channel, in which governments implement welfare measures that exceed their fiscal capacity, and the interference channel in markets, where policies disrupt the efficient allocation of resources and reduce market efficiency.

Source: Author's elaboration.

HOW DOES SOCIAL DISCONTENT INDUCE THE MIDDLE-INCOME TRAP?

THE MIDDLE-INCOME TRAP

The middle-income trap is a concept open to multiple interpretations. In some cases, it refers to the prolonged period during which a country remains at middle-income levels according to international standards without transitioning to high-income status.[37] In other cases, it is linked to the frequency of economic slowdowns that hinder sustained growth in middle-income countries.[38] Indermit Gill and Homi Kharas use the term to describe the challenges countries face when shifting their growth model from one based on factor accumulation to one driven by continuous productivity improvements.[39]

Thus, the middle-income trap refers to a situation in which a country that has reached a middle-income level becomes stuck as a result of significant obstacles preventing it from advancing to high-income status. The transition from middle to high income is a gradual process, one that takes time. It is also a convergence issue as middle-income countries strive to catch up with high-income nations.

To analyze this issue, we must address two key aspects. First, we need to define what constitutes middle-income and high-income countries. Second, we must examine the significant obstacles that may hinder the transition to higher income levels.

Regarding the first issue, a country's per capita income is typically used as a criterion for classification. For example, Michael Spence defines middle-income countries as those with a per capita income between USD 5,000 and USD 10,000, while studies such as Shekhar Aiyar et al. use a threshold of USD 1,000 to USD 12,000.[40] The most widely used classification is that of the World Bank, which categorizes countries into four groups based on per capita income thresholds expressed in dollars. These thresholds are periodically updated to account for international inflation. Using the 2019 thresholds, the four groups are: low-income countries (less than $1,025 per capita), lower-middle-income countries ($1,026 to $3,995), upper-middle-income countries ($3,996 to $12,375), and high-income countries ($12,376 or more).

Table 4.2 compares the number of countries according to the World Bank's classification for the period from 1990 to 2019. The changes have been significant. From 1990 to 2019, the number of middle-income countries increased from 76 to 107 out of a total of 218, meaning that nearly half of all countries are now in this category. According to José

Table 4.2 Number of countries by income level for 1990 and 2019

Year	Number of low-income countries	Number of medium-low-income countries	Number of medium-high-income countries	Number of high-income countries	Number of countries without classification
1990	48	48	28	41	53
2019	31	47	60	80	0
Variation	**–35.4%**	**–2.1%**	**114.3%**	**95.1%**	**-100%**

Note: The number of countries classified by income level, that is, low, medium-low, medium-high, and high, for the years 1990 and 2019. It shows a significant global shift: the number of low-income countries decreased by 35.4 percent, while medium-high and high-income countries increased by 114.3 percent and 95.1 percent, respectively. The category of unclassified countries, which included 53 nations in 1990, was eliminated by 2019.

Source: Author's elaboration based on data from José Antonio Alonso and José Antonio Ocampo, eds., *Trapped in the Middle? Developmental Challenges for Middle-Income Countries* (Oxford University Press, 2020).

Antonio Alonso and José Antonio Ocampo, in a world where middle-income countries predominate, approximately 75 percent of the global population currently lives in one.[41] This implies that three-quarters of the world's population reside in a country that is not poor in the strictest sense but remains far from being considered wealthy.

Regarding the second issue, the obstacles to reaching the high-income group can be both internal (e.g., transitioning to more productive sectors) and external (e.g., asymmetries in global markets). Alonso and Ocampo identify at least four types of obstacles: the exhaustion of surplus labor transfers from low-productivity sectors to higher-productivity sectors that countries undergo at low and even continues at middle-income levels; the difficulties countries face in shifting from productive specialization based on unskilled labor to a model where innovation, technological capabilities, and workforce qualifications play a crucial role; the challenges that arise when a middle-income country attempts to combine economic growth with a parallel process of institutional change; and the interaction between domestic weaknesses and an increasingly demanding international environment.[42]

Regarding the obstacles that countries face when transitioning to high-income status, the thesis we propose in this book is that social discontent can be an additional barrier to escaping the middle-income trap. This argument is based on the anti–growth equity channels presented in this chapter. While social discontent stems from social, political, and/or economic issues, our key point is that economic growth can be hindered when political opportunists exploit this discontent to serve their own interests. In such cases, social discontent may lead to unsustainable pro–equity policies that ultimately work against growth. In the developing world, particularly in middle-income countries, these growth slowdowns may partly delay convergence with high-income nations.

AN EXPLANATION FROM THE KUZNETS CURVE

In chapter 1, we presented the Kuznets curve model, which suggests that in the early stages of economic growth, inequality rises as the economy expands but later declines once a certain threshold is reached. In this context, the downward segment of the Kuznets curve is where every country would ideally position itself to eliminate the trade-off between equity and growth.

When analyzing the downward leg of the curve, Simon Kuznets pointed out that one factor counteracting the unequal effects of urbanization and industrialization is the growing political power of lower-income groups. As economic growth increases, these groups push for regulations in their favor, ultimately improving equity levels. In the contemporary world, such demands often manifest as social protests, as discussed in chapter 2.

For middle-income countries, it seems that demands for greater equity prevent them from reaching the downward segment of the curve. Kuznets himself was the first to suggest that the relationship could also run from equity to growth. This implies that middle-income countries experiencing social discontent remain on the upward stretch of the curve. While inequality may decline as a result of pro–equity policies, any improvement in equity comes at the cost of reduced economic growth if these countries are still in the ascending phase.

When we put all the pieces of the puzzle together, being on the upward leg of the Kuznets curve in a higher-equity mode—where greater equity leads to lower growth—means that countries in this situation face a double trap: the anti–growth equity trap and the middle-income trap. Escaping the latter requires sustained and increasing growth rates over time. However, a country that sacrifices equity for growth fails to create the necessary economic conditions to raise its overall income levels significantly.

The outlook may seem discouraging at this point, with no clear way out. In chapter 5, however, we propose a series of strategies and policies that can foster both equity and growth simultaneously. While these scenarios may appear unattainable given the challenges discussed in this chapter, they are entirely achievable in practice. Achieving equity with growth—essentially positioning a country on the downward stretch of the Kuznets curve—should be a policy objective for all nations. This approach not only facilitates escape from the middle-income trap but also does so without compromising equity.

CHAPTER 5

Pro–Growth Equity

In chapter 4, we examined the economic consequences of equity policies that exploit social discontent, including poorly designed policies where greater equity comes at the cost of lower economic growth. This does not mean that countries are incapable of fostering both equity and growth. Anti–growth equity is merely the negative side of the coin. Despite much of the world being immersed in an era of social discontent, pro–growth equity remains possible—although admittedly challenging—given the persistent social protests fueled by interest groups who use collective dissatisfaction to advance their private interests and political actors who, from the opposition, leverage conflict to discredit the government and position themselves as viable alternatives for change.

The purpose of this final chapter is to offer readers a positive and realistic perspective, demonstrating how countries can achieve pro–growth equity even amid the current climate of social discontent. We divide the chapter into three sections. The first provides a general review of how equity can serve as a meaningful foundation for economic growth. As we will see, equity has the potential to drive progress in both market dynamics and institutional frameworks—two key dimensions for fostering a country's growth.

In the second section, we narrow the focus to examine how equity functions in the context of social discontent. In chapter 4, we discussed how the inverse relationship between equity and growth can emerge through three channels: investment, ill-timed welfare states, and market interference. Here, we will argue that equity can address the challenges associated with each of these channels and thus can promote economic growth.

In the third section, we present our conclusions and offer a potential answer to one of the central questions of this book: How can pro–growth equity help countries escape the middle-income trap? In formulating this answer, we will revisit the key insights from our analysis and identify the fundamental characteristics of policies that genuinely align equity and growth as complementary objectives rather than as opposing forces.

PRO–GROWTH EQUITY POLICIES: AN OVERVIEW

In chapter 1, we noted that Simon Kuznets was fully aware that a causal relationship could run from equity to growth. He believed that a better distribution of income would have positive effects on economic growth if one viewed equity as a favorable condition for boosting a country's economy. In that same chapter, we also highlighted that Kuznets found that it was essential for modern societies to guarantee equal opportunities—both economic and political—to all segments of the population.

Building on this perspective, we can identify two broad categories of equity policies that contribute to economic growth. These categories depend on the dimension the policies target: the market dimension (what Kuznets referred to as economic opportunities) and the institutional dimension (what he called political opportunities). Over the decades, numerous studies have demonstrated that greater equity fosters growth by strengthening either market development or institutional progress.

MARKET DEVELOPMENT: BETTER ECONOMIC OPPORTUNITIES

The analysis of market dynamics requires examining the factors that influence both supply and demand. When either supply or demand increases, the expected outcome is a rise in the equilibrium quantity traded in the market. If this occurs, there is a positive effect on economic activity.

Figure 5.1 illustrates the well-known representation of a market for a given good or service, where *Y* represents the quantity of the good or service and *P* represents its price. As shown, a higher price leads to greater supply (depicted by an upward-sloping supply curve), while it reduces demand (depicted by a downward-sloping demand curve). Panel A of figure 5.1 demonstrates that when supply increases, the movement of the supply curve from O_1 to O_2 causes the quantity to be traded to be higher in the new equilibrium than in the previous equilibrium (from E_1

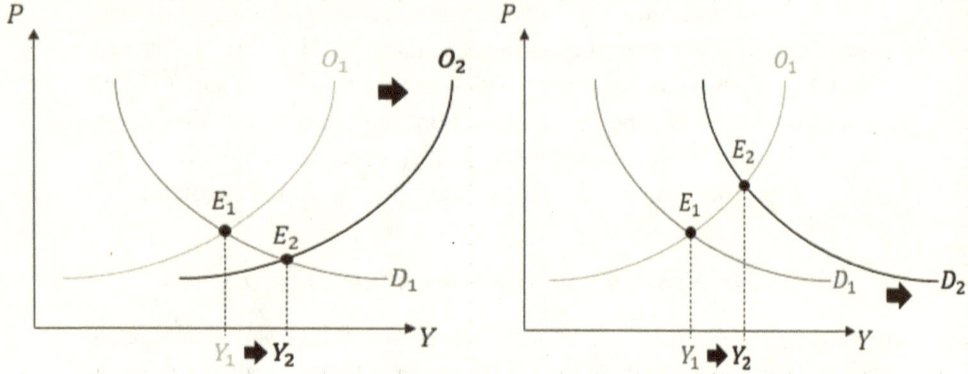

Figure 5.1 How increases in supply or demand affect market equilibrium. The graph on the left shows the effect of an increase in supply: the supply curve shifts from O_1 to O_2, leading to a reduction in the price level and an increase in output from Y_1 to Y_2, moving the equilibrium from E_1 to E_2. The graph on the right illustrates the effect of an increase in demand: the demand curve shifts from D_1 to D_2, raising both price and output and shifting the equilibrium from E_1 to E_2.

Source: Author's elaboration.

to E_2). Panel B of the same graph indicates that, in the face of an increase in demand, its respective curve also shifts to the right (from O_1 to O_2), resulting in a higher equilibrium quantity traded (shifting from E_1 to E_2). Panel B shows that when demand increases, the demand curve shifts to the right (from D_1 to D_2), also leading to a higher equilibrium quantity traded (again shifting from E_1 to E_2).

In this first dimension of the market, the key issue is what equity policies can stimulate either supply or demand, leading to economic growth. On the supply side, equity policies aimed at promoting human capital development or fostering technological innovation enhance the productive capacity of suppliers, enabling them to increase the quantity of goods or services they bring to the market. On the demand side, equity policies designed to encourage household consumption, expand financial access, or promote environmental protection boost the purchasing power of consumers, allowing them to increase their demand for goods and services. Thus, we can identify at least five equity policies that contribute to market development—two on the supply side and three on the demand side.

HUMAN CAPITAL

More equitable countries tend to have better human capital.[1] Figure 5.2 shows that lower inequality, as measured by the Gini coefficient, corresponds to a better Human Capital Index (HCI)—meaning that greater equity is associated with stronger human capital development.[2] The HCI, developed by the World Bank, reflects how improvements in current health and education outcomes shape the productivity of the next generation of workers.[3] It ranges from 0 to 1, where a value of 1 indicates that a country has fully realized its human capital potential.

Equity policies that enhance human capital not only promote social justice but also lay the foundation for stronger and more sustainable growth. This is achieved by strengthening two key components of any society—education and health—both of which are crucial determinants of human capital. Investing in schooling and skills training enables more

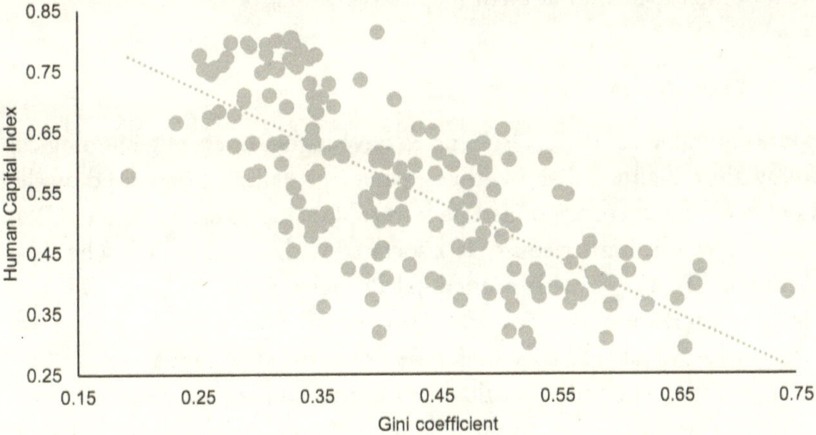

Figure 5.2 Scatterplot illustrating the relationship between the Gini coefficient and the Human Capital Index (HCI) in 2020 for a sample of 174 countries. The chart reveals a negative correlation between both variables, suggesting that countries with lower levels of income inequality tend to achieve higher levels of human capital development. The downward-sloping dotted trend line confirms this association.

Source: Author's elaboration based on data from the World Bank, "Human Capital Index," Data360, https://databank.worldbank.org/source/human-capital-index and the UNU-WIDER, "Gini Index," World Income Inequality Database, https://www.wider.unu.edu/project/wiid-world-income-inequality-database.

people to acquire the knowledge and techniques needed for better job performance, ultimately increasing labor productivity.[4] Investments in preventive measures and access to medical care reduce the burden of disease and contribute to a healthier workforce, which in turn improves labor productivity.[5] In short, a more skilled workforce tends to be more productive, and a healthier society is also a more efficient and economically dynamic one.

One of the leading countries in terms of having a low Gini coefficient and a high HCI is Finland. In 2020, its Gini coefficient was 0.28 (the eleventh lowest among the 174 countries in figure 5.2), and its HCI was 0.80 (the sixth highest). Education and health in Finland are supported by a welfare state model, where both systems have a strong equity component.[6] Education is free at all levels, from preschool to university, and medical care is universal, ensuring that all residents have access to health services regardless of their economic situation. However, it is not just about access but also about quality. In 2020, according to data from the United Nations Development Programme (UNDP), Finland ranked seventh globally in expected years of schooling (nineteen years) and twentieth in life expectancy at birth (eighty-two years).

TECHNOLOGICAL INNOVATION

More equitable countries also tend to have higher levels of technological innovation. Figure 5.3 shows that greater inequality, as measured by the Gini coefficient, corresponds to a lower Global Innovation Index (GII). In other words, higher equity is associated with a higher GII. The GII, developed by the World Intellectual Property Organization (WIPO), defines innovation as a new or improved product or process that has been made available to potential users or is used as an input in a production process.[7] The index is calculated as the simple average of two subindexes: the Innovation Input Sub-Index (which includes factors such as institutions, human capital, research, infrastructure, and market and business sophistication) and the Innovation Output Sub-Index (which captures creative outputs and knowledge and technology outputs). The GII ranges from 0 to 100, with higher values indicating a greater level of innovation.

Technological innovation is one of the key drivers of economic growth and development because it enhances efficiency, productivity, and progress across multiple sectors.[8] Therefore, equity policies that

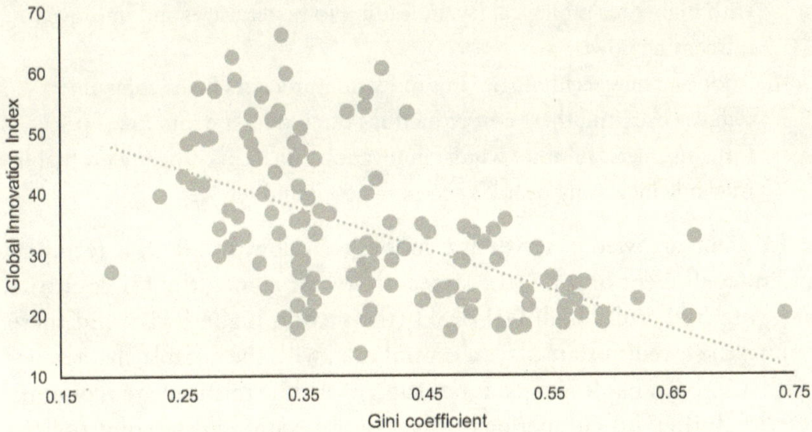

Figure 5.3 Scatterplot showing the relationship between income inequality, measured by the Gini coefficient, and the Global Innovation Index (GII) in 2020 for a sample of 131 countries. The downward-sloping trend line indicates a negative correlation between both variables, suggesting that countries with lower levels of income inequality tend to achieve higher levels of innovation.

Source: Author's elaboration based on data from the World Intellectual Property Organization (WIPO), *Global Innovation Index 2023: Innovation in the Face of Uncertainty* (WIPO, 2023) and the UNU-WIDER, "Gini Index," World Income Inequality Database, https://www.wider.unu.edu/project/wiid-world-income-inequality-database.

promote greater technological innovation also have a significant positive impact on economic growth. Equity and growth can be achieved simultaneously through technological innovation via the following four channels:

1. Innovation improves people's quality of life by providing more efficient and accessible solutions in areas such as health and education. As previously discussed, better health and education levels translate into higher economic growth.
2. Innovation leads to the creation of and access to new markets, giving consumers more options in designing their consumption plans while providing suppliers with a broader field in which to expand their economic activities.
3. Although innovation can lead to job destruction, it also generates new employment opportunities.[9] Innovation typically creates more jobs than it eliminates, with the added advantage that these new jobs are in sectors

with higher technological levels, leading to better wages and improved purchasing power.

4. Adopting new technologies in production processes helps companies reduce costs, and these cost reductions often translate into lower prices for consumers. In other words, innovation enhances company profitability while increasing people's access to goods and services.

In practice, Sweden serves as a model to follow. In 2020, it recorded a Gini coefficient of 0.29 (the sixteenth lowest among the 131 countries in figure 5.3) and a high GII of 63 (the second highest). Behind these results, the Swedish state plays a central role, with the notable characteristic that Sweden has leveraged innovation over time to stimulate economic activity during difficult periods. Waves of innovation in the country have emerged historically during times of investment slowdowns and structural crises, particularly in the 1930s, 1970s, and 2010s.[10]

Sweden's technological innovation success can be attributed to three key factors. First, both the public and private sectors allocate significant resources to research and development (R&D). For instance, according to World Bank data, Sweden's R&D expenditure as a percentage of GDP in 2021 was 3.4 percent, approximately 1.4 percentage points above the average for the European Union. Second, the state provides substantial support to innovative enterprises. Sweden offers financing and advisory services for emerging technology companies, while businesses benefit from a range of tax incentives for conducting R&D activities. Third, a strong collaboration exists between academia and industry. The Swedish government has actively promoted partnerships between academic institutions and businesses to facilitate the translation of academic research into practical applications in the corporate sector.

HOUSEHOLD CONSUMPTION

The most equitable countries tend to have higher levels of consumption per household member. Figure 5.4 shows that, as the Gini coefficient improves, per capita consumption increases. In other words, greater equity is associated with higher consumption. The data for this variable, obtained from the World Bank, capture the market value of all goods and services purchased by households, including durable products (excluding housing). It also accounts for expenditures by nonprofit institutions that provide services to households.

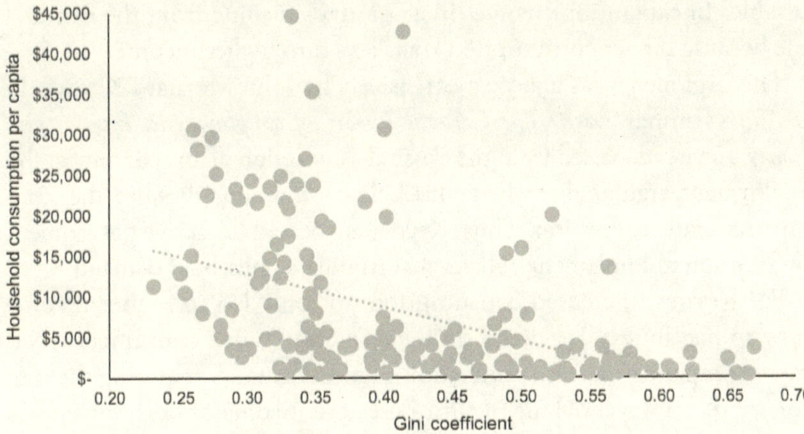

Figure 5.4 Scatterplot showing the relationship between income inequality, measured by the Gini coefficient, and household consumption per capita in 2020 for a sample of 161 countries (consumption at current USD prices). The downward-sloping trend line reveals a clear pattern: countries with lower levels of inequality tend to exhibit higher levels of household consumption per capita.

Source: Author's elaboration based on data from the World Bank, "Households and NPISHs Final Consumption Expenditure (Current US$)," Data360, https://data.worldbank.org/indicator/NE.CON.PRVT.CD; the World Bank, "Population, Total," Data360, https://data.worldbank.org/indicator/SP.POP.TOTL; and the UNU-WIDER, "Gini Index," World Income Inequality Database, https://www.wider.unu.edu/project/wiid-world-income-inequality-database.

We acknowledge that per capita consumption is not a perfectly accurate measure of actual consumption levels because there may be cases where a small segment of the population accounts for a disproportionately high share of total consumption, making the average appear higher than what most people actually experience. In the absence of a more precise metric and solely for illustrative purposes, however, we use this measure to approximate household consumption trends.

Household consumption has a dual significance. On one hand, when people have the economic capacity to access a greater quantity of goods and services, their quality of life improves, helping to reduce disparities in well-being between different population segments and thereby enhancing equity.[11] On the other hand, consumption is one of the most important variables in explaining changes in a country's income from the demand side because higher consumption translates into higher income.

This argument was analyzed extensively by John Maynard Keynes. In his 1936 seminal work, *The General Theory of Employment, Interest and Money*, Keynes departed from the classical assumption of an economy at full employment, arguing that when household consumption declines, the economy can enter a recession. Thus, Keynes advocated for active government intervention to implement policies that stimulate household demand.[12]

For Keynes, increased consumption not only led to higher income but also had multiplier effects on the economy. When consumers spend more, companies increase production to meet demand, requiring them to hire more employees. This in turn raises the income of both businesses (through higher profits) and households (through increased wages). Higher income can then fuel additional consumption, creating a virtuous cycle for the economy. In short, policies aimed at encouraging household consumption tend to foster both greater equity and economic growth.

The data suggest that special attention should be given to the case of Iceland, which in 2020 had a Gini coefficient of 0.26 (the fifth lowest among the 161 countries in figure 5.4) and a per capita consumption of USD 30,588 (the fifth highest). Throughout the twenty-first century, the welfare state has played a central role in Icelandic politics, with all political parties embracing the idea of the state as a fundamental pillar for ensuring societal well-being.[13]

Icelanders effectively applied Keynesian principles when addressing the challenges of the 2008 financial crisis. The main issues they faced included rising unemployment, declining incomes, and a heavier debt burden on households and businesses. Guðný Björk and Stefán Ólafsson documented that, given the financial constraints of the time, Iceland's welfare strategy focused on redistributing social expenditures, increasing transfers to households while cutting spending on services such as health care, education, and administration.[14] Targeting was a crucial element in preventing a significant rise in poverty. Transfers were directed toward lower-income households. What initially appeared to be a crisis with long-lasting effects on household consumption was successfully managed through Iceland's strong welfare state.

FINANCIAL DEEPENING

The most equitable countries tend to have greater financial depth. This relationship is illustrated in figure 5.5, which shows that lower Gini

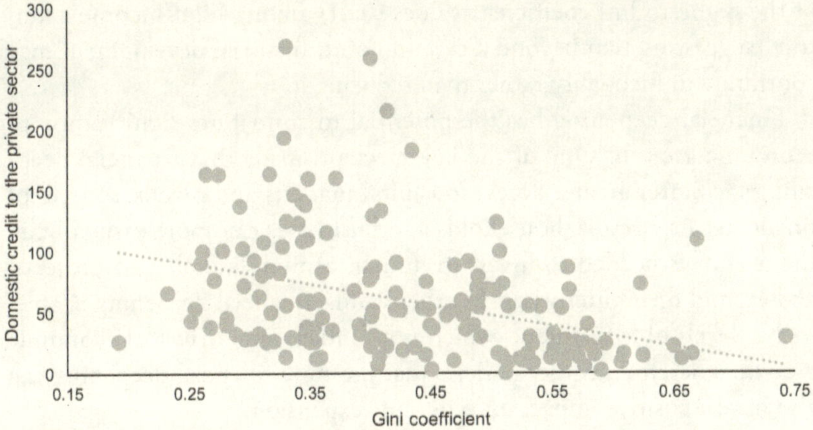

Figure 5.5 Scatterplot showing the relationship between the Gini coefficient and domestic credit to the private sector as a percentage of GDP in 2020 for a sample of 163 countries. The downward-sloping trend line indicates a negative correlation between both variables, suggesting that countries with lower levels of income inequality tend to exhibit higher levels of credit access for the private sector.

Source: Author's elaboration based on data from the World Bank, "Domestic Credit to Private Sector (% of GDP)," Data360, https://data.worldbank.org/indicator/FS.AST.PRVT.GD.ZS and the UNU-WIDER, "Gini Index," World Income Inequality Database, https://www.wider.unu.edu/project/wiid-world-income-inequality-database.

coefficient values are associated with higher levels of financial deepening. In other words, greater equity corresponds with greater financial development. Financial deepening, the main indicator of a country's financial development, measures the financial resources provided to the private sector by the financial system as a percentage of gross domestic product (GDP). It reflects the availability of credit in an economy.

Within the financial development literature, however, there is a perspective known as financialization, which examines the potential negative consequences of excessive financial deepening.[15] Chapter 1 introduced the Kuznets financial curve model, but there is also the Kuznets financial anticurve, which suggests a U-shaped relationship between financial deepening and inequality. According to this model, continued credit expansion may contribute to rising inequality beyond a certain threshold of financial development.[16]

A potential example of the negative effects of excessive financial deepening can be seen in the United States. While the United States has one of the highest levels of financial deepening (216 percent), it also has one of the highest Gini coefficient values (0.41) among high-income countries, suggesting that beyond a certain point, financial development may contribute to inequality rather than reducing it.

Financial deepening has the potential to contribute significantly to economic growth. One of the key mechanisms is that financial deepening facilitates greater access to capital markets and diverse sources of financing. As a result, households and businesses can more easily obtain the resources needed to invest in human capital, launch new projects, and expand their enterprises. In other words, financial deepening enables higher levels of investment, which is a fundamental driver of economic growth. Therefore, equity policies that promote financial deepening can also have a positive impact on economic expansion.

We can identify two key ways in which equity and finance complement each other. First, greater equity translates into expanded opportunities, including access to financial resources. This requires efforts to ensure that individuals have access to essential financial services, such as credit.[17] Second, equity can drive the creation of more inclusive financial markets, enabling diverse segments of the population to participate actively in and benefit from the financial system. This in turn fosters the development of financial services tailored to the specific needs of a broad range of people. In both cases, equity serves as a foundation for strengthening the financial system, which ultimately supports economic growth.

The case of Denmark demonstrates that it is possible to align policy objectives in both equity and finance. In 2020, Denmark recorded a Gini coefficient of 0.26 (the seventh lowest among the 163 countries in figure 5.5) and a financial deepening level of 164 percent (the seventh highest). It is important to clarify that financial deepening does not necessarily equate to financial inclusion because high levels of financial resources in an economy do not always translate into widespread access. In Denmark, however, high financial deepening has been accompanied by greater financial inclusion. A recent study by Zhong Chen et al., which is based on indicators from the World Bank's Global Findex Database, found that Denmark ranks highest globally in financial inclusion.[18] This success is attributed to policies that ensure equitable access to the financial system for all population groups, reinforced by key measures such as promoting financial education, encouraging the adoption and effective use of financial technologies, and implementing appropriate financial regulation and supervision.

ENVIRONMENT

The most equitable countries also tend to have better environmental conditions. According to figure 5.6, a lower Gini coefficient is associated with a better Environmental Performance Index (EPI), meaning that greater equity corresponds to a higher EPI. The EPI, developed by Yale and Columbia universities, ranks countries based on their performance in climate change mitigation, environmental health, and ecosystem vitality.[19] It also provides a national-level measure indicating how close countries are to achieving their environmental policy objectives. The index ranges from 0 to 100, with higher values reflecting stronger environmental sustainability performance.

In chapter 1, we discussed the Kuznets environmental curve as an attempt to explain the relationship between economic growth and environmental conditions. According to this model, the early stages of growth lead to environmental degradation. The most recent EPI report

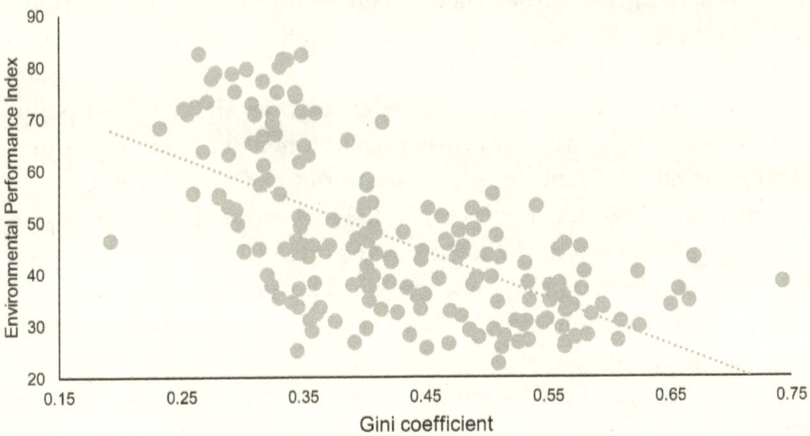

Figure 5.6 Scatterplot showing the relationship between the Gini coefficient and the Environmental Performance Index (EPI) in 2020 for a sample of 180 countries. The downward-sloping trend line indicates a negative association between both variables, suggesting that countries with lower levels of income inequality tend to achieve better environmental performance.

Source: Author's elaboration based on data from Martin Wolf, John Emerson, Daniel Esty et al., *2022 Environmental Performance Index* (Yale Center for Environmental Law & Policy, 2022) and the UNU-WIDER, "Gini Index," World Income Inequality Database, https://www.wider.unu.edu/project/wiid-world-income-inequality-database.

concludes, contrary to this theory, that industrialization and urbanization do not necessarily require sacrificing environmental sustainability.[20] While it has long been perceived that environmental protection and economic growth are in constant conflict, the reality is that a healthier environment can facilitate growth by stimulating innovation, meeting evolving consumer demands, improving resource efficiency, creating employment, and reducing risks and costs associated with environmental degradation. For instance, the need to protect the environment drives the development and adoption of green technologies, leading to investments that generate new business opportunities and jobs, thereby also fostering economic growth. Thus, environmental equity policies can serve as a catalyst for economic expansion.

At this point, it is worth highlighting two ways in which equity and the environment go hand in hand. The first is through the promotion of equitable access to natural resources. When access to these resources is distributed fairly, pressure on them can be reduced, fostering pro–growth practices such as sustainable energy generation and greater economic diversification. The second is through the pursuit of environmental justice. Marginalized communities often bear a disproportionate share of the negative effects of pollution and lack essential resources. This includes communities without access to clean drinking water and sanitation services or those exposed to high levels of pollution from industrial waste. Ensuring environmental justice means protecting the environment for all communities and guaranteeing access to fundamental services that every individual should have. As a result, human capital is strengthened and, as previously discussed, greater human capital leads to economic growth. These cases demonstrate that equity serves as a foundation for both environmental sustainability and economic progress.

In practice, the United Kingdom stands out as one of the countries with strong climate performance and moderate inequality. In 2020, the United Kingdom had an EPI of 81 (the fourth highest among the 180 countries in figure 5.6) and a Gini coefficient of 0.34 (the forty-third lowest). The country's environmental policy is built on two key strategies aimed at ensuring a healthier environment for its citizens. The first strategy focuses on significantly reducing carbon dioxide emissions. By 2020, the United Kingdom had cut emissions by approximately 50 percent from 1990 levels and committed to phasing out coal as an energy source by 2024.[21] The second strategy is the United Kingdom's robust legal framework for reducing greenhouse gas emissions. The Climate Change Act of 2008 set a legally binding target to reduce emissions by 80 percent by 2050. Since then, regulations have been strengthened, with the goal of achieving net zero emissions by 2050.

INSTITUTIONAL DEVELOPMENT

Institutions play a crucial role in shaping the structure and functioning of societies. The most widely accepted definition of institutions comes from Nobel laureate Douglass North, who describes them as the "rules of the game" that govern political, economic, and social interactions. According to North, institutions are the human-devised constraints that shape behavior, including both formal rules (such as laws and regulations) and informal norms (such as customs and traditions).[22]

Beyond their organizational role, institutions are fundamental to economic growth. North emphasizes that institutions reduce market uncertainty, influence transaction and production costs, and ultimately determine the profitability of economic activities.[23] Strong institutions create an environment where economic actors can operate with confidence, which fosters investment, innovation, and long-term development.

Daron Acemoglu and James A. Robinson's main thesis, which is very much in line with North's proposal, is that a country's success or failure is closely related to the type of institutions it has.[24] These authors distinguish between two types of institutions. The first are inclusive institutions, which encourage widespread participation in a society's economic and political activities. They are designed to provide equal rights and opportunities to all individuals, regardless of their political affiliation, ethnicity, or social class. In contrast, extractive institutions benefit a small group of elites at the expense of the majority. These institutions are structured to extract resources and wealth from society for the advantage of a select group.

Based on this classification, Acemoglu and Robinson argue that inclusive institutions are essential for economic growth, while extractive institutions lead to a country's economic and social decline because inclusive institutions promote equal opportunities, citizen participation, political transparency, and the rule of law.[25] In such environments, the necessary incentives for investment and technological innovation are present, and people are more willing to engage in various economic activities. In contrast, extractive institutions often foster harmful practices such as nepotism, corruption, and the violation of political and civil rights. These conditions create an environment with little to no incentive for investment or innovation, making it even less likely that people will actively contribute to their country's progress.

In this chapter, however, we argue that in countries with a more equitable distribution of income—where citizens enjoy better living standards—people tend to have a higher level of awareness and influence over their institutional framework. In some countries, citizens actively demand and contribute to the establishment of inclusive institutions, which in turn lead to higher-quality regulations, the proper functioning of the rule of law, and greater transparency in political processes. All these factors are fundamental components of an inclusive institutional framework and are therefore essential for economic growth. Thus, if policies that promote equity can significantly enhance institutional development, they may also serve as a catalyst for economic growth. With this possibility in mind, let's examine whether greater equity could indeed foster a more inclusive institutional environment.

INSTITUTIONAL QUALITY

The most equitable countries exhibit higher institutional quality. Figure 5.7 demonstrates that a lower Gini coefficient corresponds to a higher Institutional Quality Index (IQI), meaning that greater equity is associated with stronger institutions. The IQI, developed by the Red Liberal de América Latina (Relial, Liberal Network of Latin America), is constructed from various indicators reflecting the rule of law, government accountability, perceived corruption, protection of political and civil rights, and ease of doing business.[26] The index ranges from 0 to 1, with higher values indicating better institutional quality.

A striking example of the association between greater equity and stronger institutional development is Estonia. In 2020, Estonia had an IQI of 0.89 (the thirteenth highest among 179 countries in figure 5.7) and a Gini coefficient of 0.31 (the nineteenth lowest). Just over thirty years ago, Estonia was part of the Soviet Union, a state built on authoritarian institutions, making its current institutional quality particularly remarkable.

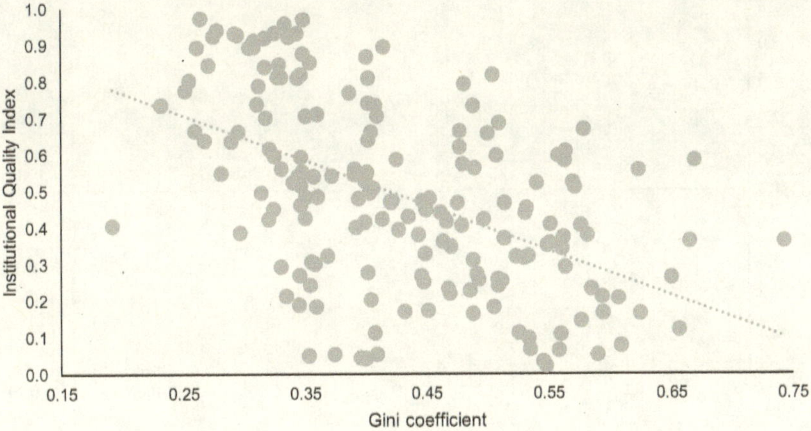

Figure 5.7 Scatterplot illustrating the relationship between the Gini coefficient and the Institutional Quality Index (IQI) in 2020 for a sample of 179 countries. The downward-sloping trend line reveals a negative correlation between both variables, indicating that countries with greater income equality tend to exhibit stronger institutional quality.

Source: Author's elaboration based on data from Red Liberal de América Latina, *Índice de Calidad Institucional 2021: La pandemia, una oportunidad para mejorar el futuro* (Relial, 2021) and the UNU-WIDER, "Gini Index," World Income Inequality Database, https://www.wider.unu.edu/project/wiid-world-income-inequality-database.

While institutional transformation is typically a slow and gradual process, Estonia has successfully implemented a strategy of institutional change toward inclusiveness. Today, its institutional framework ensures the functioning of democracy, the rule of law, human rights, and transparency in political processes.[27]

REGULATORY QUALITY

The most equitable countries exhibit better regulatory quality. According to figure 5.8, a lower Gini coefficient is associated with a higher level of regulatory quality, meaning that greater equity corresponds with stronger regulatory frameworks. This indicator, part of the World Bank's governance indicators, measures the ability of governments to formulate and implement sound policies and regulations that foster and support private sector development. It ranges from –2.5 to 2.5, with higher values indicating better regulatory quality.

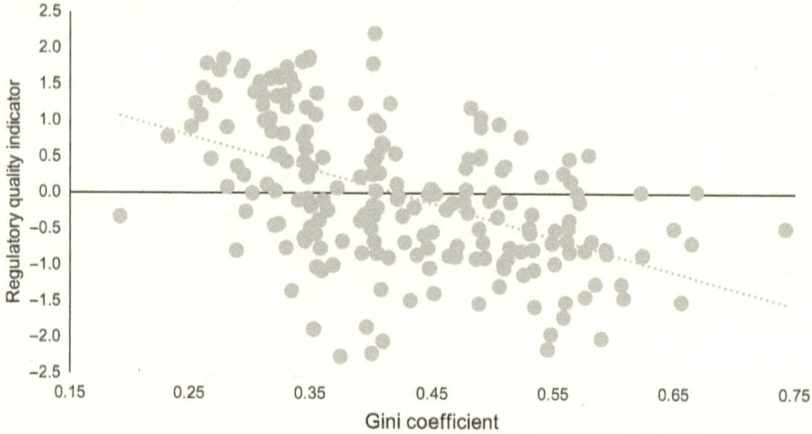

Figure 5.8 Scatterplot illustrating the relationship between the Gini coefficient and the regulatory quality indicator in 2020 for a sample of 202 countries. The downward-sloping trend line suggests a negative relationship between both variables, indicating that countries with greater income equality tend to achieve higher levels of regulatory quality.

Source: Author's elaboration based on data from the World Bank, "Regulatory Quality: Estimate," Data360, https://data.worldbank.org/indicator/RQ.EST and the UNU-WIDER, "Gini Index," World Income Inequality Database, https://www.wider.unu.edu/project/wiid-world-income-inequality-database.

Regulatory quality, as defined by the World Bank, is crucial for promoting economic growth. A clear and efficient regulatory framework reduces uncertainty, giving entrepreneurs and investors the confidence needed to develop their economic activities. By ensuring a level playing field, higher regulatory quality can also lead to a more competitive economic environment. Increased competition often drives firms to innovate to remain in the market, boosting productivity and economic growth.[28]

Macau stands out as a notable example. In 2020, it had a regulatory quality indicator of 1.74 (the ninth highest among the 202 countries in figure 5.8) and a Gini coefficient of 0.33 (the forty-fourth lowest). Macau, a special administrative region (SAR) of China, is recognized for its relatively favorable business environment and a government that has prioritized economic growth, particularly through the gaming and tourism industries. Since becoming an SAR in late 1999, Macau has maintained a high degree of autonomy in economic and political matters. This autonomy has enabled it to uphold a transparent economic system and

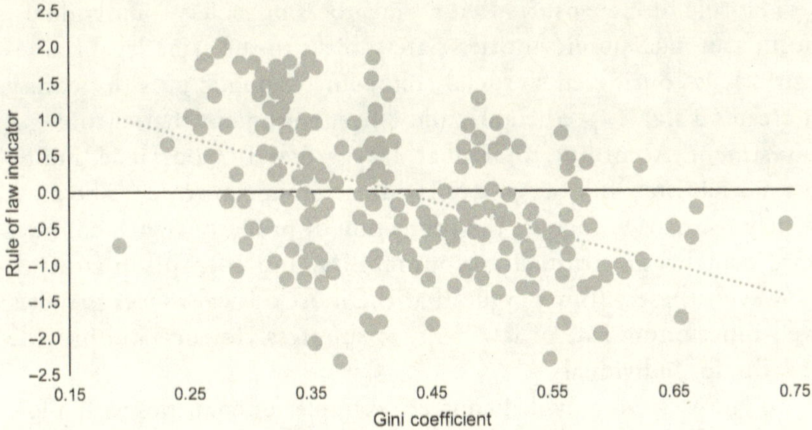

Figure 5.9 Scatterplot showing the relationship between the Gini coefficient and the rule of law (RoL) indicator in 2020 for a sample of 202 countries. The downward-sloping trend line reveals a negative correlation between both variables, suggesting that countries with more equitable income distributions tend to have a stronger rule of law.

Source: Author's elaboration based on data from the World Bank, "Rule of Law: Estimate," Data360, https://data.worldbank.org/indicator/RL.EST and the UNU-WIDER, "Gini Index," World Income Inequality Database, https://www.wider.unu.edu/project/wiid-world-income-inequality-database.

a government committed to fostering a business-friendly environment.[29] Thus, it is unsurprising that, before the COVID-19 pandemic, Macau had the seventh-highest GDP per capita in the world, according to World Bank data for 2019.

RULE OF LAW

The most equitable countries tend to have a well-functioning rule of law (RoL). Figure 5.9 shows that a lower Gini coefficient corresponds to a higher RoL indicator, meaning that greater equity is associated with stronger adherence to the rule of law. The RoL indicator, which is part of the World Bank's governance indicators, measures the extent to which people trust and abide by societal rules. It also reflects the quality of contract enforcement, the judicial system, and the likelihood of criminal activities and violence. Similar to the regulatory quality indicator, the RoL indicator ranges from −2.5 to 2.5, with higher values indicating a stronger and more effective rule of law.

The rule of law ensures that all members of society—individuals, businesses, and public entities—are subject to the same legal framework. It is considered a crucial factor for economic growth because it creates a stable, predictable, and fair environment that encourages investment. According to Stephan Haggard and Lydia Tiede, multiple mechanisms link the rule of law to economic growth.[30] The most widely recognized include the protection of property rights, contract enforcement, government accountability, and corruption control. However, these authors argue that the most critical aspect is that a well-functioning rule of law helps to suppress violence and provide security for individuals.

So far, we have provided concrete examples of countries with a low Gini coefficient that have simultaneously achieved strong market or institutional development. It is also important, however, to consider a contrasting example—one in which a weak rule of law has led to low economic growth rates. A particularly illustrative case is that of Latin America, a region historically marked by persistently high levels of inequality, making it one of the most unequal in the world. Numerous studies have examined the determinants of economic growth in Latin America, and from an institutional perspective, one of the most recent is that of Nelson Labarca and Amparo Panchana, who state:

> In Latin America, political instability—marked by frequent government changes, coups d'état, military uprisings, and the establishment of dictatorships—has led to a succession of institutional shifts toward authoritarian regimes. Even when these structures have transitioned to democratic systems, the establishment of the rule of law has not been sufficiently consistent to encourage the implementation of expansive economic policies and fiscal discipline.[31]

The aforementioned study indicates that a significant distortion has emerged in Latin America's economic activities as a result of inadequate establishment and functioning of the rule of law. For example, investors tend to prioritize financing productive processes for first-order goods—those that directly satisfy consumption needs and generate quick profits but contribute little to overall economic growth. In contrast, higher-order goods, which require significantly more financing and a longer maturation period, are more closely associated with higher economic growth rates but receive less investment.

TRANSPARENCY

More equitable countries tend to have greater transparency in their political processes. Figure 5.10 shows that a lower Gini coefficient is associated with a better Corruption Perception Index (CPI), meaning that greater equity corresponds to more transparency. The CPI ranks countries based on perceived corruption in their public sectors, with values ranging from 0 to 100, where 0 represents high corruption and 100 indicates a very transparent system. This index is crucial because corruption can significantly hinder economic performance in several ways. Albert de Vaal and Wouter Ebben highlight at least three key mechanisms: first, corruption distorts the competitive environment by favoring companies engaged in corrupt practices; second, it leads to inefficient resource allocation because resources are distributed based on bribes or political connections rather than economic efficiency; and third, it discourages investment because investors may fear the misallocation of their funds or the need to make irregular payments to conduct business.[32]

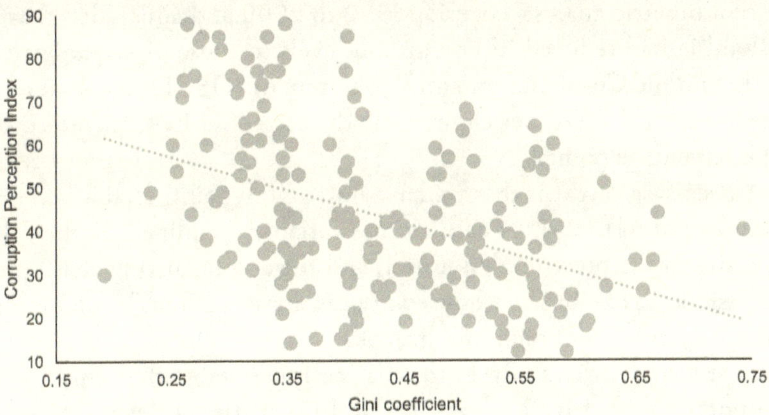

Figure 5.10 Scatterplot showing the relationship between the Gini coefficient and the Corruption Perception Index (CPI) in 2020 for a sample of 179 countries. The negative correlation between both variables suggests that countries with greater income equality tend to obtain higher CPI scores, indicating lower perceived levels of corruption. The downward-sloping dotted trend line confirms this association.

Source: Author's elaboration based on data from Transparency International, "Corruption Perceptions Index," Transparency International, https://www.transparency.org/en/cpi/2020 and the UNU-WIDER, "Gini Index," World Income Inequality Database, https://www.wider.unu.edu/project/wiid-world-income-inequality-database.

The costs of corruption can be substantial. Klaus Gründler and Niklas Potrafke analyzed data from 175 countries between 2012 and 2018, and the long-term cumulative effect of corruption on growth.[33] A roughly 17 percent decrease in real GDP per capita occurs when the inverse of the CPI increases by one standard deviation. The authors highlight that this negative relationship is more pronounced in autocracies and in countries with low government effectiveness and a weak rule of law.

An illustrative case of the link between inequality and corruption is Colombia, the fifth most unequal country in the world outside Africa. Jhorland Ayala et al. argue that Colombia's anticorruption regulations, such as Law 1474 of 2011 and Decree 734 of 2014, which were intended to strengthen prevention, investigation, and sanctions against public sector corruption, have not been as effective as expected.[34] Transparency progress has been minimal: in 2012, Colombia's CPI was 36, making the country 94th in transparency; by 2022, it had only slightly improved to 39 (91st in transparency). The economic consequences of corruption can be severe. Karoll Gómez and Santiago Galón conducted an econometric analysis covering 1990 to 2000 and concluded that if Colombia had reduced its corruption levels to those of Organisation for Economic Co-operation and Development (OECD) countries, its average annual GDP per capita growth rate could have increased by 3.14 percentage points.[35]

A necessary caveat is that we have not, at any point, established rigorous causal relationships between the variables examined. Rather, the objective of the preceding discussion and the accompanying charts and discussions was to illustrate how equity can serve as a foundation for fostering higher levels of economic growth.

In summary, the analyses in this section suggest that equity has the potential to drive both market and institutional development—two fundamental dimensions for stimulating economic growth. From a market perspective, we have observed that more equitable countries tend to exhibit more developed human capital and higher levels of technological innovation, consumption, financial deepening, and environmental protection. From an institutional standpoint, the most equitable countries also tend to have stronger institutional quality, better regulatory frameworks, a more effective rule of law, and greater transparency. Figure 5.11 summarizes the key insights from this first section of the chapter.

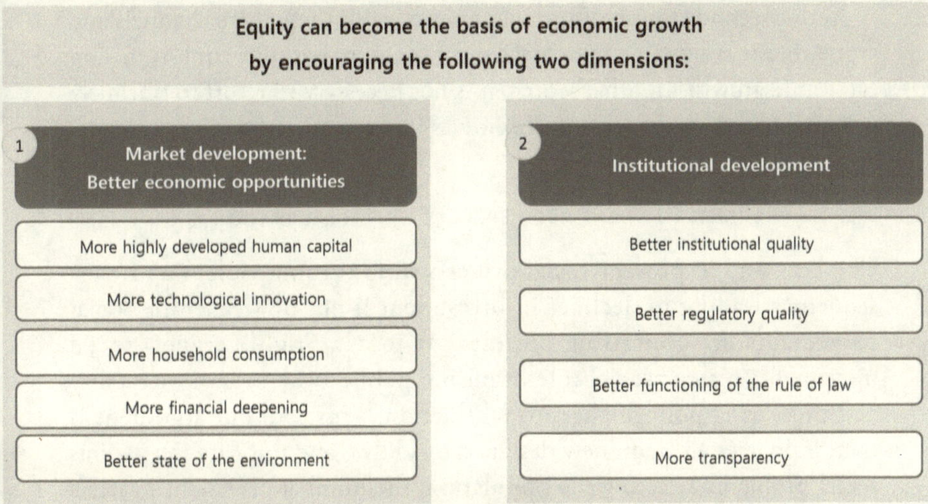

Figure 5.11 How equity can become a foundational driver of economic growth through two interrelated dimensions. The first dimension is market development, which includes improvements in human capital, technological innovation, household consumption, financial deepening, and environmental sustainability. The second dimension is institutional development, encompassing better institutional quality, improved regulatory quality, stronger rule of law, and greater transparency. These mechanisms illustrate how more equal societies can build stronger foundations for sustained and inclusive economic growth.

Source: Author's elaboration.

PRO-GROWTH EQUITY POLICIES IN THE CONTEXT OF SOCIAL DISCONTENT

In chapter 4, we argued that in a context of social discontent, economic growth is highly likely to decline through one of three channels: a direct channel, which we call the investment channel, and two indirect channels, which we call welfare states at the wrong time and market discouragement. We also pointed out that the first channel does not lead to increased equity because it is associated with capital destruction, resource misallocation, and loss of business confidence—outcomes driven by social conflict that may escalate into violence. Meanwhile, the other two channels may temporarily increase equity because they stem from opportunistic political actions that implement poorly designed equity policies; however, these policies ultimately undermine economic growth and are unsustainable in the long run.

In this second section of the chapter, we revisit these three channels and argue that it is possible to achieve greater equity without compromising economic growth. In other words, it is not necessary to resort to untimely welfare policies or to create disincentives in the markets to foster equity.

PREVENTING THE DIRECT EFFECTS OF SOCIAL DISCONTENT

The best way to prevent social protests from turning violent and consequently leading to declines in investment is not by weakening social movements or suppressing protests. As Joseph Stiglitz argues, social movements play a crucial role in raising public awareness of inequality and pressuring policymakers to take action.[36] Instead, our argument is that, if policies are genuinely designed to address and mitigate the various social problems affecting the population, the number of violent protests will likely decrease because there will be fewer significant causes fueling social discontent. In this regard, the data suggest that countries with higher levels of equity tend to have safer societies.

In figure 5.12, we illustrate the relationship between the Gini coefficient and the Social Security Index (SSI). The SSI, developed by the Institute for Economics and Peace, assesses the level of harmony within countries. To do so, it tracks various factors, including violent demonstrations, terrorist activity, crime rates, relations with neighboring countries, and the local political situation, among others.[37] The SSI ranges from 1 to 5, where lower values indicate higher levels of societal security.

However, equity policies that effectively reduce inequality and in turn diminish the unrest fueling social protests are essential. As supported by the data, such policies contribute to safer societies, fostering a more suitable environment for investment. Drawing an analogy with the discussion in chapter 4, there are three ways in which equity policies that mitigate social conflict can increase investment levels and thus promote economic growth. These three interrelated pathways are described below.

PROTECTION OF PROPERTY RIGHTS

Social conflict that escalates into acts of violence can result in the destruction of both public and private property. Domestic and foreign investors are thus more inclined to operate in countries where violent social protests are minimized. The assurance that property rights are well protected instills confidence in investors, encouraging them to allocate resources

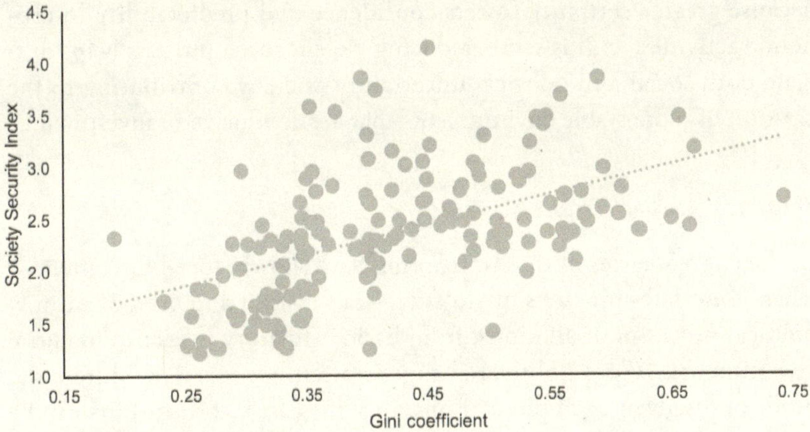

Figure 5.12 Scatterplot showing the relationship between the Gini coefficient and the Society Security Index (SSI) in 2020 for a sample of 162 countries. The upward-sloping trend line indicates a positive relationship between both variables, suggesting that higher levels of income inequality are associated with increased perceptions of social insecurity. This pattern implies that more unequal societies tend to face greater challenges related to social stability and citizen security.

Source: Author's elaboration based on data from the Institute for Economics & Peace, "Global Peace Index," Vision of Humanity, https://www.visionofhumanity.org/maps/#/ and the UNU-WIDER, "Gini Index," World Income Inequality Database, https://www.wider.unu.edu/project/wiid-world-income-inequality-database.

to a given country because they know that their investments will be safeguarded by law. The protection of property rights also facilitates access to financing because investors can use their assets as collateral to secure various funding sources. In societies with strong property rights protections, economic agents are motivated to invest in innovation and the development of new goods, services, and processes because they can trust that the institutional framework will ensure that they, rather than third parties, reap the benefits of their efforts.

CREATING CERTAINTY ENVIRONMENTS

In chapter 4, we stated that, in a society with high levels of uncertainty, there is a significant likelihood that investment projects will be postponed or even abandoned as investors seek more stable destinations. While it is impossible to eliminate uncertainty from any society completely, creating environments of greater certainty is essential for stimulating investment because greater certainty fosters confidence and predictability in economic activities. In this sense, reducing violent social protests helps mitigate both social and political uncertainty, thereby contributing to the creation of more stable environments that are conducive to investment.

STABILITY AND POLITICAL CONTINUITY

As the consequences of the Arab Spring have shown, social discontent—when it escalates into acts of violence—can disrupt and even overthrow political processes of all kinds, from basic regulatory measures to entire governments. While political change is often necessary to address the needs of disadvantaged populations, in some cases, abrupt shifts can be counterproductive because medium- and long-term political stability is often crucial for ensuring policy continuity and credibility, both of which are essential for sustaining economic growth.

In short, when equity policies successfully reduce social discontent, they create a more favorable investment climate. This relationship extends beyond just social stability; it also affects economic stability. By mitigating social violence, equity policies help prevent disruptions in the production and distribution of goods and services, which in turn fosters a more predictable economic environment.

Reduced social violence as a result of higher equity translates into a lower perceived risk for investments. This is particularly important when considering the two main types of investment: those independent of interest rates and those directly influenced by them. Because investment decisions that depend on interest rates are sensitive to risk levels, a higher perceived risk leads to higher interest rates, which raises borrowing costs and ultimately discourages investment. Therefore, equity policies that contribute to reducing social unrest and economic risk can also help lower interest rates, making capital more accessible and supporting higher levels of investment and economic growth.

An example comparing Spain and Sweden highlights how social protest can influence investment dynamics, particularly through the availability of credit (see figure 5.13). Spain, which experienced significantly more protests than Sweden between 2009 and 2019, also saw a substantial decline in credit granted to the private sector—falling from nearly 174 percent of GDP to about 94 percent. In contrast, Sweden, with far fewer protests, saw an increase in credit from 124 percent to 131 percent of GDP over the same period.

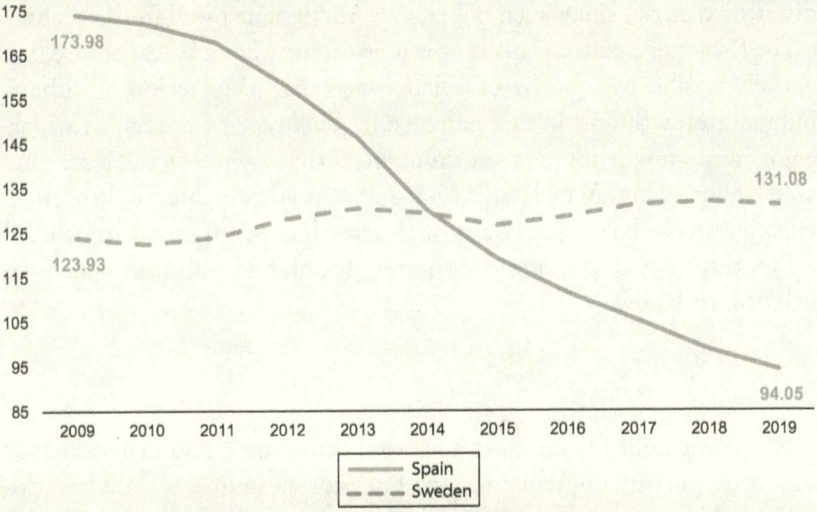

Figure 5.13 Comparison of the evolution of domestic credit granted by banks to the private sector as a percentage of GDP in Spain (solid line) and Sweden (dashed line) from 2009 to 2019. Spain experienced a substantial decline in credit levels, falling from 173.98 percent of GDP in 2009 to 94.05 percent in 2019, while Sweden maintained a relatively stable and slightly increasing trend, rising from 123.93 percent to 131.08 percent.

Source: Author's elaboration based on data from the World Bank, "Domestic Credit to Private Sector by Banks (% of GDP)," Data360, https://data.worldbank.org/indicator/FD.AST.PRVT.GD.ZS.

While multiple factors influence credit availability, the data suggest that heightened social unrest can contribute to economic uncertainty, which discourages banks from extending credit and businesses from making long-term investments. This underscores the importance of maintaining social stability through well-designed equity policies. A stable environment fosters investor confidence, sustains credit flow, and ultimately supports economic growth.

ALTERNATIVES TO THE SIDE EFFECTS OF SOCIAL DISCONTENT

SUSTAINABLE WELFARE STATES

In chapter 4, we also pointed out that political opportunism often manifests through the adoption of welfare states at the wrong time—a situation in which equity policies are implemented to win the support of dissatisfied citizens, but such policies are not designed well from a technical or fiscal perspective. This is only a possibility, not a rule, because it is entirely feasible to conceive of welfare states that increase equity without reducing growth and in fact enhance it. This type of model, in which equity and growth are pursued simultaneously, is what we call a sustainable welfare state. We classify such states as sustainable because their effectiveness in balancing equity with growth depends on their viability across three key dimensions: economic, social, and political, which we will explore below.

ECONOMIC SUSTAINABILITY

Every public policy requires, as a necessary condition, a source of financing to support its implementation. The more resources a state has, the more public programs it can implement and the better the quality of such programs. To carry out equity policies, a welfare state needs a solid economic foundation for financing, with the specific requirement that this foundation be built on strong equity principles. A state's financing comes from its tax structure, and when it is aligned with a sustainable welfare state, it consists of a set of taxes and fiscal policies that distribute the tax burden proportionally among taxpayers according to their economic capacities. Equity in the tax structure means that those with greater economic capacity contribute more to state financing, while the tax burden on the economically vulnerable is alleviated. This approach not only addresses the main issue of ill-timed welfare states—namely, the eventual emergence of fiscal unsustainability in the implemented policies—but also ensures that the welfare state's financing is rooted in equity principles.

SOCIAL SUSTAINABILITY

Two key aspects, in principle, guarantee the social sustainability of a welfare state. The first is that a welfare state must be designed with the genuine intention of addressing the problems affecting the population rather than merely seeking electoral support. While each society has its own specific challenges, welfare states should generally begin by developing strategies to support quality education, health care, labor protection, social security, and affordable housing, among other needs. The second aspect concerns the role of citizens because a socially sustainable welfare state also involves its citizens in decision making and policymaking. Citizens' active participation is essential because it fosters and strengthens trust in public institutions—an important factor because the welfare state requires public acceptance to enable state intervention in key aspects of daily life.

POLITICAL SUSTAINABILITY

The political sustainability of a welfare state includes two key points. The first is the respect for and effective implementation of the system of checks and balances. It is incorrect to assume that a welfare state inherently concentrates political power in a single figure. Preventing abuses of power and the misallocation of public resources is essential for a sustainable welfare state, particularly because such states must have transparent oversight and evaluation mechanisms to ensure that public funds are used efficiently and fulfill the objectives set by equity policies. The second point concerns political consensus on equity policies. In a sustainable welfare state, these policies should not be subject to dismantling in the short term because of shifts in political leadership. Equity policies must remain independent of political parties because, if well designed and genuinely aimed at serving the most vulnerable populations, they should garner broad consensus on their benefits, and thus their continuity should be ensured over time. A politically sustainable welfare state is one whose existence depends not on the party in power but on the effectiveness of the measures it implements.

If a welfare state is established based on the criteria of economic, social, and political sustainability that we have just outlined, greater equity will likely lead to increased economic growth. This aligns with the discussion in the first section of this chapter, where we explained how improvements in health care, education, attention to societal issues, and more effective institutions are fundamental drivers of economic growth. It is also evident that meeting these criteria can be challenging in practice, although they remain essential for building a truly sustainable welfare state. It is reasonable to expect that results will not be achieved overnight. Unlike the temporary equity brought about by the welfare policies of a political opportunist, the equity ensured by a sustainable welfare state may take time to materialize. Unlike the former, however, it will endure over time. Figure 5.14 summarizes the most relevant aspects of this discussion.

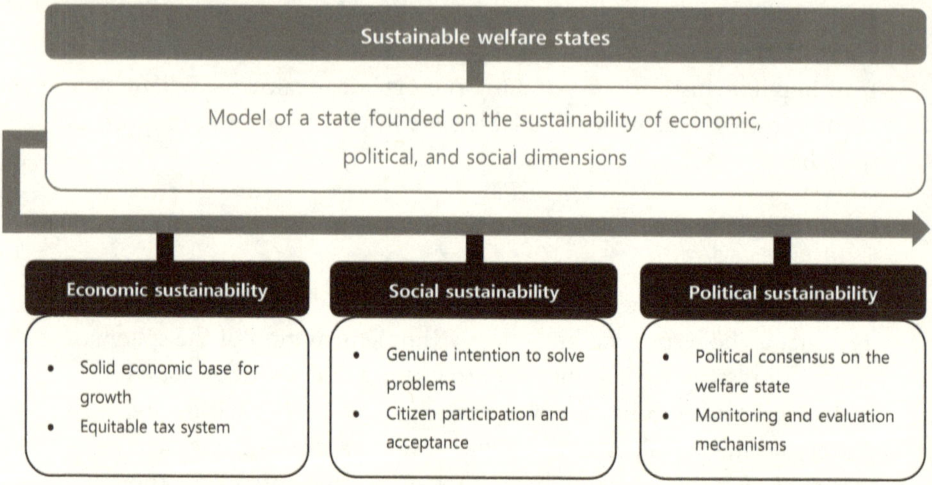

Figure 5.14 Dimensions of sustainable welfare states. The model presents a state framework grounded in the sustainability of economic, social, and political dimensions. Economic sustainability includes a solid base for growth and an equitable tax system. Social sustainability involves a genuine commitment to addressing social problems and the participation and acceptance of citizens. Political sustainability is based on political consensus regarding the welfare state and the existence of monitoring and evaluation mechanisms to ensure the long-term viability of welfare policies.

Source: Author's elaboration.

It is useful to revisit the case of Colombia. As we concluded in chapter 4, Colombia has not developed a welfare state at an inappropriate time. On the contrary, the country has implemented several measures in an effort to resemble what we have defined as a sustainable welfare state. The most recent of these is the 2022 tax reform, called Tax Reform for Equality and Social Justice. Colombia has historically been characterized by high and persistent levels of poverty and inequality. In 2022 alone, the country recorded 18,331,941 people living in monetary poverty,[38] representing more than one-third of the population.[39] Using the Gini coefficient as a measure, data from the World Income Inequality Database indicate that, apart from African nations, Colombia is the fifth most unequal country in the world in terms of income. The purpose of the 2022 tax reform was precisely to help reduce the country's long-standing debt to its citizens regarding poverty and inequality.

From an economic perspective, the tax reform was designed with clear sustainability criteria. On one hand, the initial proposal estimated revenue of 25 billion pesos (1.72 percent of Colombia's GDP), which was intended to establish a solid source of funding for social and productive development programs aimed at reducing poverty and inequality. On the other hand, tax collection was structured to be equitable because the core principle of the reform was that those who have more should contribute more. With this premise, the reform proposed eliminating tax benefits for individuals and sectors with extensive exemptions, thereby increasing the tax burden on higher-income individuals. It also introduced a wealth tax, taxes on windfall profits in the oil and coal sectors, and taxes on junk food.

Sustainability was also addressed from a social perspective. As mentioned, the ambitious revenue from the tax reform was largely intended to finance social and productive development programs aimed at alleviating the country's socioeconomic challenges. For example, the reform would help fund initiatives such as cash transfers to the most vulnerable groups, including single mothers who are heads of households, low-income families, impoverished elderly individuals without pensions, and young people seeking to continue their higher education. At the same time, the 2022 tax reform stood out as one of the most widely agreed-upon regulations in history. To finalize its version, the bill underwent extensive discussions between the central government, the economic sectors affected by the reform, and Colombian citizens at large.

The greatest challenge will always come from the political sphere, however, because it is often the most complex dimension when discussing sustainability—and tax reform is no exception. There is no guarantee that, with a political shift, the principles of equity and social justice on which the 2022 tax reform was designed will be upheld when a new tax law is introduced. The goal of the reform was to reduce poverty and inequality significantly. If this goal is successfully achieved in practice, it should be sufficient justification for maintaining equity and social justice as fundamental principles in future tax reforms.

EFFICIENT ALLOCATION OF MARKETS

According to the principles of orthodox economic theory, any form of subsidy or transfer in a market disrupts the efficient allocation of resources. However, this is an extreme perspective. In reality, subsidies and transfers can lead to both efficient and inefficient resource allocation. In chapter 4, we examined a specific case where the market allocated resources inefficiently as a result of political opportunism. When a subsidy or transfer is designed to gain electoral support rather than to assist a population that genuinely needs public sector support, the market is likely to lose efficiency in resource allocation. Now, it is time to explore situations where well-designed equity policies—implemented through subsidies or transfers—actually contribute to the efficient allocation of resources and thus to greater economic growth. For this to occur, government measures must align with the principles outlined below.

FOCUS ON THE CORRECT TARGET POPULATION

Let's begin with a counterexample that we discussed in chapter 4. Some economic analysts argue that, in Colombia, the gasoline subsidy for taxi drivers lacks justification because higher-income individuals are the primary users of taxi services and could afford a higher fare to cover the increased cost of gasoline. As a result, the subsidy would be misdirected because it would lead to an inefficient allocation of resources in the market.

Proper targeting is essential to ensure that resources are used efficiently and that the benefits of government measures reach those who genuinely need them. This condition of correct targeting is desirable because the focus on the population facing serious socioeconomic challenges (1) maximizes the impact of the measures, (2) prevents the waste of public resources spent on those who do not require government assistance, and (3) enhances the legitimacy and public support of government decisions.

GENERATE POSITIVE INCENTIVES

We return again to a counterexample discussed in chapter 4. State-provided economic support is often conditional on beneficiaries not exceeding a certain income threshold. As mentioned, this requirement can lead individuals to opt for underemployment or even voluntary unemployment to avoid losing public assistance. In this scenario, state support creates perverse incentives that discourage active participation in the economy. A well-designed subsidy or transfer policy should avoid such perverse incentives and instead promote positive incentives that encourage beneficiaries to use state aid as a stepping stone to improving their socioeconomic situation.

ALIGN STAKEHOLDER INCENTIVES

Although state measures are directed at a specific population segment, policymakers must not overlook the potential impacts that subsidies or transfers may have on other societal actors. Equity policies should be designed in a way that does not negatively affect the economic activity of those who are not direct beneficiaries. These policies should encourage overall economic growth and support the broader objectives that equity measures aim to achieve.

When the target population is properly identified, the state can improve the quality of life for many people, contributing to the growth of human capital—an essential factor for economic development. When positive incentives are created, individuals benefit from state support while also actively contributing to their society's economic growth.

When public policy successfully aligns the incentives of all agents affected by state support, collective efforts increase and become interconnected through a shared objective. Under these conditions, equity that promotes the efficient allocation of resources in markets serves as the foundation for greater economic growth. Figure 5.15 summarizes the conditions just described in this section of the chapter.

At this point, it is worth highlighting the example of the planning and execution of housing policy in Colombia between 2019 and 2022. The data indicate that Colombia had never seen such a high volume of new home purchases as that between 2019 and 2022. According to Cámara Colombiana de la Construcción (CAMACOL), over this four-year period, more than 874,000 new homes were purchased. In 2021 alone—despite the ongoing COVID-19 pandemic—the country broke its national record for home purchases in a single year, with over 250,000 homes acquired. As a result, in 2021, Colombia became one of the countries with the highest number of home purchases per million inhabitants.[40]

In Colombia, housing is classified as Viviendas de Interés Social (VIS, Social Interest Housing) and Non–Social Interest Housing (non-VIS) based on its market value. VIS refers to lower-priced housing designed to meet the needs of low-income individuals, while non-VIS includes higher-priced housing typically acquired by people with higher incomes. Figure 5.16 highlights a noteworthy trend: the success of the housing sector in Colombia is largely attributable to the growing importance of VIS housing. In 2010, the proportion of VIS and non-VIS home purchases was fairly similar. From 2019 to 2022, however, VIS

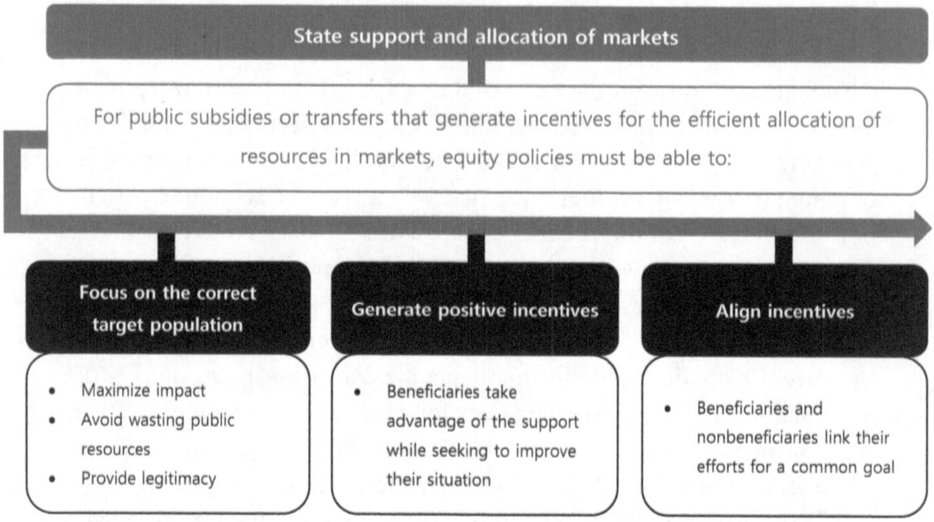

Figure 5.15 Necessary conditions for public subsidies or transfers to promote efficient market allocation through equity policies. Public policies should focus on the correct target population to maximize impact, avoid waste of public resources, and provide legitimacy. They should also generate positive incentives so that beneficiaries use the support as a springboard to improve their situation, and align incentives by encouraging both beneficiaries and nonbeneficiaries to coordinate efforts toward a shared objective.

Source: Author's elaboration.

housing gained significant relevance. In 2021, seven out of every ten homes sold were VIS.

This was no coincidence because the housing policy from 2019 to 2022 was characterized by a strong boost to VIS housing. An equity-focused subsidy policy called *Mi Casa Ya* (MCY, My House Now) was the reason. It was based on the three conditions that ensure an efficient allocation of resources in the market—in this case, the housing market. These subsidies targeted the demand side, financing a significant portion of the price of VIS homes and providing lower interest rates on mortgage loans. The most remarkable feature of MCY was its targeted approach. From its inception, it was designed to address the housing needs of the lowest-income households. To qualify for the program, households had to demonstrate that their monthly income did not exceed a threshold of four minimum wages. Between 2019 and 2022, more than 200,000

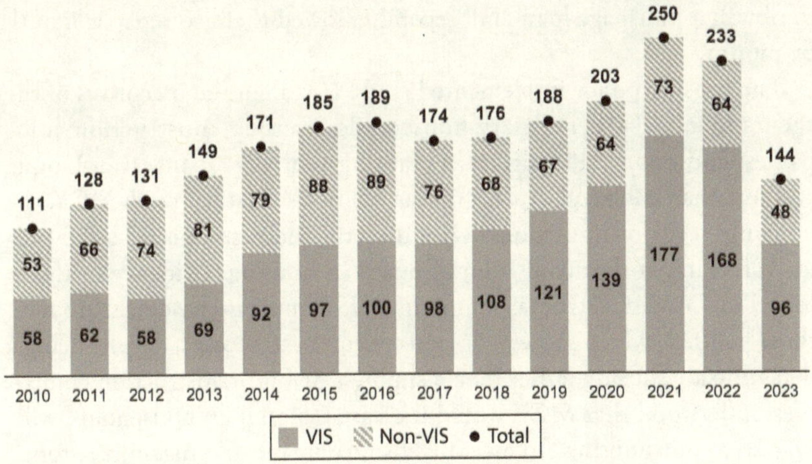

Figure 5.16 The number of new home purchases in Colombia between 2010 and 2023 (thousands of units), disaggregated into Viviendas de Interés Social (VIS, Social Interest Housing) (solid bars) and Non–Social Interest Housing (non-VIS) (patterned bars). The figure shows a steady increase in total housing purchases (black dots) from 2010 to 2021, reaching a peak of 250,000 units in 2021. VIS housing consistently represents a significant share of purchases, with 2021 and 2022 recording the highest VIS volumes during the period. The decline in 2023 reflects a broader slowdown across both housing categories.

Source: Author's elaboration based on data from Cámara Colombiana de la Construcción (CAMACOL), "Tabla de Coyuntura—Unidades," Coordenada Urbana, https://camacol.co/descargable/tablas-de-coyuntura-unidades-corte-noviembre-2025.

MCY subsidies were allocated, with over 70 percent directed to households earning up to two minimum wages—representing the country's lowest-income segment.[41]

Nor was there any room for a perverse incentive. It is true that the crucial requirement for MCY was the income level of potential beneficiaries, but this did not encourage them, for example, to choose underemployment or voluntary unemployment to access the subsidy because MCY financed only part of the home's value, not its entirety. Therefore, the beneficiary had to demonstrate to their financial institution that they had a sufficient income stream to meet the obligations of the mortgage loan they acquired. The beneficiary was also responsible for making monthly mortgage payments. Under both considerations, households that accessed MCY had to engage in some economic activity that, first, enabled them to obtain a mortgage loan and, second, allowed them to repay it month by month.

The subsidy policy implemented could also align the incentives of the agents involved—beneficiary households, housing construction companies, and financial institutions granting mortgage loans. Iván Duque and Jonathan Malagón explain this as follows.[42] First, through MCY, the housing needs of households were directly addressed because the program facilitated the acquisition of new VIS housing. Evidence of this is found in CAMACOL data: comparing VIS home purchases in 2018 with those in 2022, which shows a 56 percent increase. Second, despite being a demand-side subsidy rather than a supply-side one, construction companies understood that MCY would increase Colombian households' willingness to buy housing. To meet this rising demand and maximize profits, they had to expand their economic activity. CAMACOL data show that VIS housing initiations in 2022 grew by 63 percent compared to 2018. Housing construction served as a strong driver of other economic sectors, to the extent that, in Colombia, the construction sector developed productive chains with thirty-four economic activities,[43] representing 50 percent of the sectors in the country's productive apparatus.[44] Third, the primary activity of banks—lending money—grew significantly because the number of households requiring credit increased. As a result, according to Departamento Administrativo Nacional de Estadística (DANE) figures, the balance of the VIS housing mortgage portfolio rose by 86 percent from 2018 to 2022. Colombia's housing policy demonstrated that it is possible to overcome the dilemma between equity and growth by fostering more egalitarian societies while giving the economy a productive boost with a significant impact across various sectors.

HOW TO PROMOTE PRO-GROWTH EQUITY AND HOW THESE POLICIES CONTRIBUTE TO ESCAPING THE MIDDLE-INCOME TRAP

Up to this point in the chapter, our goal has been to present a series of arguments justifying that equity can be a solid foundation for economic growth: if people have access to quality health care and education systems, decent and affordable housing, well-paying jobs, and effective and transparent institutions, they will surely have the necessary conditions to contribute to the economic growth of their society. As an important instrument of social justice that leads to higher growth rates, equity is also a powerful engine capable of generating the additional growth needed by countries mired in the middle-income trap to escape economic stagnation. With this in mind, our next and final step is to determine how we can move into the downward leg of the Kuznets curve, where both greater equity and higher growth are policy objectives that can be achieved simultaneously, and how this could enable countries to break free from the middle-income trap.

Based on the discussions in the previous two sections of this chapter, we present a series of recommendations with the hope that, in one way or another, countries can make significant progress toward their goal of becoming high-income nations. These recommendations address specifically the technical details of pro–growth equity policies, their orientation, and how they should be implemented.

LESS RHETORIC AND MORE TECHNICAL FOUNDATION

As we mentioned in chapter 3, in times of social discontent, there is a threat of political opportunists entering the scene. To win the support of the citizenry, they often promise simple solutions to complex problems. This situation should raise alarms throughout society because these types of solutions rely more on the opportunist's power of persuasion than on a proper technical analysis of the issues. In other words, they are solutions based on rhetoric that lack a solid technical foundation. Because this foundation is absent, the measures implemented by the opportunist fail to solve the problems plaguing society and often lead to serious challenges regarding the sustainability of public finances. Both outcomes can ultimately cause the public to feel disappointed in their government, allowing social discontent to continue to grow.

In principle, for equity policies to be technically well designed, they must meet at least the following three conditions. The first is that they must be policies designed to address the problems that society faces. Although this may seem like an obvious condition, it is unfortunately difficult to fulfill in practice, especially when dealing with political opportunists. Taking action requires thorough research by policymakers to understand social issues. Collecting data; consulting with entities and experts; and, above all, engaging in dialogue with multiple and diverse communities to understand their needs are fundamental tasks for this purpose. It also implies keeping in mind that the environment is constantly changing, so equity policies must be flexible enough to adapt to the social dynamics of their context. Uncertainty will always be a factor that governments must deal with because it is impossible to predict everything. Therefore, it is crucial to be able to adjust policies according to the changing needs and problems of the population. Governments must avoid being influenced or controlled by the objectives of interest groups. While these groups should be listened to and considered in public policy, their needs cannot override the needs of society as a whole.

The second condition is that equity policies must be fiscally sustainable. By fiscal sustainability, we refer to a government's ability to ensure the long-term viability of its public policies and maintain healthy levels of debt. In this context, fiscal sustainability aims to avoid excessive budget deficits and the uncontrolled accumulation of debt, but it also seeks to ensure that public policies are viable and can adapt over time. On this issue, we consider one of the most precise guidelines to be that prepared by Alberto Arenas, former Minister of Finance of Chile. According to Arenas, the foundation of fiscal sustainability for policies that address inequality involves the efficient management of what he calls the four dimensions of public finances: public revenues, public expenditures, fiscal institutions, and the political economy of public finances.[45]

The efficient management of public revenues occurs when tax reforms are designed based on solid technical and progressive criteria, enabling them to serve as a key social instrument for financing public policies and advancing equity. On the expenditure side, management should aim to solve society's problems through various programs while keeping in mind the restrictions posed by the government's income and level of indebtedness. Efficient fiscal institutions require a system for evaluating and controlling the budget cycle. And the political economy of public finances refers to the ever-present interaction between the economy and politics. Efficient management begins by recognizing the distribution of powers in any society and then aims to establish fiscal pacts. These are important because they seek to generate consensus among citizens, encouraging people and companies to recognize the importance of certain policies—even when they directly affect their personal interests, such as income taxes or taxes on economic activities that pollute the environment.

The third condition is that policies must be designed according to the context in which they will be implemented. Equity policies that work well in some countries do not necessarily work equally well in others. Each country has its own particularities and must find its own path to becoming a high-income nation. If equity policies do not account for the special conditions of each country when they are designed, there is a risk that these policies will not achieve their objective of increasing equity levels. As an example, Jonathan Malagón and José Antonio Ocampo, in the case of Latin America, conclude that fiscal policy contributes to improving income distribution, but this is achieved to a greater extent through spending rather than taxation.[46] Unlike developed economies, however, many Latin American countries have not yet achieved universal access to basic services such as health care or education, which are fundamental determinants of equity. Given this, the most effective policies to improve income distribution are those that aim to guarantee the universalization of basic services and provide income transfers to poor households. This does not mean that taxation should be ruled out because, according to the results of Nora Lustig, Valentina Martinez and Carola Pessino, both direct and indirect taxes have helped reduce inequality in Latin America.[47] Given the region's context, however, the general objective of Latin American social policy should, at first, focus on the universalization of basic services.

Regarding taxes, it is essential to carefully review the composition of tax revenues and their evolution over time because this exercise allows each country to identify the measures that have had the greatest distributional impact, providing a useful basis for designing future distributive policies. Looking again at the case of Latin America, Malagón and Ocampo point out that direct taxes have strengthened, especially those levied on firms.[48] Table 5.1 shows that revenues from direct taxes increased from representing an average of 3.3 percent of GDP in 1993 to 7.0 percent in 2022. This is significantly more than the growth of indirect taxes, which rose from 7.5 percent to 9.1 percent of GDP and continued to be the main source of tax revenues. Some economies exhibit more striking growth; in Chile, for example, direct tax revenues increased from 4.0 percent of GDP in 1993 to 10.9 percent in 2022. It is not by chance that direct taxes in the region have been strengthened, as Malagón and Ocampo explain, because the distributive impact of fiscal policy in Latin America has improved over time.[49]

When designing equity policies, one must consider the specific context of each country, but it also means recognizing and anticipating that the magnitude of the impacts will not be the same for all countries. Numerous studies support this assertion, particularly those comparing the distributional impacts of fiscal policies in Latin American countries with those in developed OECD countries. The studies of Edwin Goñi, Humberto López, and Luis Servén; David Jesuit and Vincent Mahler; and Rodrigo Cubero and Ivanna Vladkova allow us to conclude that the distributional

Table 5.1 Composition of central national government tax revenues, as a percentage of GDP, for a sample of seventeen Latin American and Caribbean economies

Country	1993					2022				
	Taxes			Social security	Total	Taxes			Social security	Total
	Direct	*Indirect*	*Other*			*Direct*	*Indirect*	*Other*		
Argentina	1.1	5.4	0.7	5.0	**12.2**	4.0	5.9	0.5	4.5	**14.8**
Bolivia	0.6	9.7	1.3	1.2	**12.8**	3.7	12.1	1.2	5.7	**22.6**
Brazil	6.0	5.3	0.3	6.7	**18.4**	10.4	5.0	0.1	7.3	**22.7**
Chile	4.0	11.6	0.9	1.4	**17.9**	10.9	10.6	-0.1	1.0	**22.3**
Colombia	3.9	4.2	0.2	0.0	**8.3**	7.7	7.0	0.1	2.0	**16.8**
Costa Rica	3.3	9.0	0.3	5.4	**18.0**	7.1	7.8	0.5	8.0	**23.4**
Ecuador	1.1	4.9	0.0	2.1	**8.1**	5.1	10.2	0.0	5.0	**20.4**
El Salvador	2.8	7.7	0.2	0.0	**10.7**	8.5	11.3	0.0	0.0	**19.7**
Guatemala	2.0	6.1	0.2	0.2	**8.5**	4.4	8.4	0.0	0.4	**13.2**
Honduras	3.2	7.9	0.0	0.0	**11.1**	6.9	10.4	0.0	0.0	**17.2**
Mexico	4.4	4.4	0.3	2.3	**11.5**	8.0	5.5	0.3	2.4	**16.3**
Nicaragua	1.7	7.0	0.0	1.4	**10.1**	9.0	10.8	0.0	6.3	**26.1**
Panama	4.8	5.9	0.3	6.1	**17.1**	4.4	3.5	0.0	5.2	**13.0**
Paraguay	1.9	6.0	0.2	0.8	**8.9**	3.0	7.0	0.1	1.2	**11.4**
Peru	2.4	9.3	0.9	2.0	**14.6**	7.8	8.6	0.5	1.9	**18.8**
Dominican Republic	2.1	8.7	0.2	0.1	**11.1**	5.2	8.7	0.0	0.1	**14.0**
Uruguay	2.5	9.9	0.1	7.4	**19.8**	8.3	10.0	0.0	6.7	**25.1**
Average	**2.8**	**7.2**	**0.4**	**2.5**	**12.9**	**6.7**	**8.4**	**0.2**	**3.4**	**18.7**

Note: The composition of tax revenues disaggregated into direct taxes, indirect taxes, other revenues, and social security contributions, as a percentage of GDP, in 1993 and 2022 for seventeen Latin American and Caribbean countries. The data show a general increase in total tax revenues, with the average rising from 12.9 percent in 1993 to 18.7 percent in 2022. The structure of taxation still relies mostly on indirect taxes, although the contribution of direct taxes has increased significantly, on average, from 2.8 percent to 6.7 percent.

Source: Author's elaboration based on data from the Economic Commission for Latin America and the Caribbean, "Tax Revenue by Type of Taxes as a Percentage of GDP (Latin America and the Caribbean)," CEPALSTAT, https://statistics.cepal.org/portal/cepalstat/dashboard.html?theme=2&lang=en.

impact of equity policies in Latin America is considerably lower than that in developed OECD countries.[50] From the aforementioned studies, it is found that, through tax policy and public transfers, Latin America manages to reduce the Gini coefficient by an equivalent of 0.039 points, while the developed OECD countries reduce it by 0.167 points. In the case of taxes, we can see in figure 5.17 that their distributional impact in the OECD (0.040 points of the Gini coefficient) is more than thirteen times that of Latin America (0.003 points of the Gini coefficient).

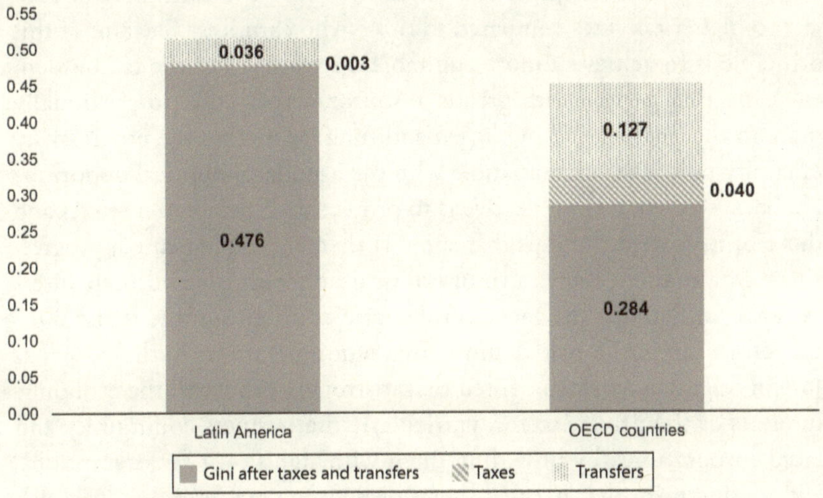

Figure 5.17 The redistributive effect of fiscal policy in Latin American countries and OECD countries, measured through the Gini coefficient before and after taxes and transfers. In Latin American countries, the Gini coefficient after fiscal interventions (solid bar) stands at 0.476, with transfers (dotted bar) contributing only 0.036 and taxes (patterned bar) reducing inequality by merely 0.003 points. In contrast, OECD countries show a Gini coefficient of 0.284 after taxes and transfers (solid bar), with transfers (dotted bar) reducing inequality by 0.127 points and taxes (patterned bar) reducing inequality by 0.040 points. The chart illustrates the limited redistributive power of fiscal policy in Latin American countries compared to OECD countries. The countries included in the Latin American group are Argentina, Bolivia, Brazil, Chile, Colombia, Costa Rica, El Salvador, Guatemala, Honduras, Mexico, Nicaragua, Panama, and Peru. The OECD countries are Australia, Belgium, Canada, Denmark, Finland, France, Germany, Ireland, the Netherlands, Norway, Sweden, Switzerland, the United Kingdom, and the United States.

Source: Author's elaboration based on data from Edwin Goñi, Humberto López, and Luis Servén, "Fiscal Redistribution and Income Inequality in Latin America," World Bank Policy Research Paper, no. 4487 (World Bank, 2008); David Jesuit and Vincent Mahler, "State Redistribution in Comparative Perspective: A Cross-National Analysis of the Developed Countries," LIS Working Paper, no. 392 (Luxembourg Income Study, 2004); Rodrigo Cubero and Ivanna Vladkova, "Equity and Fiscal Policy: The Income Distribution Effects of Taxation and Social Spending in Central America," IMF Working Paper, no. 112 (International Monetary Fund, 2010).

LESS REGRESSIVITY AND MORE PROGRESSIVITY

Progressive taxation requires that those who have and earn more be subject to higher tax rates compared to those who earn less. The aim of this principle is to achieve a more equitable distribution of the tax burden, ensuring that people with greater resources contribute proportionally more to the financing of public expenditures. Note that the progressivity of equity policies is incompatible with the agenda of political opportunists because their main objective is to protect their personal interests and those of the interest groups that support them. If implemented, progressivity would affect the wealth of political opportunists and their interest groups. Perhaps the most emblematic counterexample is the 2017 tax reform under Donald Trump's first administration. Authors such as Joseph Stiglitz have documented that it strongly protected the economic interests of the private sector, particularly the business community and large corporations, by providing them with significant tax exemptions, eliminating taxes that harmed them, or defining tax rates that were disproportionately low relative to their resources.[51]

It is expected that, if policies are progressively oriented, equity will tend to increase because we are talking about a fair allocation of fiscal responsibilities among the economic groups of society. Countries that want to escape the middle-income trap should consider the following recommendations when designing a progressively oriented tax system. Such a system should, on the one hand, raise resources equitably to finance public sector actions and, on the other, support the implementation of pro–growth equity policies.

First, on the public funding side, sectors with high profit margins and high incomes should contribute more. This means that sectors such as real estate, pharmaceuticals, finance, and large multinational corporations should be evaluated to determine whether it is appropriate to impose a proportionally higher tax burden on them. Guided by erroneous precepts from free market advocates, however, many countries have historically granted these sectors tax exemptions and low or even negligible tax burdens.

Second, sectors that benefit most from the resources provided by the environment should also contribute more. For example, sectors that heavily exploit natural resources, such as oil extraction and mining, could be subject to progressive taxation to ensure an equitable distribution of benefits. Higher taxes should also be applied to those sectors that generate negative externalities for society, such as environmental pollution or the production of goods harmful to health, in order to internalize the social costs of these externalities.

Starting from a progressive scheme also requires conducting more in-depth evaluations and addressing more specific aspects. For example, in most cases, inheritance taxes are viewed as progressive measures because they help prevent the excessive intergenerational accumulation of wealth. The progressive agenda is also ideally complemented by exemptions or subsidies for sectors that generate more progress for society, such as health care and education.

The principle of progressivity should not be limited solely to the area of tax collection, however; it should extend to how the resources the government has collected are invested equitably. A progressive allocation of public resources is based on addressing the needs and priorities of society. We can distinguish at least six areas in which governments could invest to generate the equity that would lead to additional growth, which is also necessary to escape the middle-income trap.

The first two areas are health care and education. As we have already discussed at length in this chapter, health care and education are fundamental to strengthening the human capital of any society. Better education and health-care facilities, more competitive salaries for health-care and education workers, and subsidies to help the most vulnerable people access these basic services are some of the equity policies needed in these two areas.

The third area consists of R&D, essential determinants for the generation and dissemination of knowledge, a primary source of innovation. This is a key area because there are projects in which the private sector will not invest as a result of the high levels of risk. Many of these projects are crucial for progress in health care and education, as mentioned in the previous point, but also in many other areas. In this sense, public investment in R&D boosts economic competitiveness by creating new market opportunities while also promoting general prosperity by strengthening areas that have a direct impact on the well-being of societies.

This third area deserves even more attention from public policy designers, especially considering that technological innovation could exacerbate levels of economic inequality. Drawing on the discussions put forward by Daron Acemoglu and Simon Johnson, if we analyze the potential implications of automation and artificial intelligence (AI), we may encounter a stark contrast between two population groups.[52] On one hand are individuals with high technological skills and capabilities who will reap significant benefits in the labor market because they can access the highest-paying jobs. On the other hand are individuals with low qualifications who will most likely face unemployment as a result of the replacement of their roles by more advanced technologies or better-trained individuals. If they do manage to find employment, it will most likely be in the lowest-paid positions. This imbalance between these two groups would ultimately lead to higher levels of inequality.

Given this scenario, governments must anticipate and seek solutions to mitigate these potential negative impacts. One possible solution is the implementation of a universal basic income, a proposal that is increasingly debated in public policy discussions and is advocated by figures such as Guy Standing, a professor at the University of London who has studied the implementation of a universal basic income for many years. Based on Standing's work, a universal basic income could provide low-skilled workers with an economic safety net, granting them the stability needed to acquire new technological skills and adapt to emerging labor roles.[53] To make this possible, it is also crucial that, alongside the introduction of such an income, educational systems adapt and offer comprehensive programs that provide technological training from the early grades, such as primary and secondary education, complemented by specialized technical programs and continuous skills training for adults.

A universal basic income has been the subject of multiple criticisms, however, particularly regarding its fiscal feasibility. The main concern is where to find the necessary resources to fund a universal basic income. One of the most discussed solutions is the implementation of taxes on companies that replace workers with technologies such as automation and AI. Another potential source of funding could be the reallocation of public funds, redirecting resources from government programs that are failing to achieve their intended outcomes toward the implementation of a universal basic income.

The fourth area is infrastructure. Investing in infrastructure has two positive and desirable impacts. First, better public services, roads, and railways improve people's quality of life. Second, it directly boosts economic growth by facilitating economic activities such as the transportation of goods.

The fifth area is affordable housing. To ensure higher levels of equity, it is essential to have programs that make access to decent housing possible, not only from a quantitative point of view (i.e., meeting the needs of households without a home) but also from a qualitative point of view (i.e., addressing the needs of households that, despite having a home, require repairs and improvements to live in it properly).

The sixth area relates to environmental protection. A portion of public resources should be allocated to this purpose because environmental destruction leads to more people facing health problems and depletes the resources needed in the future to sustain economic activities. Without healthy people and available resources, it is impossible to achieve growth rates commensurate with a high-income level.

Although the redistributive initiatives we have just outlined have the potential to help countries escape the middle-income trap, their implementation faces significant challenges that cannot be ignored. One of the most critical challenges is the political and social resistance that these measures often generate, especially when sectors with a certain degree of power and influence are affected by higher tax burdens or the elimination of tax exemptions. Another challenge is related to the negative perception that certain segments of the population have toward redistributive initiatives, which, in many cases, limits the social acceptance required for their implementation. This negative perception is often shaped by narratives that label progressivity as an obstacle to economic growth or even as a penalty for success. In such scenarios, fostering transparent dialogue among all stakeholders becomes essential to explain how redistributive initiatives can benefit the majority of the population.

An additional challenge concerns the administrative and technical capacities of each government. To implement redistributive initiatives effectively and in a timely manner, governments must have strong, efficient, and transparent tax systems that minimize serious issues such as tax evasion. Redistributive initiatives must be supported by robust oversight and control mechanisms to prevent or, if necessary, combat any acts of corruption. This is by no means a negligible challenge, particularly considering that countries trapped in the middle-income trap often lack the human, technological, and financial resources necessary to strengthen their tax systems. To overcome these challenges, a crucial first step for countries seeking to escape the middle-income trap is to prioritize public resources for the modernization of their tax systems. This entails training personnel, acquiring new technologies, and adopting open governance practices, among other initiatives.

We conclude our analysis of policy guidance with the following. Tax collection and public spending are two sides of the same coin: they are the fundamental tools available to any country's fiscal policy. For pro-growth equity to take place, we believe that fiscal policy should have a progressive orientation because this would generate the socioeconomic opportunities people often need to escape poverty and contribute more significantly to the economic growth of their country.

At the same time, we contend that, if an essential objective of politics is to escape the middle-income trap, regressivity cannot even be considered as an option because it leads to unfavorable scenarios like the so-called trickle-down economy. This concept is based on the false belief that, if the rich and higher-income sectors are relieved of all tax liability, the well-being they enjoy will eventually benefit the rest of society. In reality, the trickle-down economy tends to perpetuate inequality instead of reducing it because there is no guarantee that the most privileged will effectively distribute their well-being with the rest of society.

LESS RELIANCE ON THE FREE MARKET, A MORE ACTIVE ROLE OF THE STATE

THE FREE MARKET

The free market is an economic system in which transactions occur with minimal state intervention. Under this system, economic variables such as production levels and prices are determined by the interaction between supply and demand rather than being regulated or controlled by the state. In economic theory, the free market has been the dominant concept that has significantly influenced economic policies throughout history, especially during the development of the capitalist system and the rise of economic liberalism in the nineteenth and twentieth centuries.

Classical economists and then neoclassical economists have defended the free market as a mechanism for allocating resources efficiently. Among the most prominent of these economists are Adam Smith, who formulated the idea of the invisible hand, according to which the individual pursuit of self-interest leads to collective well-being under a free market system; Friedrich Hayek, who warned of the dangers of collectivism and emphasized the importance of competition and decentralization in economic decision making to preserve individual freedom; and Milton Friedman, who strongly defended individual freedom and markets free of state intervention as means to achieve a more prosperous society.[54]

Despite all the apparent benefits that the free market brings, the truth is that it is an economic system that entails serious socioeconomic problems for any society, as experience has shown. Let's start by reviewing what happens with inequality. Under the free market, competition can lead to considerable differences in both income generation and wealth accumulation. At the same time, agents with more resources often have initial advantages, which can result in the concentration of economic power in the hands of a few. This leads to a lack of economic and social mobility, creating serious disparities between the members of a society. In relation to economic crises, the absence of regulation that characterizes the free market can lead to risky behaviors in financial markets, such as a lack of transparency and excessive speculation, which can create financial bubbles that adversely affect economic stability.

We also have the case of the provision of public goods. Because these types of goods often do not have clear direct benefits for the private sector, free market forces may not be sufficient to guarantee the supply needed to meet the quantity demanded by the population. The real problem is that many of these goods are essential for general welfare, such as education, health care, and infrastructure.

Given this series of problems, it is questionable whether the free market is capable of implementing the equity measures that countries need to escape the middle-income trap.

ALTERNATIVES FOR IMPLEMENTING PRO-GROWTH EQUITY POLICIES

If we cannot fully rely on the free market to generate the equity that societies demand and need, then we must explore other alternatives. The first alternative that comes to mind is its counterpart: state intervention. In its most extreme form, the state intervenes in most aspects of people's lives. As the experiences of the Soviet Union and North Korea have shown, however, this can lead to the establishment of institutions that threaten equity and growth. An intermediate option was proposed by Keynes, who advocated for state intervention but did not call for it in all situations or at all times, only in specific cases where the market failed.[55]

We could say that Keynes's approach is, to a certain extent, associated with the idea of a social democratic system. Figures such as Eduard Bernstein, one of the most renowned Marxist theorists, conceive a social democratic system as the combination of socialist principles with those of a market economy.[56] By "social democracy," we mean a political ideology that seeks to combine socialist principles with a democratic system and a market economy. It focuses on achieving goals of equality and socioeconomic justice through democratic means and state intervention but without completely abolishing the market system or private property. Note that, with this conception, a social democratic system distinguishes itself from more extreme forms of state intervention by accepting the existence of the free market while also advocating for significant regulation and redistribution to mitigate existing inequalities in society.

Throughout the twentieth century, social democracy became a major force in several European nations, including Sweden, Denmark, and Finland, where social democratic parties came to power and implemented policies that combined the best of the market economy with a strong and clear welfare state. Through this approach, these nations adopted measures of wealth redistribution, universal health care, free education, and other policies aimed at improving equality and social welfare. It is no coincidence, therefore, that these were the countries we used as examples in the first section of this chapter to show how equity can become the foundation for growth.

We argue, as Keynes and Bernstein do, that when the market is incapable of performing a task effectively, the state should intervene to address what the market cannot achieve on its own. For our particular purposes, the market alone cannot implement measures in favor of equity. Therefore, the active role of the state is required, one that, with the highest level of technical detail, designs the equity policies that societies demand. In addition to failing to implement progressive measures, the market can exacerbate inequality by favoring the interests of a privileged few. In this case, state intervention to implement progressive policies is crucial if the goal is to achieve higher levels of equity.

Again, at no point are we proposing the abolition of the market to be replaced by the absolute domination of the state. However, because the private sector has shown that it is incapable, on its own, of being the engine of innovation as a result of its high aversion to risk,[57] or of addressing the challenges posed by globalization and neoliberalism in a way that benefits the majority,[58] the leadership of the state is essential for the design and implementation of pro–growth equity policies. Although it may seem contradictory, state intervention can be compatible with the promotion of the free market if it is implemented in a balanced and strategic way. For example, the state complements the free market when it intervenes to correct market failures such as negative externalities, monopolies, oligopolies, and information asymmetries. There are also synergies when state regulations help, first, to shield the economy from risky behaviors that lead to severe crises, and second, to preserve market competition by prohibiting or punishing anticompetitive practices.

Finally, we acknowledge that the proposal of a social democratic system is not an infallible formula in itself. Just as with the free market, state intervention also comes with certain shortcomings that, according to public choice theory, can lead to what is known as government failures. According to Julian Le Grand, these failures manifest in three main areas: provision, subsidies, and regulation.[59] Regarding the provision of goods and services, public entities tend to operate as monopolies, which can reduce market competition and ultimately result in inefficiencies such as higher operating and production costs or lower-quality goods and services. As for subsidies, they may generate excessive demand and an inefficient allocation of resources, disproportionately benefiting certain groups instead of promoting widespread equity. In terms of regulation, the state faces two significant challenges that often hinder its ability to act optimally. On the one hand, there is the lack of adequate information for decision making; on the other, the alliances that emerge between legislators and interest groups could result in the favoritism of a select few at the expense of collective well-being. A major source of social discontent arises when governments fail to address the concerns of those who elected them; however, a decisive way to prevent government failures is through the active role of citizens. Voting conscientiously and staying constantly informed about political affairs are crucial actions for the proper functioning of democracy and the overall well-being of society. It is our collective responsibility to critically examine the government plans presented during electoral periods, carefully analyze the technical content of policy promises, and objectively and continuously evaluate the performance of those who represent us in power. In democratic systems, this is the only way to prevent political opportunism from seizing control and leading our societies either toward growth-inhibiting equity scenarios or, even worse, toward scenarios lacking both equity and growth.

NOTES

1. THE DILEMMA BETWEEN EQUITY AND GROWTH

1. Lucas Chancel, Thomas Piketty, Emmanuel Saez, and Gabriel Zucman, *World Inequality Report 2022* (World Inequality Lab, 2022).

2. A. W. Phillips, "The Relation Between Unemployment and the Rate of Change of Money Wages in the United Kingdom, 1861–1957," *Economica* 25, no. 100 (1958): 283–99.

3. Phillips, "The Relation Between Unemployment and the Rate of Change," 283–99; Paul Samuelson and Robert Solow, "Analytical Aspects of Anti-Inflation Policy," *American Economic Review, Papers and Proceedings* 50, no. 2 (1960): 177–94.

4. Jude Wanniski, "Taxes, Revenues and the Laffer Curve," *Public Interest* 50 (1978): 3–16.

5. Arthur Laffer, *The Laffer Curve: Past, Present, and Future* (Heritage Foundation, 2004).

6. Simon Kuznets, *Shares of Upper Income Groups in Income and Savings* (National Bureau of Economic Research, 1953).

7. Thomas Piketty, *Capital in the Twenty-First Century* (Harvard University Press, 2014).

8. Simon Kuznets, "Economic Growth and Income Inequality," *American Economic Review* 45, no. 1 (1955): 1–28.

9. Kuznets, "Economic Growth and Income Inequality," 10.

10. Raghuram G. Rajan and Luigi Zingales, *Saving Capitalism from the Capitalists: Unleashing the Power of Financial Markets to Create Wealth and Spread Opportunity* (Princeton University Press, 2004).

11. Rajan and Zingales, *Saving Capitalism from the Capitalists.*

12. Jonathan Malagón and Luis Triveño, "Estructura y acabados: 30 ideas sobre cómo mejorar la política de vivienda en Colombia, aplicables al mundo emergente," *Coyuntura Económica: Investigación Económica y Social* 52 (2022): 65–92.

13. Jorge González, Clara Ramírez, and Alfredo Sarmiento, *Reflexiones en torno a la distribución del ingreso, el crecimiento y el gasto público* (Universidad Externado de Colombia, 2003), 7.

14. Simon Kuznets, as cited in Jorge González, "Juan Luis Londoño: Ideas para la acción," *Revista de Economía Institucional* 5, no. 8 (2003): 229.

15. Simon Kuznets, "Quantitative Aspects of the Economic Growth of Nations: VIII. Distribution of Income by Size," *Economic Development and Cultural Change* 11, no. 2 (1963): 1–80.

16. González, "Juan Luis Londoño," 229.

17. Kuznets, "Economic Growth and Income Inequality," 26.

18. Piketty, *Capital in the Twenty-First Century*, 29.

19. Ivan Lyubimov, "Income Inequality Revisited 60 Years Later: Piketty vs Kuznets," *Russian Journal of Economics* 3, no. 1 (2017): 42–53.

20. Lyubimov, "Income Inequality Revisited 60 Years Later," 45.

21. Piketty, *Capital in the Twenty-First Century*.

22. Piketty, *Capital in the Twenty-First Century*.

23. Chancel et al., *World Inequality Report 2022*.

24. See, for example, Deirdre McCloskey, "Measured, Unmeasured, Mismeasured, and Unjustified Pessimism: A Review Essay of Thomas Piketty's *Capital in the Twenty-First Century*," *Erasmus Journal for Philosophy and Economics* 7, no. 2 (2014): 73–115; Phillip Magness and Robert Murphy, "Challenging the Empirical Contribution of Thomas Piketty's *Capital in the 21st Century*," *Journal of Private Enterprise* 30, no. 2 (2015): 1–34.

25. Branko Milanovic, *The Haves and the Have-Nots: A Brief and Idiosyncratic History of Global Inequality* (Basic Books, 2011).

26. Laura Policardo, Lionello Punzo, and Edgar Sánchez, "¿Desigualdad insostenible? Evidencia empírica para países de América Latina," in *América Latina en la larga historia de la desigualdad*, ed. Martín Puchet and Alicia Puyana (FLACSO, 2018), 177–205.

27. Gary Fields, "Income Distribution and Economic Growth," in *The State of Development Economics: Progress and Perspectives*, ed. Gustav Ranis and T. Paul Schultz (Basil Blackwell, 1988), 459–81.

28. Gary Fields, *Distribution and Development: A Summary of the Evidence for the Developing World* (World Bank, 1999), 23.

29. See, for example, Laszlo Matyas, Laszlo Konya, and Lachlan MacQuarie, "The Kuznets U-Curve Hypothesis: Some Panel Data Evidence," *Applied Economics Letters* 5, no. 11 (1998): 693–97.

30. Federico Cingano, "Trends in Income Inequality and Its Impact on Economic Growth," OECD Social, Employment and Migration Working Papers, no. 163 (Organisation for Economic Co-operation and Development, 2014).

31. Donald Harris, "Economic Growth and Equity: Complements or Opposites?," *Review of Black Political Economy* 21, no. 3 (1993): 65–72.

32. Joseph E. Stiglitz, "Inequality and Economic Growth," *Political Quarterly* 86, no. 51 (2015): 134–55.

33. Stiglitz, "Inequality and Economic Growth."

34. John Gallup, *Is There a Kuznets Curve?* (Portland State University, 2012).

35. Gallup, *Is There a Kuznets Curve?*

36. Gallup, *Is There a Kuznets Curve?*

37. Piketty, *Capital in the Twenty-First Century*.

38. Diya Rattan, "Exploring the Kuznets Curve and the 'Latin American Effect' in Latin America," in *International Economic Review: Post Recession Challenges and Analysis*, ed. Kishore Kulkarni (Matrix, 2012), 271–87.

39. See Klaus Deininger and Lyn Squire, "Measuring Income Inequality: A New Data-Base," *World Bank Economic Review* 10, no. 3 (1996): 565–91; Klaus Deininger and Lyn Squire, "New Ways of Looking at Old Issues: Inequality and Growth," *Journal of Development Economics* 57 (1998): 259–87.

40. Deininger and Squire, "Measuring Income Inequality."

41. Deininger and Squire, "New Ways of Looking at Old Issues."

42. Rattan, "Exploring the Kuznets Curve and the 'Latin American Effect' "; José Gabriel Palma, "Homogeneous Middles vs. Heterogeneous Tails, and the End of the 'Inverted-U': It's All About the Share of the Rich," *Development and Change* 42, no. 1 (2011): 87–153.

43. Palma, "Homogeneous Middles vs. Heterogeneous Tails."

44. Roland Bénabou, "Inequality and Growth," *NBER Macroeconomics Annual* 11 (1996): 11–92.

45. Bénabou, "Inequality and Growth."

46. Philippe Aghion, Eve Caroli, and Cecilia García-Peñalosa, "Inequality and Economic Growth: The Perspective of the New Growth Theories," *Journal of Economic Literature* 37, no. 4 (1999): 1615–60.

47. Andrew Berg, Jonathan Ostry, Charalambos G. Tsangarides, and Yorbol Yakhshilikov, "Redistribution, Inequality, and Growth: New Evidence," *Journal of Economic Growth* 23, no. 3 (2018): 259–305.

48. Berg et al., "Redistribution, Inequality, and Growth."

49. Alberto Alesina and Dani Rodrik, "Distributive Politics and Economic Growth," *Quarterly Journal of Economics* 109, no. 2 (1994): 465–90; Giuseppe Bertola, "Factor Shares and Savings in Endogenous Growth," *American Economic Review* 83, no. 5 (1993): 1184–99.

50. Moheddine Younsi and Marwa Bechtini, "Economic Growth, Financial Development, and Income Inequality in BRICS Countries: Does Kuznets' Inverted U-Shaped Curve Exist?," *Journal of the Knowledge Economy* 11, no. 2 (2018): 721–42.

51. Donghyun Park and Kwanho Shin, "Economic Growth, Financial Development, and Income Inequality," *Emerging Markets Finance and Trade* 53, no. 12 (2017): 2794–2825.

52. Leandro Prados de la Escosura, "Inequality, Poverty, and the Kuznets Curve in Spain, 1850–2000," *European Review of Economic History* 12, no. 3 (2008): 287–324.

53. Prados de la Escosura, "Inequality, Poverty, and the Kuznets Curve in Spain."

54. Robert J. Barro, "Inequality and Growth Revisited," Working Paper Series on Regional Economic Integration, no. 11 (Asian Development Bank, 2008).

55. Barro, "Inequality and Growth Revisited."

56. Julio Alonso and Ángela González, "Evaluación de la hipótesis de Kuznets para Colombia, 1977–2005," *Apuntes del CENES* 36, no. 63 (2017): 43–62.

57. José Antonio Ocampo and Carmen Astrid Romero, *Crecimiento económico colombiano y sus efectos sobre el desarrollo social y regional, 1905–2019* (Central Bank of Colombia, 2023).

58. Gene M. Grossman and Alan B. Krueger, "Environmental Impacts of a North American Free Trade Agreement," NBER Working Paper, no. 3914 (National Bureau of Economic Research, 1991).

59. Grossman and Krueger, "Environmental Impacts of a North American Free Trade Agreement."

60. Patricio Crespo, *Decisiones ambientales y liberalismo* (Ediciones Abya-Yala, 2008).

61. Kuheli Dutt, "Governance, Institutions, and the Environment Income Relationship: Across Country Study," *Environment, Development and Sustainability* 11, no. 4 (2009): 705–23.

62. See, for example, Soumyananda Dinda, "Environmental Kuznets Curve Hypothesis: A Survey," *Ecological Economics* 49, no. 4 (2004): 431–55; Fander Falconí, Rafael Burbano, and Pedro Cango, *La discutible curva de Kuznets* (FLACSO Ecuador, 2016).

63. See, for example, Haisheng Yang, Jie He, and Shaoling Chen, "The Fragility of the Environmental Kuznets Curve: Revisiting the Hypothesis with Chinese Data via an 'Extreme Bound Analysis,'" *Ecological Economics* 109 (2014): 41–58.

64. Jeremy Greenwood and Boyan Jovanovic, "Financial Development, Growth, and the Distribution of Income," *Journal of Political Economy* 98, no. 5 (1990): 1076–1107.

65. Greenwood and Jovanovic, "Financial Development, Growth, and the Distribution of Income"; Zlatko Nikoloski, "Financial Sector Development and Inequality: Is There a Financial Kuznets Curve?," *Journal of International Development* 25, no. 7 (2012): 897–911.

66. Onur Özdemir, "Rethinking the Financial Kuznets Curve in the Framework of Income Inequality: Empirical Evidence on Advanced and Developing Economies," *Economic and Business Letters* 8, no. 4 (2019): 176–90.

67. Nikoloski, "Financial Sector Development and Inequality"; Özdemir, "Rethinking the Financial Kuznets Curve."

2. THE ERA OF SOCIAL DISCONTENT

1. Economic Commission for Latin America and the Caribbean (ECLAC), *Social Panorama of Latin America 2020* (ECLAC, 2021), 221.

2. Joseph E. Stiglitz, *People, Power, and Profits: Progressive Capitalism for an Age of Discontent* (Norton, 2019).

3. Stiglitz, *People, Power, and Profits*, 8.

4. See John Komlos, "Reaganomics: una línea divisoria," *Tiempo y Economía* 6, no. 1 (2019): 47–76.

5. Stiglitz, *People, Power, and Profits.*

6. Joseph E. Stiglitz, *Globalization and Its Discontents* (Norton, 2002).

7. Nesrine Malik, *We Need New Stories: Challenging the Toxic Myths Behind Our Age of Discontent* (Weidenfeld & Nicolson, 2019).

8. ECLAC, *Social Panorama of Latin America 2020.*

9. Mancur Olson, *The Logic of Collective Action: Public Goods and the Theory of Groups* (Harvard University Press, 1971).

10. See Alberto Alesina and Paola Giuliano, "Preferences for Redistribution," NBER Working Paper, no. 14825 (National Bureau of Economic Research, 2009).

11. Sidney Tarrow, *Power in Movement: Social Movements and Contentious Politics* (Cambridge University Press, 2011); Víctor Barrera and Carlos Hoyos, "¿Violenta y desordenada? Análisis de los repertorios de la protesta social en Colombia," *Análisis Político* 33, no. 98 (2020): 167–90.

12. See Catalina Restrepo, "Redes sociales y participación política en las elecciones presidenciales de 2022 en Colombia," *Análisis Político* 36, no. 106 (2023): 133–64.

13. Ernesto Calvo and Natalia Aruguete, *Fake News, Trolls y Otros Encantos: Cómo Funcionan (para Bien y para Mal) las Redes Sociales* (Siglo XXI, 2020).

14. Byung-Chul Han, *Infocracy: Digitization and the Crisis of Democracy* (Polity, 2022).

15. David Clark and Patrick Regan, *Mass Mobilization Protest Data* (Harvard Dataverse, 2016).

16. Adam Smith, *Wealth of Nations* (Wordsworth, 2012).

17. See Theodore Schultz, "Capital Formation by Education," *Journal of Political Economy* 68, no. 6 (1960): 571–83; Theodore Schultz, "Investment in Human Capital," *American Economic Review* 51, no. 1 (1961): 1–17; Gary Becker, *Human Capital: A Theoretical and Empirical Analysis, with Special Reference to Education* (Columbia University Press, 1964).

18. United Nations Development Programme (UNDP), *Human Development Report 2021/2022: Uncertain Times, Unsettled Lives: Shaping Our Future in a Transforming World* (UNDP, 2022).

19. Amartya Sen, *Development as Freedom* (Knopf, 1999).

20. See Pablo Pinto, David Hammond, Steve Killelea, and Andrew Etchell, *The Paradox of Progress with Polarization* (United Nations Development Programme, 2023).

21. Isabel Ortiz, Sara Burke, Mohamed Berrada, and Hernán Cortés, *World Protests: A Study of Key Protest Issues in the 21st Century* (Palgrave McMillan, 2022).

22. A similar upward trend in the number of protests can be observed when comparing figure 2.2 with figure 2.14. However, the absolute number of protests per year differs between the two graphs. This discrepancy arises because the databases used—Clark and Regan, *Mass Mobilization Protest Data*, and Ortiz et al., *World Protests*—apply different criteria for identifying social protests and analyze different country samples. For instance, while the first database includes 160 countries, the second focuses on a sample of 101 countries.

23. Ortiz et al., *World Protests.*

24. UN Women and United Nations Department of Economic and Social Affairs, *Progress on the Sustainable Development Goals: The Gender Snapshot 2022* (UN Women and United Nations Department of Economic and Social Affairs, 2022).

25. Marina Nord, Martin Lundstedt, David Altman et al., *Democracy Report 2024: Democracy Winning and Losing at the Ballot* (University of Gothenburg, V-Dem Institute, 2024).

26. See Noam Lupu, "Weak Parties and the Inequality Trap in Latin America," III Working Papers, no. 137 (International Inequalities Institute, London School of Economics and Political Science, 2024).

27. Alfredo Ramírez, "Crisis de la representación, crisis económica e ideología alternativa: Los conceptos de ruptura estática y ruptura dinámica," *Estudios de Deusto* 62, no. 1 (2014): 235–59.

28. Fernán González, "La crisis de representación de la sociedad colombiana: Un intento de análisis político del Paro Nacional de 2021," *Revista Controversia* 218 (2022): 87–125.

29. Clark and Regan, *Mass Mobilization Protest Data.*

30. See "How a Slap Sparked Tunisia's Revolution," February 22, 2011, *CBS News*, https://www.cbsnews.com/news/how-a-slap-sparked-tunisias-revolution-22-02-2011/.

31. Tesbih Habbal and Muzna Hasnawi, "In the Midst of Chaos, an Invincible Arab Spring," *The Nation*, 2019.

32. See Zidane Zeraoui, "A una década de la Primavera Árabe: ¿Hacia dónde va el mundo árabe?," *Relaciones Internacionales* 30, no. 60 (2021): 49–72; Ezequiel Kopel, "¿El tercer capítulo de la Primavera Árabe?," *Nueva Sociedad* 286 (2020): 129–40.

33. "Egipto desaparece del mapa de Internet," *El País*, January 28, 2011.

34. See Maria Roque, "Los jóvenes en la Primavera Árabe," *Ankulegi* 19 (2015): 11–24.

35. See David Reher and Miguel Requena, "Un perfil demográfico del mundo árabe," *Afkar/Ideas* 30 (2011): 28–31.

36. Zeraoui, "A una década de la Primavera Árabe."

37. See Habibul Khondker, "The Impact of the Arab Spring on Democracy and Development in the MENA Region," *Sociology Compass* 13, no. 9 (2019): e12726.

38. María Quiroga and Ana Magrini, "Protestas sociales y cuestión social en América Latina contemporánea," *Revista Temas Sociológicos* 27 (2020): 282.

39. Quiroga and Magrini, "Protestas sociales y cuestión social."

40. As shown in figure 2.7, Africa is also highly unequal. In addition, there is no data for countries in the Middle East, where inequality is also very high. See Nora Lustig, "Desigualdad y descontento social en América Latina," *Nueva Sociedad* 286 (2020): 53–61.

41. See "Protestas en Chile: La histórica marcha de más de un millón de personas que tomó las calles de Santiago," *BBC News Mundo*, 2019.

42. See Joaquín Rozas and Nicolás Somma, "Determinantes de la protesta juvenil en Chile," *Revista Mexicana de Sociología* 82, no. 3 (2020): 673–703.

43. See Benjamín Ugalde, Felipe Schwember, and Valentina Verbal, eds., *El octubre chileno: Reflexiones sobre democracia y libertad* (Ediciones Democracia y Libertad, 2020).

44. See Claudia Heiss, *¿Por qué necesitamos una nueva Constitución?* (Aguilar, 2020).

45. See Guillermo Rivera and Luis Jiménez, "Resistencias desde el Sur: Algunas reflexiones sobre los jóvenes y el octubre chileno," *Journal of Socially-Engaged Art Criticism*, no. 15 (2020).

46. See Senado de la República de México, *Comisión para la Igualdad de Género respalda reformas para combatir violencia feminicida* (Senado de la República de México, 2023).

47. Maristella Svampa, "Consenso de los *commodities*, giro ecoterritorial y pensamiento crítico en América Latina," *Revista del Observatorio Social de América Latina* 13, no. 32 (2012): 19.

48. See Global Witness, *Nueva información revela que 197 personas defensoras de la tierra y el medioambiente han sido asesinadas en 2017* (Global Witness, 2018).

49. Alejandro Alvarado, "La criminalización de la protesta social: Un estado de la cuestión," *Revista Rupturas* 10, no. 1 (2020): 25–43.

50. See Florencia Arancibia and Renata Motta, "Estrategias de lucha y contra-experiencia en el juicio por las fumigaciones con agrotóxicos en Ituzaingó, Córdoba," in *Naturaleza y conocimientos en tensión: Aportes al debate ambiental desde las ciencias sociales*, ed. Laura Mombello and Ana Spivak (Teseo, 2020), 357–404.

51. Diego Escobari and Gary Hoover, *Evo Morales and Electoral Fraud in Bolivia: A Natural Experiment and Discontinuity Evidence* (Social Science Research Network, 2020).

52. Observatorio Venezolano de Conflictividad Social (OVCS), *Informe de conflictividad social en Venezuela en 2021* (OVCS, 2022).

3. SOCIAL DISCONTENT AND POLITICS

1. Sidney Tarrow, *Power in Movement: Social Movements and Contentious Politics* (Cambridge University Press, 2011).

2. Doug McAdam, Sidney Tarrow, and Charles Tilly, *Dynamics of Contention* (Cambridge University Press, 2001).

3. Alberto Melucci, *Nomads of the Present: Social Movements and Individual Needs in Contemporary Society* (Temple University Press, 1989); Amy Bartholomew and Margit Mayer, "Nomads of the Present: Melucci's Contribution to 'New Social Movement' Theory," *Theory, Culture & Society* 9, no. 4 (1992): 141–59.

4. Melucci, *Nomads of the Present.*

5. Doug McAdam, *Political Process and the Development of Black Insurgency, 1930–1970* (University of Chicago Press, 1982); Frances Piven and Richard Cloward, *Regulating the Poor: The Functions of Public Welfare* (Pantheon, 1971).

6. See Nathaniel Persily and Charles Stewart, "The Miracle and Tragedy of the 2020 U.S. Election," *Journal of Democracy* 32, no. 2 (2021): 159–78.

7. See Roger Biles, "Robert F. Wagner, Franklin D. Roosevelt, and Social Welfare Legislation in the New Deal," *Presidential Studies Quarterly* 28, no. 1 (1998): 139–52; Andreu Espasa, *Historia del New Deal: Conflicto y reforma durante la Gran Depresión* (Los Libros de la Catarata, 2021).

8. See Anthony Downs, *An Economic Theory of Democracy* (Harper & Row, 1957), James Buchanan and Gordon Tullock, *The Calculus of Consent: Logical Foundations*

of Constitutional Democracy (Liberty Fund, 1962); William A. Niskanen, *Bureaucracy and Representative Government* (Routledge, 1971).

9. See José Ayala, *Instituciones y economía: Una introducción al neoinstitucionalismo económico* (Fondo de Cultura Económica, 1999).

10. See Margaret Canovan, "Trust the People! Populism and the Two Faces of Democracy," *Political Studies* 47, no. 1 (1999): 2–16.

11. Carlos de la Torre, "Populismo, ciudadanía y Estado de derecho," in *El retorno del pueblo: Populismo y nuevas democracias en América Latina*, ed. Carlos de la Torre and Enrique Peruzzotti (FLACSO and Ministerio de Cultura del Ecuador, 2008), 24.

12. See Gustavo Coronel, *Corrupción, administración deficiente y abuso de poder en la Venezuela de Hugo Chávez* (CATO Institute, 2006); Steve Ellner, "La primera década del gobierno de Hugo Chávez: Logros y desaciertos," *Cuadernos del Cendes* 27, no. 74 (2010): 27–50.

13. Marton Gera, " 'Here, the Hungarian People Will Decide How to Raise Our Children': Populist Rhetoric and Social Categorization in Viktor Orbán's Anti-LGBTQ Campaign in Hungary," *New Perspectives: Interdisciplinary Journal of Central & East European Politics and International Relations* 31, no. 2 (2023): 104–29.

14. Daniel Béland, "Right-Wing Populism and the Politics of Insecurity: How President Trump Frames Migrants as Collective Threats," *Political Studies Review* 18, no. 2 (2020): 162–77.

15. Paolo Moncagatta and Ana Poveda, "La creciente polarización ideológica en Ecuador bajo el Gobierno de Rafael Correa," *Estado y Comunes, Revista de Políticas y Problemas Públicos* 1, no. 12 (2021): 57–71.

16. See Luis Jorge Garay, Eduardo Salcedo, Isaac de León-Beltrán, and Bernardo Guerrero, *La captura y reconfiguración cooptada del Estado en Colombia* (Fundación Método, Fundación Avina y Transparencia por Colombia, 2008).

17. Mancur Olson, *The Rise and Decline of Nations: Economic Growth, Stagflation, and Social Rigidities* (Yale University Press, 1982).

18. Manuel Funke, Moritz Schularick, and Christoph Trebesch, "Populist Leaders and the Economy," *American Economic Review* 113, no. 12 (2023): 3249–88.

4. ANTI-GROWTH EQUITY

1. See Adam Smith, *Wealth of Nations* (Wordsworth, 2012).

2. Robert Solow, "A Contribution to the Theory of Economic Growth," *Quarterly Journal of Economics* 70, no. 1 (1956): 65–94.

3. Roy F. Harrod, "An Essay in Dynamic Theory," *Economic Journal* 49, no. 193 (1939): 14–33; Evsey Domar, "Capital Expansion, Rate of Growth, and Employment," *Econometrica* 14, no. 2 (1946): 137–47.

4. Frank Ramsey, "A Mathematical Theory of Saving," *Economic Journal* 38, no. 152 (1928): 543–59.

5. David Cass, "Optimum Growth in an Aggregative Model of Capital Accumulation," *Review of Economic Studies* 32, no. 3 (1965): 233–40; Tjalling Koopmans, "On the Concept of Optimal Economic Growth," in *The Econometric Approach to Development Planning* (North Holland Publishing, 1965), 225–87.

6. Paul Romer, "Endogenous Technological Change," *Journal of Political Economy* 98, no. 5 (1990): 71–102.

7. Robert Lucas, "On the Mechanics of Economic Development," *Journal of Monetary Economics* 22, no. 1 (1988): 3–42.

8. See Fernando Mayoral, *Revisión histórica de los modelos poskeynesianos de crecimiento y distribución del ingreso* (Flacso Ecuador, 2019).

9. Harrod, "An Essay in Dynamic Theory"; Domar, "Capital Expansion, Rate of Growth, and Employment." See John Maynard Keynes, *The General Theory of Employment, Interest and Money* (Harcourt and Brace, 1936).

10. See Nicholas Kaldor, *Causes of the Slow Rate of Growth of the United Kingdom* (Cambridge University Press, 1966); Nicholas Kaldor, "Economic Growth and the Verdoorn Law: A Comment on Mr. Rowthorn's Article," *Economic Journal* 85, no. 340 (1975): 891–96; Nicholas Kaldor, *Further Essays in Economic Theory* (Duckworth, 1978). For an analysis of its possible application to the Colombian case, see Álvaro Moreno, "Las Leyes del Desarrollo Económico Endógeno de Kaldor: El Caso Colombiano," *Revista de Economía Institucional* 10, no. 18 (2008): 129–47.

11. See in particular the aforementioned essay by Kaldor, "Economic Growth and the Verdoorn Law."

12. See José Antonio Ocampo, ed., *Economía poskeynesiana* (Fondo de Cultura Económica, 1988). Besides, in an initial essay by the editor, titled "From Keynes to Post-Keynesian Analysis," the history of this school of thought is examined.

13. Albert Hirschman, *The Strategy of Economic Development* (Yale University Press, 1958).

14. Donella Meadows, Dennis Meadows, Jørgen Randers, and William W. Behrens III, *The Limits to Growth: A Report for the Club of Rome's Project on the Predicament of Mankind* (Universe Books, 1972), 23.

15. Nicholas Georgescu-Roegen, *The Entropy Law and the Economic Process* (Harvard University Press, 1971).

16. Entropy is an elementary concept in thermodynamics that is used as a measure of the disorder of a system. This means that, when entropy increases, things are getting messier.

17. Herman Daly, *Steady-State Economics: The Economics of Biophysical Equilibrium and Moral Growth* (Freeman, 1977).

18. Gro Harlem Brundtland, *Our Common Future: Report of the World Commission on Environment and Development* (United Nations, 1987).

19. Serge Latouche, *Le pari de la décroissance* (Librairie Arthème Fayard, 2006).

20. Latouche, *Le pari de la décroissance.*

21. Verónica Amarante and Gioia de Melo, "Crecimiento económico y desigualdad: Una revisión bibliográfica," Serie Documentos de Trabajo Working Paper, no. 2/04 (Instituto de Economía, 2004).

22. Robert J. Barro, "Inequality, Growth, and Investment," NBER Working Paper, no. 7038 (National Bureau of Economic Research, 1999).

23. Alberto Alesina and Robert Perotti, "Income Distribution, Political Instability, and Investment," *European Economic Review* 40, no. 6 (1996): 1203–28; Philip Keefer

and Stephen Knack, "Polarization, Politics and Property Rights: Links Between Inequality and Growth," *Public Choice* 111, no. 1/2 (2002): 127–54.

24. For illustrative purposes, we assign a linear functional form to the investment function. However, the relationship between investment and the interest rate can take forms other than the linear one. The analyses presented below hold regardless of the functional form.

25. This inverse relationship between the interest rate and investment is expected in most cases. As John Maynard Keynes warned, however, depending on the state of investors' expectations, a decrease in the interest rate may not necessarily lead to an increase in investment. For the purposes of this chapter, we will assume the standard relationship between the interest rate and investment.

26. Alberto Alesina and Dani Rodrik, "Distributive Politics and Economic Growth," *Quarterly Journal of Economics* 109, no. 2 (1994): 465–90; Torsten Persson and Guido Tabellini, "Is Inequality Harmful for Growth?," *American Economic Review* 84, no. 3 (1994): 600–621. These models help analyze how politicians and parties adjust their positions to maximize electoral support. The fundamental premise of such models is that politicians tend to adopt positions close to the median of the political spectrum because this enables them to attract the largest number of voters.

27. Tax revenues come from the following items: goods and services taxes, personal and corporate income taxes, social security contributions, property taxes, payroll taxes, and other levies.

28. See Sustainable Development Goal (SDG) 4, entitled "Ensure inclusive and equitable quality education and promote lifelong learning opportunities for all."

29. In Colombia, socioeconomic strata are an official classification system that groups households into levels (from 1 to 6) based on housing and neighborhood characteristics. This system is primarily used to target social subsidies and determine eligibility for public benefits and services.

30. Milton Friedman and Rose D. Friedman, *Free to Choose: A Personal Statement* (Harcourt Brace Jovanovich, 1980).

31. Robert Moffitt, "Incentive Effects of the U.S. Welfare System: A Review," *Journal of Economic Literature* 30, no. 1 (1992): 1–61.

32. Rafael Ribas and Fábio Soares, *Is the Effect of Conditional Transfer on Labor Supply Negligible Everywhere?* (University of Amsterdam and International Policy Centre for Inclusive Growth, 2011); Alan de Brauw, Daniel O. Gilligan, John Hoddinott, and Shalini Roy, "Bolsa Família and Household Labor Supply," *Economic Development and Cultural Change* 63, no. 3 (2013): 423–57.

33. Johannes Koettl and Michael Weber, "Does Formal Work Pay? The Role of Labor Taxation and Social Benefit Design in the New EU Member States," IZA Discussion Paper, no. 6313 (Institute of Labor Economics, 2012).

34. Stefano Farné, David Rodríguez, and Paola Ríos, *Impacto de los subsidios estatales sobre el mercado laboral en Colombia*, Cuadernos de Trabajo del Observatorio del Mercado de Trabajo y la Seguridad Social de la Universidad Externado de Colombia, no. 17 (Universidad Externado de Colombia, 2016); Carlos Castañeda and Lorena Trujillo, *Evaluación del impacto de los subsidios sobre el mercado laboral colombiano* (Departamento Nacional de Planeación, 2017).

35. Moffitt, "Incentive Effects of the U.S. Welfare System."

36. See Asociación Nacional de Instituciones Financieras (ANIF), *Subsidio a los taxis: Borrar con el codo lo que hace la mano* (ANIF, 2023).

37. See Jesús Felipe, Arnelyn Abdon, and Utsav Kumar, "Tracking the Middle-Income Trap: What Is It, Who Is in It, and Why?," Levy Economics Institute Working Paper, no. 715 (Levy Economics Institute, 2012); Fernando Im and David Rosenblatt, "Middle-Income Traps: A Conceptual and Empirical Survey," Policy Research Working Paper, no. 6594 (World Bank, 2013).

38. See Shekhar Aiyar, Romain Duval, Damien Puy, Yiqun Wu, and Longmei Zhang, "Growth Slowdowns and the Middle-Income Trap," IMF Working Paper, no. 13/71 (International Monetary Fund, 2013).

39. Indermit Gill and Homi Kharas, *An East Asian Renaissance: Ideas for Economic Growth* (World Bank, 2007); Indermit Gill and Homi Kharas, "The Middle-Income Trap Turns Ten," Policy Research Working Paper, no. 7403 (World Bank, 2015).

40. Michael Spence, *The Next Convergence: The Future of Economic Growth in a Multispeed World* (Farrar, Straus and Giroux, 2011); Aiyar et al., "Growth Slowdowns and the Middle-Income Trap."

41. José Antonio Alonso and José Antonio Ocampo, eds., *Trapped in the Middle? Developmental Challenges for Middle-Income Countries* (Oxford University Press, 2020).

42. Alonso and Ocampo, eds., *Trapped in the Middle?*

5. PRO-GROWTH EQUITY

1. Human capital refers to the skills, knowledge, health, and abilities that individuals acquire through education, training, and experience, which enhance their productivity and economic potential. It is widely recognized as a key factor for economic growth and social development.

2. The Gini coefficient data we have presented so far were obtained from the World Inequality Database (WID), but the data shown in figure 5.2 were obtained from the World Income Inequality Database (WIID), produced by United Nations University World Institute for Development Economics Research (UNU-WIDER). The difference between the two databases is that the former calculates the Gini coefficient with income before taxes (as Kuznets conceived it), while the latter calculates it with income after taxes. For that reason, the WIID's Gini coefficients are lower than those reported by the WID. We decided to use the WIID data because they incorporate the impact that taxes have on countries' inequality, so the analyses we carry out with this database allow a better understanding of the impact of equity policies to stimulate economic growth.

3. See World Bank, *The Human Capital Index 2020 Update: Human Capital in the Time of Covid-19* (World Bank, 2021).

4. See Economic Commission for Latin America and the Caribbean (ECLAC) and Organization of Ibero-American States for Education, Science and Culture, *Educación, juventud y trabajo: Habilidades y competencias necesarias en un contexto cambiante* (ECLAC, 2020).

5. See Pablo Monterubbianesi, "El rol de la salud en el proceso de crecimiento económico: Una revisión de literatura," *Cuadernos de Economía* 33, no. 62 (2013): 91–121.

6. Julián Flórez, "La política pública de educación en Colombia y Finlandia: Elementos para la construcción de una educación pública en época de Reformas Educativas Globales," *Papel Político* 24, no. 2 (2019): 1–15.

7. See World Intellectual Property Organization (WIPO), *Global Innovation Index 2023: Innovation in the Face of Uncertainty* (WIPO, 2023).

8. See Joseph A. Schumpeter, *The Theory of Economic Development: An Inquiry Into Profits, Capital, Credit, Interest, and the Business Cycle* (Harvard University Press, 1934).

9. See Andrés Oppenheimer, *¡Sálvese quien pueda! El futuro del trabajo en la era de la automatización* (Penguin Random House, 2019).

10. See Josef Taalbi, "Innovation in the Long Run: Perspectives on Technological Transitions in Sweden 1908–2016," *Environmental Innovation and Societal Transitions* 40 (2021): 222–48.

11. See Warren Bilkey, "Equality of Income Distribution and Consumption Expenditures," *Review of Economics and Statistics* 38, no. 1 (1956): 81–87.

12. See John Maynard Keynes, *The General Theory of Employment, Interest and Money* (Harcourt and Brace, 1936).

13. See Guðmundur Jónsson, "The Evolving Concept of the Welfare State in Iceland Politics," in *The Changing Meanings of the Welfare State: Histories of a Key Concept in the Nordic Countries*, ed. Nils Edling (Berghahn, 2019), 276–314.

14. Guðný Björk and Stefán Ólafsson, "Iceland: Welfare in a Deep Economic Crisis," in *Challenges to European Welfare Systems*, ed. Klaus Schubert, Paloma de Villota, and Johanna Kuhlmann (Springer, 2016), 371–94.

15. See Thomas Palley, "Financialization: What It Is and Why It Matters," Working Paper, no. 525 (Levy Economics Institute of Bard College, 2007).

16. See Ibrahim N. Khatatbeh, Wasfi Al Salamat, Mohammed N. Abu-Alfoul, and Jamil J. Jaber, "Is There Any Financial Kuznets Curve in Jordan? A Structural Timer Series Analysis," *Cogent Economics & Finance* 10, no. 1 (2022): 1–17.

17. See Eduardo Arce, "Democratización del crédito y economía popular," in *Inclusión financiera y economía popular: Alternativas en la era digital* (Asobancaria, 2023), 87–107.

18. Zhong Chen, Sajid Ali, Majid Lateef, Ahmad Imran Khan, and Muhammad Khalid Anser, "The Nexus Between Asymmetric Financial Inclusion and Economic Growth: Evidence from the Top 10 Financially Inclusive Economies," *Borsa Istanbul Review* 23, no. 2 (2023): 368–77.

19. See Zachary Wendling, John Emerson, Alex de Sherbinin et al., *2020 Environmental Performance Index* (Yale Center for Environmental Law & Policy, 2020).

20. See Martin Wolf, John Emerson, Daniel Esty et al., *2022 Environmental Performance Index* (Yale Center for Environmental Law & Policy, 2022).

21. See UK Climate Change Committee, *Progress in Reducing Emissions: 2021 Report to Parliament* (UK Climate Change Committee, 2021); United Kingdom,

End of Coal in Sight as UK Secures Ambitious Commitments at COP26 Summit (Department for Business, Energy and Industrial Strategy, 2021).

22. Douglass North, "Institutions," *Journal of Economic Perspectives* 5, no. 1 (1991): 97–112.

23. North, "Institutions."

24. Daron Acemoglu and James A. Robinson, *Why Nations Fail: The Origins of Power, Prosperity, and Poverty* (Crown, 2012). Here, we refer to the conceptual framework proposed by these authors rather than their classification of countries into one of these two categories, which remains a subject of considerable debate.

25. Acemoglu and Robinson, *Why Nations Fail.*

26. See Red Liberal de América Latina, *Índice de Calidad Institucional 2021: La pandemia, una oportunidad para mejorar el futuro* (Relial, 2021).

27. See Wisuwat Wannamakok, Yu-Yu Chang, and Marge Täks, "The Relationship Between Institutional Environments and Entrepreneurial Intention in Estonia: Mediating Roles of Desirability and Feasibility," *Entrepreneurial Business and Economics Review* 8, no. 2 (2020): 111–26

28. See Cornelius Dube, "Competition Policy and Economic Growth—Is There a Causal Factor?," C-CIER Briefing Paper, no. 4 (Centre for Competition, Investment and Economic Regulation, 2008).

29. See Yufan Hao, Li Sheng, and Guanjin Pan, *Political Economy of Macao Since 1999: The Dilemma of Success* (Palgrave Macmillan, 2017).

30. Stephan Haggard and Lydia Tiede, "The Rule of Law and Economic Growth: Where Are We?," *World Development* 39, no. 5 (2011): 673–85.

31. Nelson Labarca and Amparo Panchana, "Crecimiento económico en América Latina: Algunos determinantes desde la perspectiva austriaca," *Revista de Ciencias Sociales* 28, no. 1 (2022): 228.

32. Albert de Vaal and Wouter Ebben, "Institutions and the Relation Between Corruption and Economic Growth," *Review of Development Economics* 15, no. 1 (2011): 108–23.

33. Klaus Gründler and Niklas Potrafke, "Corruption and Economic Growth: New Empirical Evidence," *European Journal of Political Economy* 60 (2019): 101801.

34. Jhorland Ayala, Jaime Bonet, Gerson Pérez, Eduardo Heilbron, and Jéssica Suret, "La corrupción en Colombia: Un análisis integral," *Documentos de Trabajo sobre Economía Regional y Urbana* 307 (2022): 1–42.

35. Karoll Gómez and Santiago Galón, "El impacto de la corrupción sobre el crecimiento económico colombiano, 1990–1999," *Lecturas de Economía* 57 (2022): 51–85.

36. Joseph E. Stiglitz, *The Price of Inequality: How Today's Divided Society Endangers Our Future* (Norton, 2012).

37. See Institute for Economics & Peace, *Global Peace Index 2023: Measuring Peace in a Complex World* (Institute for Economics & Peace, 2023).

38. In Colombia, monetary poverty measures the percentage of the population with an income below the minimum monthly income defined as necessary to cover their basic needs.

39. See Departamento Administrativo Nacional de Estadística, *Press release: En 2022, en el total nacional, la pobreza monetaria fue de 36,6 percent y la pobreza monetaria extrema fue del 13,8 percent* (Departamento Administrativo Nacional de Estadística, 2023).

40. See Jonathan Malagón and Luis Triveño, "Estructura y acabados: 30 ideas sobre cómo mejorar la política de vivienda en Colombia, aplicables al mundo emergente," *Coyuntura Económica: Investigación Económica y Social* 52 (2022): 65–92.

41. See Ministerio de Vivienda, Ciudad y Territorio (MVCT), *Política de vivienda integral: Equidad, inclusión y formalización* (MVCT, 2022).

42. Iván Duque and Jonathan Malagón, eds., *Libertad y equidad: El ADN de la política de vivienda y agua en Colombia* (Planeta, 2022).

43. Productive chains refer to the links between different groups of companies within a product or service's value chain that interact to achieve mutual benefits.

44. See Malagón and Triveño, "Estructura y acabados."

45. Alberto Arenas, *Sostenibilidad fiscal y reformas tributarias en América Latina* (ECLAC, 2016).

46. Jonathan Malagón and José Antonio Ocampo, "El tamaño del Estado y su impacto redistributivo en América Latina," *Coyuntura Económica: Investigación Económica y Social* 44, no. 1 (2014): 15–76.

47. Nora Lustig, Valentina Martinez, and Carola Pessino, "Fiscal Policy, Income Redistribution, and Poverty Reduction in Latin America," LACIR Working Paper, no. 115 (Latin America and Caribbean Inequality Review, 2023).

48. Jonathan Malagón and José Antonio Ocampo, "Los efectos distributivos de la política fiscal en América Latina," *Pensamiento Iberoamericano* 10 (2012): 71–104.

49. Malagón and Ocampo, "Los efectos distributivos."

50. Edwin Goñi, Humberto López, and Luis Servén, "Fiscal Redistribution and Income Inequality in Latin America," World Bank Policy Research Paper, no. 4487 (World Bank, 2008); David Jesuit and Vincent Mahler, "State Redistribution in Comparative Perspective: A Cross-National Analysis of the Developed Countries," LIS Working Paper, no. 392 (Luxembourg Income Study, 2004); Rodrigo Cubero and Ivanna Vladkova, "Equity and Fiscal Policy: The Income Distribution Effects of Taxation and Social Spending in Central America," IMF Working Paper, no. 112 (International Monetary Fund, 2010).

51. Joseph E. Stiglitz, *People, Power, and Profits: Progressive Capitalism for an Age of Discontent* (Norton, 2019).

52. Daron Acemoglu and Simon Johnson, *Power and Progress: Our Thousand-Year Struggle Over Technology and Prosperity* (PublicAffairs, 2023).

53. See Guy Standing, *Basic Income: And How We Can Make It Happen* (Pelican, 2017); Guy Standing, *Battling Eight Giants: Basic Income Now* (Tauris, 2020).

54. See Adam Smith, *Wealth of Nations* (Wordsworth, 2012); Friedrich A. Hayek, *The Road to Serfdom* (Routledge, 1944); Milton Friedman, *Capitalism and Freedom* (University of Chicago Press, 1962).

55. Keynes, *The General Theory of Employment, Interest and Money.*

56. See Eduard Bernstein, *Las premisas del socialismo y las tareas de la socialdemocracia* (Siglo Veintiuno Editores, 1982).

57. See Mariana Mazzucato, *The Entrepreneurial State: Debunking Public vs. Private Sector Myths* (Anthem, 2013).

58. See Dani Rodrik, *The Globalization Paradox: Democracy and the Future of the World Economy* (Norton, 2011).

59. Julian Le Grand, "The Theory of Government Failure," *British Journal of Political Science* 21, no. 4 (1991): 423–42. There are additional studies that have explored government failures, including Anne Krueger, "Government Failures in Development," *Journal of Economic Perspectives* 4, no. 3 (1990): 9–23. Krueger proposes that these can be classified into two categories: failures of omission, which occur when the state fails to intervene to correct market failures, and failures of commission, which arise when state intervention moves away from, rather than approaching, the Pareto equilibrium point.

BIBLIOGRAPHY

Acemoglu, Daron, and Simon Johnson. *Power and Progress: Our Thousand-Year Struggle Over Technology and Prosperity*. PublicAffairs, 2023.

Acemoglu, Daron, and James A. Robinson. *Why Nations Fail: The Origins of Power, Prosperity, and Poverty*. Crown, 2012.

Aghion, Philippe, Eve Caroli, and Cecilia García-Peñalosa. "Inequality and Economic Growth: The Perspective of the New Growth Theories." *Journal of Economic Literature* 37, no. 4 (1999): 1615–60.

Aiyar, Shekhar, Romain Duval, Damien Puy, Yiqun Wu, and Longmei Zhang. "Growth Slowdowns and the Middle-Income Trap." IMF Working Paper, no. 13/71. International Monetary Fund, 2013.

Alesina, Alberto, and Paola Giuliano. "Preferences for Redistribution." NBER Working Paper, no. 14825. National Bureau of Economic Research, 2009.

Alesina, Alberto, and Robert Perotti. "Income Distribution, Political Instability, and Investment." *European Economic Review* 40, no. 6 (1996): 1203–28.

Alesina, Alberto, and Dani Rodrik. "Distributive Politics and Economic Growth." *Quarterly Journal of Economics* 109, no. 2 (1994): 465–90.

Alonso, José Antonio, and José Antonio Ocampo, eds. *Trapped in the Middle? Developmental Challenges for Middle-Income Countries*. Oxford University Press, 2020.

Alonso, Julio, and Ángela González. "Evaluación de la hipótesis de Kuznets para Colombia, 1977–2005." *Apuntes del CENES* 36, no. 63 (2017): 43–62.

Alvarado, Alejandro. "La criminalización de la protesta social: Un estado de la cuestión." *Revista Rupturas* 10, no. 1 (2020): 25–43.

Amarante, Verónica, and Gioia de Melo. "Crecimiento económico y desigualdad: Una revisión bibliográfica." Serie Documentos de Trabajo Working Paper, no. 2/04. Instituto de Economía, 2004.

Arancibia, Florencia, and Renata Motta. "Estrategias de lucha y contra-experiencia en el juicio por las fumigaciones con agrotóxicos en Ituzaingó, Córdoba." In *Naturaleza y conocimientos en tensión: Aportes al debate ambiental desde las ciencias sociales*, ed. Laura Mombello and Ana Spivak, 357–404. Teseo, 2020.

Arce, Eduardo. "Democratización del crédito y economía popular." In *Inclusión financiera y economía popular: Alternativas en la era digital*, 87–107. Asobancaria, 2023.

Arenas, Alberto. *Sostenibilidad fiscal y reformas tributarias en América Latina*. ECLAC, 2016.

Asociación Nacional de Instituciones Financieras (ANIF). *Subsidio a los taxis: Borrar con el codo lo que hace la mano*. ANIF, 2023.

Ayala, Jhorland, Jaime Bonet, Gerson Pérez, Eduardo Heilbron, and Jéssica Suret. "La corrupción en Colombia: Un análisis integral." *Documentos de Trabajo sobre Economía Regional y Urbana* 307 (2022): 1–42.

Ayala, José. *Instituciones y economía: Una introducción al neoinstitucionalismo económico*. Fondo de Cultura Económica, 1999.

Barrera, Víctor, and Carlos Hoyos. "¿Violenta y desordenada? Análisis de los repertorios de la protesta social en Colombia." *Análisis Político* 33, no. 98 (2020): 167–90.

Barro, Robert J. "Inequality and Growth Revisited." Working Paper Series on Regional Economic Integration, no. 11. Asian Development Bank, 2008.

Barro, Robert J. "Inequality, Growth, and Investment." NBER Working Paper, no. 7038. National Bureau of Economic Research, 1999.

Bartholomew, Amy, and Margit Mayer. "Nomads of the Present: Melucci's Contribution to 'New Social Movement' Theory." *Theory, Culture & Society* 9, no. 4 (1992): 141–59.

Becker, Gary. *Human Capital: A Theoretical and Empirical Analysis, with Special Reference to Education*. Columbia University Press, 1964.

Béland, Daniel. "Right-Wing Populism and the Politics of Insecurity: How President Trump Frames Migrants as Collective Threats." *Political Studies Review* 18, no. 2 (2020): 162–77.

Bénabou, Roland. "Inequality and Growth." *NBER Macroeconomics Annual* 11 (1996): 11–92.

Berg, Andrew, Jonathan Ostry, Charalambos G. Tsangarides, and Yorbol Yakhshilikov. "Redistribution, Inequality, and Growth: New Evidence." *Journal of Economic Growth* 23, no. 3 (2018): 259–305.

Bernstein, Eduard. *Las premisas del socialismo y las tareas de la socialdemocracia*. Siglo Veintiuno Editores, 1982.

Bertola, Giuseppe. "Factor Shares and Savings in Endogenous Growth." *American Economic Review* 83, no. 5 (1993): 1184–99.

Biles, Roger. "Robert F. Wagner, Franklin D. Roosevelt, and Social Welfare Legislation in the New Deal." *Presidential Studies Quarterly* 28, no. 1 (1998): 139–52.

Bilkey, Warren. "Equality of Income Distribution and Consumption Expenditures." *Review of Economics and Statistics* 38, no. 1 (1956): 81–87.

Björk, Guðný, and Stefán Ólafsson. "Iceland: Welfare in a Deep Economic Crisis." In *Challenges to European Welfare Systems*, ed. Klaus Schubert, Paloma de Villota, and Johanna Kuhlmann, 371–94. Springer, 2016.

Brundtland, Gro Harlem. *Our Common Future: Report of the World Commission on Environment and Development*. United Nations, 1987.

Buchanan, James, and Gordon Tullock. *The Calculus of Consent: Logical Foundations of Constitutional Democracy*. Liberty Fund, 1962.

Calvo, Ernesto, and Natalia Aruguete. *Fake News, Trolls y Otros Encantos: Cómo Funcionan (para Bien y para Mal) las Redes Sociales*. Siglo XXI, 2020.

Canovan, Margaret. "Trust the People! Populism and the Two Faces of Democracy." *Political Studies* 47, no. 1 (1999): 2–16.

Cass, David. "Optimum Growth in an Aggregative Model of Capital Accumulation." *Review of Economic Studies* 32, no. 3 (1965): 233–40.

Castañeda, Carlos, and Lorena Trujillo. *Evaluación del impacto de los subsidios sobre el mercado laboral colombiano*. Departamento Nacional de Planeación, 2017.

Chen, Zhong, Sajid Ali, Majid Lateef, Ahmad Imran Khan, and Muhammad Khalid Anser. "The Nexus Between Asymmetric Financial Inclusion and Economic Growth: Evidence from the Top 10 Financially Inclusive Economies." *Borsa Istanbul Review* 23, no. 2 (2023): 368–77.

Cingano, Federico. "Trends in Income Inequality and Its Impact on Economic Growth." OECD Social, Employment and Migration Working Papers, no. 163. Organisation for Economic Co-operation and Development, 2014.

Chancel, Lucas, Thomas Piketty, Emmanuel Saez, and Gabriel Zucman. *World Inequality Report 2022*. World Inequality Lab, 2022.

Clark, David, and Patrick Regan. *Mass Mobilization Protest Data*. Harvard Dataverse, 2016.

Coronel, Gustavo. *Corrupción, administración deficiente y abuso de poder en la Venezuela de Hugo Chávez*. CATO Institute, 2006.

Crespo, Patricio. *Decisiones ambientales y liberalismo*. Ediciones Abya-Yala, 2008.

Cubero, Rodrigo, and Ivanna Vladkova. "Equity and Fiscal Policy: The Income Distribution Effects of Taxation and Social Spending in Central America." IMF Working Paper, no. 112. International Monetary Fund, 2010.

Daly, Herman. *Steady-State Economics: The Economics of Biophysical Equilibrium and Moral Growth*. Freeman, 1977.

De Brauw, Alan, Daniel O. Gilligan, John Hoddinott, and Shalini Roy. "Bolsa Família and Household Labor Supply." *Economic Development and Cultural Change* 63, no. 3 (2013): 423–57.

Deininger, Klaus, and Lyn Squire. "Measuring Income Inequality: A New Data-Base." *World Bank Economic Review* 10, no. 3 (1996): 565–91.

Deininger, Klaus, and Lyn Squire. "New Ways of Looking at Old Issues: Inequality and Growth." *Journal of Development Economics* 57 (1998): 259–87.

De la Torre, Carlos. "Populismo, ciudadanía y Estado de derecho." In *El retorno del pueblo: Populismo y nuevas democracias en América Latina*, ed. Carlos de la Torre and Enrique Peruzzotti, 23–54. FLACSO and Ministerio de Cultura del Ecuador, 2008.

Departamento Administrativo Nacional de Estadística. *Press release: En 2022, en el total nacional, la pobreza monetaria fue de 36,6 percent y la pobreza monetaria extrema fue del 13,8 percent*. Departamento Administrativo Nacional de Estadística, 2023.

De Vaal, Albert, and Wouter Ebben. "Institutions and the Relation Between Corruption and Economic Growth." *Review of Development Economics* 15, no. 1 (2011): 108–23.

Dinda, Soumyananda. "Environmental Kuznets Curve Hypothesis: A Survey." *Ecological Economics* 49, no. 4 (2004): 431–55.

Domar, Evsey. "Capital Expansion, Rate of Growth, and Employment." *Econometrica* 14, no. 2 (1946): 137–47.

Downs, Anthony. *An Economic Theory of Democracy*. Harper & Row, 1957.

Dube, Cornelius. "Competition Policy and Economic Growth—Is There a Causal Factor?" C-CIER Briefing Paper, no. 4. Centre for Competition, Investment and Economic Regulation, 2008.

Duque, Iván, and Jonathan Malagón, eds. *Libertad y equidad: El ADN de la política de vivienda y agua en Colombia*. Planeta, 2022.

Dutt, Kuheli. "Governance, Institutions, and the Environment Income Relationship: Across Country Study." *Environment, Development and Sustainability* 11, no. 4 (2009): 705–23.

Economic Commission for Latin America and the Caribbean (ECLAC). *Social Panorama of Latin America 2020*. ECLAC, 2021.

Economic Commission for Latin America and the Caribbean (ECLAC) and Organization of Ibero-American States for Education, Science and Culture. *Educación, juventud y trabajo: Habilidades y competencias necesarias en un contexto cambiante*. ECLAC, 2020.

"Egipto desaparece del mapa de Internet." *El País*, January 28, 2011.

Ellner, Steve. "La primera década del gobierno de Hugo Chávez: Logros y desaciertos." *Cuadernos del Cendes* 27, no. 74 (2010): 27–50.

Escobari, Diego, and Gary Hoover. *Evo Morales and Electoral Fraud in Bolivia: A Natural Experiment and Discontinuity Evidence*. Social Science Research Network, 2020.

Espasa, Andreu. *Historia del New Deal: Conflicto y reforma durante la Gran Depresión*. Los Libros de la Catarata, 2021.

Falconí, Fander, Rafael Burbano, and Pedro Cango. *La discutible curva de Kuznets*. FLACSO Ecuador, 2016.

Farné, Stefano, David Rodríguez, and Paola Ríos. *Impacto de los subsidios estatales sobre el mercado laboral en Colombia*. Cuadernos de Trabajo del Observatorio del Mercado de Trabajo y la Seguridad Social de la Universidad Externado de Colombia, no. 17. Universidad Externado de Colombia, 2016.

Felipe, Jesús, Arnelyn Abdon, and Utsav Kumar. "Tracking the Middle-Income Trap: What Is It, Who Is in It, and Why?" Levy Economics Institute Working Paper, no. 715. Levy Economics Institute, 2012.

Fields, Gary. *Distribution and Development: A Summary of the Evidence for the Developing World*. World Bank, 1999.

Fields, Gary. "Income Distribution and Economic Growth." In *The State of Development Economics: Progress and Perspectives*, ed. Gustav Ranis and T. Paul Schultz, 459–81. Basil Blackwell, 1988.

Flórez, Julián. "La política pública de educación en Colombia y Finlandia: Elementos para la construcción de una educación pública en época de Reformas Educativas Globales." *Papel Político* 24, no. 2 (2019): 1–15.

Friedman, Milton. *Capitalism and Freedom*. University of Chicago Press, 1962.

Friedman, Milton, and Rose D. Friedman. *Free to Choose: A Personal Statement.* Harcourt Brace Jovanovich, 1980.

Funke, Manuel, Moritz Schularick, and Christoph Trebesch. "Populist Leaders and the Economy." *American Economic Review* 113, no. 12 (2023): 3249–88.

Gallup, John. *Is There a Kuznets Curve?* Portland State University, 2012.

Garay, Luis Jorge, Eduardo Salcedo, Isaac de León-Beltrán, and Bernardo Guerrero. *La captura y reconfiguración cooptada del Estado en Colombia.* Fundación Método, Fundación Avina y Transparencia por Colombia, 2008.

Georgescu-Roegen, Nicholas. *The Entropy Law and the Economic Process.* Harvard University Press, 1971.

Gera, Marton. "'Here, the Hungarian People Will Decide How to Raise Our Children': Populist Rhetoric and Social Categorization in Viktor Orbán's Anti-LGBTQ Campaign in Hungary." *New Perspectives: Interdisciplinary Journal of Central & East European Politics and International Relations* 31, no. 2 (2023): 104–29.

Gill, Indermit, and Homi Kharas. *An East Asian Renaissance: Ideas for Economic Growth.* World Bank, 2007.

Gill, Indermit, and Homi Kharas. "The Middle-Income Trap Turns Ten." Policy Research Working Paper, no. 7403. World Bank, 2015.

Global Witness. *Nueva información revela que 197 personas defensoras de la tierra y el medioambiente han sido asesinadas en 2017.* Global Witness, 2018.

Gómez, Karoll, and Santiago Galón. "El impacto de la corrupción sobre el crecimiento económico colombiano, 1990–1999." *Lecturas de Economía* 57 (2022): 51–85.

González, Fernán. "La crisis de representación de la sociedad colombiana: Un intento de análisis político del Paro Nacional de 2021." *Revista Controversia* 218 (2022): 87–125.

González, Jorge. "Juan Luis Londoño: Ideas para la acción." *Revista de Economía Institucional* 5, no. 8 (2003): 223–39.

González, Jorge, Clara Ramírez, and Alfredo Sarmiento. *Reflexiones en torno a la distribución del ingreso, el crecimiento y el gasto público.* Universidad Externado de Colombia, 2003.

Goñi, Edwin, Humberto López, and Luis Servén. "Fiscal Redistribution and Income Inequality in Latin America." World Bank Policy Research Paper, no. 4487. World Bank, 2008.

Greenwood, Jeremy, and Boyan Jovanovic. "Financial Development, Growth, and the Distribution of Income." *Journal of Political Economy* 98, no. 5 (1990): 1076–1107.

Grossman, Gene M., and Alan B. Krueger. "Environmental Impacts of a North American Free Trade Agreement." NBER Working Paper, no. 3914. National Bureau of Economic Research, 1991.

Gründler, Klaus, and Niklas Potrafke. "Corruption and Economic Growth: New Empirical Evidence." *European Journal of Political Economy* 60 (2019): 101801.

Habbal, Tesbih, and Muzna Hasnawi. "In the Midst of Chaos, an Invincible Arab Spring." *The Nation*, 2019.

Haggard, Stephan, and Lydia Tiede. "The Rule of Law and Economic Growth: Where Are We?" *World Development* 39, no. 5 (2011): 673–85.

Han, Byung-Chul. *Infocracy: Digitization and the Crisis of Democracy*. Polity, 2022.

Hao, Yufan, Li Sheng, and Guanjin Pan. *Political Economy of Macao Since 1999: The Dilemma of Success*. Palgrave Macmillan, 2017.

Harris, Donald. "Economic Growth and Equity: Complements or Opposites?" *Review of Black Political Economy* 21, no. 3 (1993): 65–72.

Harrod, Roy F. "An Essay in Dynamic Theory." *Economic Journal* 49, no. 193 (1939): 14–33.

Hayek, Friedrich A. *The Road to Serfdom*. Routledge, 1944.

Heiss, Claudia. *¿Por qué necesitamos una nueva Constitución?* Aguilar, 2020.

Hirschman, Albert. *The Strategy of Economic Development*. Yale University Press, 1958.

"How a Slap Sparked Tunisia's Revolution." February 22, 2011, *CBS News*. https://www.cbsnews.com/news/how-a-slap-sparked-tunisias-revolution-22-02-2011/.

Im, Fernando, and David Rosenblatt. "Middle-Income Traps: A Conceptual and Empirical Survey." Policy Research Working Paper, no. 6594. World Bank, 2013.

Institute for Economics & Peace. *Global Peace Index 2023: Measuring Peace in a Complex World*. Institute for Economics & Peace, 2023.

Jesuit, David, and Vincent Mahler. "State Redistribution in Comparative Perspective: A Cross-National Analysis of the Developed Countries." LIS Working Paper, no. 392. Luxembourg Income Study, 2004.

Jónsson, Guðmundur. "The Evolving Concept of the Welfare State in Iceland Politics." In *The Changing Meanings of the Welfare State: Histories of a Key Concept in the Nordic Countries*, ed. Nils Edling, 276–314. Berghahn, 2019.

Kaldor, Nicholas. *Causes of the Slow Rate of Growth of the United Kingdom*. Cambridge University Press, 1966.

Kaldor, Nicholas. "Economic Growth and the Verdoorn Law: A Comment on Mr. Rowthorn's Article." *Economic Journal* 85, no. 340 (1975): 891–96.

Kaldor, Nicholas. *Further Essays in Economic Theory*. Duckworth, 1978.

Keefer, Philip, and Stephen Knack. "Polarization, Politics and Property Rights: Links Between Inequality and Growth." *Public Choice* 111, no. 1/2 (2002): 127–54.

Keynes, John Maynard. *The General Theory of Employment, Interest and Money*. Harcourt and Brace, 1936.

Khatatbeh, Ibrahim N., Wasfi Al Salamat, Mohammed N. Abu-Alfoul, and Jamil J. Jaber. "Is There Any Financial Kuznets Curve in Jordan? A Structural Timer Series Analysis." *Cogent Economics & Finance* 10, no. 1 (2022): 1–17.

Khondker, Habibul. "The Impact of the Arab Spring on Democracy and Development in the MENA Region." *Sociology Compass* 13, no. 9 (2019): e12726.

Koettl, Johannes, and Michael Weber. "Does Formal Work Pay? The Role of Labor Taxation and Social Benefit Design in the New EU Member States." IZA Discussion Paper, no. 6313. Institute of Labor Economics, 2012.

Komlos, John. "Reaganomics: una línea divisoria." *Tiempo y Economía* 6, no. 1 (2019): 47–76.

Koopmans, Tjalling. "On the Concept of Optimal Economic Growth." In *The Econometric Approach to Development Planning*, 225–87. North Holland Publishing, 1965.

Kopel, Ezequiel. "¿El tercer capítulo de la Primavera Árabe?" *Nueva Sociedad* 286 (2020): 129–40.

Krueger, Anne. "Government Failures in Development." *Journal of Economic Perspectives* 4, no. 3 (1990): 9–23.

Kuznets, Simon. "Economic Growth and Income Inequality." *American Economic Review* 45, no. 1 (1955): 1–28.

Kuznets, Simon. "Quantitative Aspects of the Economic Growth of Nations: VIII. Distribution of Income by Size." *Economic Development and Cultural Change* 11, no. 2 (1963): 1–80.

Kuznets, Simon. *Shares of Upper Income Groups in Income and Savings.* National Bureau of Economic Research, 1953.

Labarca, Nelson, and Amparo Panchana. "Crecimiento económico en América Latina: Algunos determinantes desde la perspectiva austriaca." *Revista de Ciencias Sociales* 28, no. 1 (2022): 216–33.

Laffer, Arthur. *The Laffer Curve: Past, Present, and Future.* Heritage Foundation, 2004.

Latouche, Serge. *Le pari de la décroissance.* Librairie Arthème Fayard, 2006.

Le Grand, Julian. "The Theory of Government Failure." *British Journal of Political Science* 21, no. 4 (1991): 423–42.

Lucas, Robert. "On the Mechanics of Economic Development." *Journal of Monetary Economics* 22, no. 1 (1988): 3–42.

Lupu, Noam. "Weak Parties and the Inequality Trap in Latin America." III Working Papers, no. 137. International Inequalities Institute, London School of Economics and Political Science, 2024.

Lustig, Nora. "Desigualdad y descontento social en América Latina." Nueva Sociedad 286 (2020): 53–61.

Lustig, Nora, Valentina Martinez, and Carola Pessino. "Fiscal Policy, Income Redistribution, and Poverty Reduction in Latin America." LACIR Working Paper, no. 115. Latin America and Caribbean Inequality Review, 2023.

Lyubimov, Ivan. "Income Inequality Revisited 60 Years Later: Piketty vs Kuznets." *Russian Journal of Economics* 3, no. 1 (2017): 42–53.

Magness, Phillip, and Robert Murphy. "Challenging the Empirical Contribution of Thomas Piketty's *Capital in the 21st Century.*" *Journal of Private Enterprise* 30, no. 2 (2015): 1–34.

Malagón, Jonathan, and José Antonio Ocampo. "Los efectos distributivos de la política fiscal en América Latina." *Pensamiento Iberoamericano* 10 (2012): 71–104.

Malagón, Jonathan, and José Antonio Ocampo. "El tamaño del Estado y su impacto redistributivo en América Latina." *Coyuntura Económica: Investigación Económica y Social* 44, no. 1 (2014): 15–76.

Malagón, Jonathan, and Luis Triveño. "Estructura y acabados: 30 ideas sobre cómo mejorar la política de vivienda en Colombia, aplicables al mundo emergente." *Coyuntura Económica: Investigación Económica y Social* 52 (2022): 65–92.

Malik, Nesrine. *We Need New Stories: Challenging the Toxic Myths Behind Our Age of Discontent.* Weidenfeld & Nicolson, 2019.

Matyas, Laszlo, Laszlo Konya, and Lachlan MacQuarie. "The Kuznets U-Curve Hypothesis: Some Panel Data Evidence." *Applied Economics Letters* 5, no. 11 (1998): 693–97.

Mayoral, Fernando. *Revisión histórica de los modelos poskeynesianos de crecimiento y distribución del ingreso*. Flacso Ecuador, 2019.

Mazzucato, Mariana. *The Entrepreneurial State: Debunking Public vs. Private Sector Myths*. Anthem, 2013.

McAdam, Doug. *Political Process and the Development of Black Insurgency, 1930–1970*. University of Chicago Press, 1982.

McAdam, Doug, Sidney Tarrow, and Charles Tilly. *Dynamics of Contention*. Cambridge University Press, 2001.

McCloskey, Deirdre. "Measured, Unmeasured, Mismeasured, and Unjustified Pessimism: A Review Essay of Thomas Piketty's *Capital in the Twenty-First Century*." *Erasmus Journal for Philosophy and Economics* 7, no. 2 (2014): 73–115.

Meadows, Donella, Dennis Meadows, Jørgen Randers, and William W. Behrens III. *The Limits to Growth: A Report for the Club of Rome's Project on the Predicament of Mankind*. Universe Books, 1972.

Melucci, Alberto. *Nomads of the Present: Social Movements and Individual Needs in Contemporary Society*. Temple University Press, 1989.

Milanovic, Branko. *The Haves and the Have-Nots: A Brief and Idiosyncratic History of Global Inequality*. Basic Books, 2011.

Ministerio de Vivienda, Ciudad y Territorio (MVCT). *Política de vivienda integral: Equidad, inclusión y formalización*. MVCT, 2022.

Moffitt, Robert. "Incentive Effects of the U.S. Welfare System: A Review." *Journal of Economic Literature* 30, no. 1 (1992): 1–61.

Moncagatta, Paolo, and Ana Poveda. "La creciente polarización ideológica en Ecuador bajo el Gobierno de Rafael Correa." *Estado y Comunes, Revista de Políticas y Problemas Públicos* 1, no. 12 (2021): 57–71.

Monterubbianesi, Pablo. "El rol de la salud en el proceso de crecimiento económico: Una revisión de literatura." *Cuadernos de Economía* 33, no. 62 (2013): 91–121.

Moreno, Álvaro. "Las Leyes del Desarrollo Económico Endógeno de Kaldor: El Caso Colombiano." *Revista de Economía Institucional* 10, no. 18 (2008): 129–47.

Nikoloski, Zlatko. "Financial Sector Development and Inequality: Is There a Financial Kuznets Curve?" *Journal of International Development* 25, no. 7 (2012): 897–911.

Niskanen, William A. *Bureaucracy and Representative Government*. Routledge, 1971.

Nord, Marina, Martin Lundstedt, David Altman et al. *Democracy Report 2024: Democracy Winning and Losing at the Ballot*. University of Gothenburg, V-Dem Institute, 2024.

North, Douglass. "Institutions." *Journal of Economic Perspectives* 5, no. 1 (1991): 97–112.

Observatorio Venezolano de Conflictividad Social (OVCS). *Informe de conflictividad social en Venezuela en 2021*. OVCS, 2022.

Ocampo, José Antonio, ed. *Economía poskeynesiana*. Fondo de Cultura Económica, 1988.

Ocampo, José Antonio, and Carmen Astrid Romero. *Crecimiento económico colombiano y sus efectos sobre el desarrollo social y regional, 1905–2019*. Central Bank of Colombia, 2023.

Olson, Mancur. *The Logic of Collective Action: Public Goods and the Theory of Groups*. Harvard University Press, 1971.

Olson, Mancur. *The Rise and Decline of Nations: Economic Growth, Stagflation, and Social Rigidities*. Yale University Press, 1982.

Oppenheimer, Andrés. *¡Sálvese quien pueda! El futuro del trabajo en la era de la automatización*. Penguin Random House, 2019.

Ortiz, Isabel, Sara Burke, Mohamed Berrada, and Hernán Cortés. *World Protests: A Study of Key Protest Issues in the 21st Century*. Palgrave McMillan, 2022.

Özdemir, Onur. "Rethinking the Financial Kuznets Curve in the Framework of Income Inequality: Empirical Evidence on Advanced and Developing Economies." *Economic and Business Letters* 8, no. 4 (2019): 176–90.

Palley, Thomas. "Financialization: What It Is and Why It Matters." Working Paper, no. 525. Levy Economics Institute of Bard College, 2007.

Palma, José Gabriel. "Homogeneous Middles vs. Heterogeneous Tails, and the End of the 'Inverted-U': It's All About the Share of the Rich." *Development and Change* 42, no. 1 (2011): 87–153.

Park, Donghyun, and Kwanho Shin. "Economic Growth, Financial Development, and Income Inequality." *Emerging Markets Finance and Trade* 53, no. 12 (2017): 2794–2825.

Persily, Nathaniel, and Charles Stewart. "The Miracle and Tragedy of the 2020 U.S. Election." *Journal of Democracy* 32, no. 2 (2021): 159–78.

Persson, Torsten, and Guido Tabellini. "Is Inequality Harmful for Growth?" *American Economic Review* 84, no. 3 (1994): 600–621.

Phillips, A. W. "The Relation Between Unemployment and the Rate of Change of Money Wages in the United Kingdom, 1861–1957." *Economica* 25, no. 100 (1958): 283–99.

Piketty, Thomas. *Capital in the Twenty-First Century*. Harvard University Press, 2014.

Pinto, Pablo, David Hammond, Steve Killelea, and Andrew Etchell. *The Paradox of Progress with Polarization*. United Nations Development Programme, 2023.

Piven, Frances, and Richard Cloward. *Regulating the Poor: The Functions of Public Welfare*. Pantheon, 1971.

Policardo, Laura, Lionello Punzo, and Edgar Sánchez. "¿Desigualdad insostenible? Evidencia empírica para países de América Latina." In *América Latina en la larga historia de la desigualdad*, ed. Martín Puchet and Alicia Puyana, 177–205. FLACSO, 2018.

Prados de la Escosura, Leandro. "Inequality, Poverty, and the Kuznets Curve in Spain, 1850–2000." *European Review of Economic History* 12, no. 3 (2008): 287–324.

"Protestas en Chile: La histórica marcha de más de un millón de personas que tomó las calles de Santiago." *BBC News Mundo*, 2019.

Quiroga, María, and Ana Magrini. "Protestas sociales y cuestión social en América Latina contemporánea." *Revista Temas Sociológicos* 27 (2020): 275–308.

Rajan, Raghuram G., and Luigi Zingales. *Saving Capitalism from the Capitalists: Unleashing the Power of Financial Markets to Create Wealth and Spread Opportunity*. Princeton University Press, 2004.

Ramírez, Alfredo. "Crisis de la representación, crisis económica e ideología alternativa: Los conceptos de ruptura estática y ruptura dinámica." *Estudios de Deusto* 62, no. 1 (2014): 235–59.

Ramsey, Frank. "A Mathematical Theory of Saving." *Economic Journal* 38, no. 152 (1928): 543–59.

Rattan, Diya. "Exploring the Kuznets Curve and the 'Latin American Effect' in Latin America." In *International Economic Review: Post Recession Challenges and Analysis*, ed. Kishore Kulkarni, 271–87. Matrix, 2012.

Red Liberal de América Latina. *Índice de Calidad Institucional 2021: La pandemia, una oportunidad para mejorar el futuro*. Relial, 2021.

Reher, David, and Miguel Requena. "Un perfil demográfico del mundo árabe." *Afkar/Ideas* 30 (2011): 28–31.

Restrepo, Catalina. "Redes sociales y participación política en las elecciones presidenciales de 2022 en Colombia." *Análisis Político* 36, no. 106 (2023): 133–64.

Ribas, Rafael, and Fábio Soares. *Is the Effect of Conditional Transfer on Labor Supply Negligible Everywhere?* University of Amsterdam and International Policy Centre for Inclusive Growth, 2011.

Rivera, Guillermo, and Luis Jiménez. "Resistencias desde el Sur: Algunas reflexiones sobre los jóvenes y el octubre chileno." *Journal of Socially-Engaged Art Criticism*, no. 15 (2020).

Rodrik, Dani. *The Globalization Paradox: Democracy and the Future of the World Economy*. Norton, 2011.

Romer, Paul. "Endogenous Technological Change." *Journal of Political Economy* 98, no. 5 (1990): 71–102.

Roque, Maria. "Los jóvenes en la Primavera Árabe." *Ankulegi* 19 (2015): 11–24.

Rozas, Joaquín, and Nicolás Somma. "Determinantes de la protesta juvenil en Chile." *Revista Mexicana de Sociología* 82, no. 3 (2020): 673–703.

Samuelson, Paul, and Robert Solow. "Analytical Aspects of Anti-Inflation Policy." *American Economic Review, Papers and Proceedings* 50, no. 2 (1960): 177–94.

Schultz, Theodore. "Capital Formation by Education." *Journal of Political Economy* 68, no. 6 (1960): 571–83.

Schultz, Theodore. "Investment in Human Capital." *American Economic Review* 51, no. 1 (1961): 1–17.

Schumpeter, Joseph A. *The Theory of Economic Development: An Inquiry Into Profits, Capital, Credit, Interest, and the Business Cycle*. Harvard University Press, 1934.

Sen, Amartya. *Development as Freedom*. Knopf, 1999.

Senado de la República de México. *Comisión para la Igualdad de Género respalda reformas para combatir violencia feminicida*. Senado de la República de México, 2023.

Smith, Adam. *Wealth of Nations*. Wordsworth, 2012.

Solow, Robert. "A Contribution to the Theory of Economic Growth." *Quarterly Journal of Economics* 70, no. 1 (1956): 65–94.

Spence, Michael. *The Next Convergence: The Future of Economic Growth in a Multispeed World.* Farrar, Straus and Giroux, 2011.

Standing, Guy. *Basic Income: And How We Can Make It Happen.* Pelican, 2017.

Standing, Guy. *Battling Eight Giants: Basic Income Now.* Tauris, 2020.

Stiglitz, Joseph E. *Globalization and Its Discontents.* Norton, 2002.

Stiglitz, Joseph E. "Inequality and Economic Growth." *Political Quarterly* 86, no. 51 (2015): 134–55.

Stiglitz, Joseph E. *People, Power, and Profits: Progressive Capitalism for an Age of Discontent.* Norton, 2019.

Stiglitz, Joseph E. *The Price of Inequality: How Today's Divided Society Endangers Our Future.* Norton, 2012.

Svampa, Maristella. "Consenso de los *commodities*, giro ecoterritorial y pensamiento crítico en América Latina." *Revista del Observatorio Social de América Latina* 13, no. 32 (2012): 15–38.

Taalbi, Josef. "Innovation in the Long Run: Perspectives on Technological Transitions in Sweden 1908–2016." *Environmental Innovation and Societal Transitions* 40 (2021): 222–48.

Tarrow, Sidney. *Power in Movement: Social Movements and Contentious Politics.* Cambridge University Press, 2011.

Ugalde, Benjamín, Felipe Schwember, and Valentina Verbal, ed. *El octubre chileno: Reflexiones sobre democracia y libertad.* Ediciones Democracia y Libertad, 2020.

UK Climate Change Committee. *Progress in Reducing Emissions: 2021 Report to Parliament.* UK Climate Change Committee, 2021.

United Kingdom. *End of Coal in Sight as UK Secures Ambitious Commitments at COP26 Summit.* Department for Business, Energy and Industrial Strategy, 2021.

United Nations Development Programme (UNDP). *Human Development Report 2021/2022: Uncertain Times, Unsettled Lives: Shaping Our Future in a Transforming World.* UNDP, 2022.

UN Women and United Nations Department of Economic and Social Affairs. *Progress on the Sustainable Development Goals: The Gender Snapshot 2022.* UN Women and United Nations Department of Economic and Social Affairs, 2022.

Wannamakok, Wisuwat, Yu-Yu Chang, and Marge Täks. "The Relationship Between Institutional Environments and Entrepreneurial Intention in Estonia: Mediating Roles of Desirability and Feasibility." *Entrepreneurial Business and Economics Review* 8, no. 2 (2020): 111–26.

Wanniski, Jude. "Taxes, Revenues and the Laffer Curve." *Public Interest* 50 (1978): 3–16.

Wendling, Zachary, John Emerson, Alex de Sherbinin et al. *2020 Environmental Performance Index.* Yale Center for Environmental Law & Policy, 2020.

Wolf, Martin, John Emerson, Daniel Esty et al. *2022 Environmental Performance Index.* Yale Center for Environmental Law & Policy, 2022.

World Bank. *The Human Capital Index 2020 Update: Human Capital in the Time of Covid-19.* World Bank, 2021.

World Intellectual Property Organization (WIPO). *Global Innovation Index 2023: Innovation in the Face of Uncertainty.* WIPO, 2023.

Yang, Haisheng, Jie He, and Shaoling Chen. "The Fragility of the Environmental Kuznets Curve: Revisiting the Hypothesis with Chinese Data via an 'Extreme Bound Analysis.'" *Ecological Economics* 109 (2014): 41–58.

Younsi, Moheddine, and Marwa Bechtini. "Economic Growth, Financial Development, and Income Inequality in BRICS Countries: Does Kuznets' Inverted U-Shaped Curve Exist?" *Journal of the Knowledge Economy* 11, no. 2 (2018): 721–42.

Zeraoui, Zidane. "A una década de la Primavera Árabe: ¿Hacia dónde va el mundo árabe?" *Relaciones Internacionales* 30, no. 60 (2021): 49–72.

INDEX

GPSR Authorized Representative: Easy Access System Europe, Mustamäe tee 50, 10621 Tallinn, Estonia, gpsr.requests@easproject.com

www.ingramcontent.com/pod-product-compliance
Lightning Source LLC
LaVergne TN
LVHW091514200926
848483LV00008B/459/J

* 9 7 8 0 2 3 1 2 2 2 9 1 4 *